Waiting on the Weather
Making Movies with Akira Kurosawa

DERSU UZALA

Waiting on the Weather
Making Movies with Akira Kurosawa

Teruyo Nogami
Foreword by
Donald Richie

Translated by Juliet Winters Carpenter

Stone Bridge Press • Berkeley, California

Published by
Stone Bridge Press
P.O. Box 8208
Berkeley, CA 94707
TEL 510-524-8732 • sbp@stonebridge.com • www.stonebridge.com

The publisher gratefully acknowledges the support of the Japan Foundation and the Suntory Foundation in the translation and production of this book.

Thanks also to Canadian filmmaker Marty Gross, who brought this project to our attention and worked tirelessly on its behalf.

The word order of Japanese names follows Western usage, family name last.

All illustrations by the author.

Tenki Machi by Teruyo Nogami. © 2001 Teruyo Nogami. Original Japanese edition published by Bungei Shunju Ltd., Japan. English translation rights arranged with Bungei Shunju Ltd., through Japan Foreign-Rights Centre.

English translation © 2006 Juliet Winters Carpenter.

All rights reserved.

No part of this book may be reproduced in any form without permission from the publisher.

Printed in the United States of America.

2010 2009 2008 2007 2006   10 9 8 7 6 5 4 3 2 1

LIBRARY OF CONGRESS CATALOGING-IN-PUBLICATION DATA
Nogami, Teruyo, 1927–
 [Tenki machi. English]
 Waiting on the weather: making movies with Akira Kurosawa / Teruyo Nogami; foreword by Donald Richie; translated by Juliet Winters Carpenter.
    p. cm.
 Includes bibliographical references.
 ISBN-13: 978-1-933330-09-9.
 1. Nogami, Teruyo, 1927–. 2. Script clerks—Japan—Biography. 3. Kurosawa, Akira, 1910–1998. I. Title.
PN1998.3.N64A3 2006
791.4302'33—dc22
[B]
2006032033

Contents

Foreword by Donald Richie 7

1 **Mansaku Itami, My First Mentor**   16
   Letters 16 • Listening to Memories 21 • A Female Muhomatsu 25 • Images 30 • *The Life of a Giant* 34 • Face to Face with Death 39

2 **Life in Miniature: At the Daiei Kyoto Studios**   44
   Inside a Small Arena 44 • An Apprentice 48 • Eyes on the Goal 53 • Black-Market Cigarettes 57

3 **Smiled on by Lady Luck:** *Rashomon*   63
   Akira Kurosawa Arrives 63 • Dancing on Mount Wakakusa 68 • The Camera Work is 100+ 73 • Shooting the Sun 77 • Get the Negative, the Negative! 82 • Lady Luck 88 • Farewell to Kyoto 93

4 **Toho Paradise**   99
   The Fountain 99 • Script Supervisor 104 • Cinematography 109 • Art Direction 115 • The Assistant Director and the Ants 120

5 **The Past Won't Return: Remembering** *Dersu Uzala*   127
   Off to Siberia 127 • Ticks, Mosquitoes, and Outdoor Toilets 132 • Feeling like Napoleon 139 • Bone-Freezing Night Shoots 144 • *Dosvidanya, Sayonara* 149

6 **Kurosawa and Animals**   157
   Tigers 157 • Horses 164 • Crows 172

7 **Kurosawa and Music**   183
   A Solo Conductor 183 • Fumio Hayasaka 188 • Masaru Sato 193 • Toru Takemitsu 201

8 **Sentimental Recollections**   210
   Death Notices 210 • Kamatari Fujiwara 215 • Junzaburo Ban and Bokuzen Hidari 220 • Takashi Shimura and Toshiro Mifune 225 • Mifune's Embarrassment 230 • Remembering Juzo Itami 234

9 **Observing the Kurosawa Group**   244
   Director Toshiro Mifune 244 • The Petition 247 • What Really Happened with Shintaro Katsu on *Kagemusha* 251 • Footfalls of a Giant 261 • Parting Sadness: Director Akira Kurosawa 265 • Kurosawa and Mifune after *Red Beard* 268

10 **Akira Kurosawa and World Filmmakers**   277
   John Ford 278 • Laurence Olivier 280 • Jean Renoir 281 • Foreign Filmmakers Offer Support 281 • Jean-Luc Godard and John Milius 282 • Werner Herzog 282 • Martin Scorsese 283 • William Friedkin 284 • Sidney Lumet 284 • Francis F. Coppola 284 • George Lucas 285 • John Cassavetes and Jim Jarmusch 286 • The Directors Guild of America 287

Afterword 288
Afterword to the English Edition 291
Notes and Sources 293

Foreword

Behind every great man, intones the adage, is a woman. Teruyo Nogami would not like it said that she was in any way responsible for Akira Kurosawa's greatness, but she did stand behind him—all the way from *Rashomon* to *Madadayo* and beyond.

She began as a continuity assistant (or script girl) on the 1951 *Rashomon* and continued in that position through *Ikiru* and all the rest of Kurosawa's pictures until *Dodeskaden*, when she became assistant producer, a position continued during the production of *Dersu Uzala* and *Kagemusha*. For *Ran*, in 1985, she was a production manager, a position she held for all the final films—*Dreams, Rhapsody in August*, and *Madadayo*.

Script girls, assistant producers, and production managers alike are devoted to realizing the wishes of the directors for whom they work. They are responsible for continuity and for everything else that goes into the complications which result in a film. Without such help even the greatest director is helpless. There is too much to do and too much can go wrong.

Consequently Kurosawa came to rely greatly on Nogami: on her care, her memory, her quickness, her probity. What she did was sometimes invisible but her suggestions were always there, incorporated. And accepted with a degree of appreciation rare in the director, who could be quite difficult. During my own association with Kurosawa, on and off the set, the single person whom he did not criticize and with whom he never lost his temper was Nogami.

Not that things did not go wrong. In filmmaking things invariably go wrong. The negative of *Rashomon* is threatened by fire, the ants in *Rhapsody in August* refuse to behave, and—always—is the expense and frustration of waiting for good weather.

Yet, at the same time, as she writes, "During shooting it's nice to have to wait for sunny weather. You can sit back and relax. As soon as the lighting man, his contrast filter to his eye, looks up at the sky and opines, 'Yup, it's gonna be a while,' your time is yours."

When Nogami decided to collect her memories of working with Kurosawa she began with the above sentence. And she began, not with Kurosawa but with the first director who showed her what films could do. This was Mansaku Itami, one of Japan's finest filmmakers, and Nogami was at the time only in her second year of high school.

She had seen one of his films, *Akanishi Kakita*, and had never known that Japanese films could be so exciting. So she wrote him a fan letter, and he answered it. Thus began the correspondence between the ill and dying man and the young schoolgirl whose life he would completely change.

School finished, other jobs (librarian, newspaper reporter) tried on and discarded, Nogami applied to a studio for film work and ended up working with Kurosawa on *Rashomon*. This was good fortune for both of them. She would continue throughout her life to discover the joys and frustrations of filmmaking and he would have someone who made his difficult work not just easier but, in some cases, possible.

Her reminiscences, *Waiting on the Weather*, appeared in Japanese in 2001 and occasioned lively interest. She was at the same time still helping Kurosawa with his posthumous productions, including *After the Rain*, based on his script. With its straightforward style, its fascinating stories, its deep understanding of the man she stood behind, *Waiting on the Weather* is perhaps the most human record we have of Kurosawa, and certainly the most detailed telling of how he worked. At the same time it is a portrait of Nogami herself—devoted, critical, funny, and faithful.

Donald Richie
Tokyo, September 2006

Waiting on the Weather
Making Movies with Akira Kurosawa

RASHOMON *(top, bottom)*

THE SEVEN SAMURAI

DERSU UZALA *(below, right)*

KAGEMUSHA

RAN

KAGEMUSHA

TERUYO NOGAMI, 2001

1

Mansaku Itami, My First Mentor

LETTERS

During shooting it's nice to have to wait for sunny weather. You can sit back and relax. As soon as the lighting man, his contrast filter to his eye, looks up at the sky and opines, "Yup, it's gonna be a while," your time is yours. If the sun has gone behind an enormous cloud, right away everyone begins hunting around for something to sit on. Three men might manage to sit back to back on a little toolbox. I remember a new assistant getting scolded for trying to perch on a baby tripod.

Today, most crews can't afford to take time out to wait for the sun, but it's one of the things the Akira Kurosawa unit was known for. Of course, we sometimes waited for the clouds as well. There are times, after all, when a clear blue sky just isn't what's wanted. And so someone would say, "Let's wait and shoot the scene after that cloud goes in back of that mountain." It may seem an extravagant waste of time, but that's how you made a movie in those days.

When he was still an assistant director, one day Kurosawa visited the open set where Sadao Yamanaka was shooting *Humanity and Paper Balloons* (Ninjo Kamifusen, 1937). It was the scene where the unemployed *ronin* (masterless samurai) Matajuro, played by Chojuro Kawarazaki, tries to hand over a letter of entreaty to a senior official. What Kurosawa never forgot about that day was that even though the weather was perfectly fine, everybody was just standing around idly, peering up at the sky. He learned they were waiting for a cloud to waft over a warehouse on the set.

During such breaks, while waiting for the weather to cooperate, we killed time gossiping. Nowadays people watch afternoon TV shows for much the same reason, but back then we would eagerly trade information about the latest romantic breakups or entanglements, or compare stories about how we got started in the business. Listening to each other's life stories was always a good way of passing the time.

I have no intention of going into my life story in much depth here, since it is no particular interest, but I'd like to relate how one film changed the course of my life. It was the comic film *Kakita Akanishi* (Akanishi Kakita), which Mansaku Itami directed in 1936—although I must have first seen it around 1941.

It was my father who told me about the film, having seen it favorably reviewed in an economic journal. I remember going to see it in a movie theater with the odd name of Tokyo Club. I was only a young girl at the time, in my second year at a girls' higher school, so it surprises me that I would have gone by myself. It must have been my fondness for the writings of Naoya Shiga that drew me, as the movie was based on one of his short stories.

Seen from above, two oiled-paper umbrellas move together

"Waiting on the weather" is pleasant. Such scenes are rare nowadays.

through the rain. Rain beats on a roof-tile imprinted with a seal depicting a sparrow and bamboo. A stray cat seeks shelter. The two samurai carrying the umbrellas walk along toward their lodgings, speaking of the new fellow, Akanishi.

Never had I known that a Japanese movie could be so fascinating. In my excitement, I sat down and composed a fan letter to Itami, who was living in Kyoto. Wonder of wonders, I not only received a prompt reply from the ailing director, but also a copy of his book, *Notes on Film*.[1] Upon opening the dark blue covers, I saw my name inscribed beside his in elegant calligraphic strokes, and my heart leaped.

From then on he and I corresponded, but to my unending sorrow I no longer have any of his letters. I read and reread them so many times, though, that I can summon up clearly what he wrote—both the look of his calligraphy and entire sentences. Once he wrote this:

You never use the wrong characters in your letters, and you never ask me for anything.... You are my disciple, but if you asked me what I mean to teach you, I couldn't say. I suppose there's nothing wrong in having a disciple who gets taught nothing at all.

My own letters were filled with innocent chatter about a funny mistake the teacher had made in school, or a stray cat I'd picked up in a field and then released again. He sometimes would include a short poem in his letters, and I remember one to the effect that the cat might have preferred being left alone to being picked up, only to be set back down. Pasted in the margin was a snapshot inscribed, "This is my cat Teko."

The letters he sent were always written on fine-quality art paper with spaces for 400 characters per page, ruled in red, with his name centered at the top. When wartime privations grew severe, the paper would be cut in half, with his beautifully penciled characters filling every inch of space on front and back.

In the darkening war years, from February 1943 to May 1944, Itami moved to the countryside to continue his convalescence after a bout of tuberculosis, staying with relatives on the southern island of Oshima in Yamaguchi Prefecture. He wrote me a letter filled with concern for his family: "I cannot sit still for worry when I hear that in Kyoto, today's food ration consisted of a single leek." His anxiety was acute.

I graduated and underwent a year's training at a school for librarians in Ueno, Tokyo. In the spring of 1945 I finally managed to get away from the air raids myself, working in the library of my father's alma mater, Yamaguchi Higher School. I was there when the war ended in August. Before moving back to Tokyo, I took advantage of a friend's recent marriage to an Oshima native to pay the place a visit. It was just a small island, so I had no trouble finding where Itami's relatives lived, but he had already returned to Kyoto.

Postwar Tokyo was a chaotic whirl of confusion and bustle and excitement. I was soon absorbed in work at a left-leaning paper, the *Jinmin Shinbun*. With so much else going on then in my life, I can remember nothing about any further correspondence with Itami until the day I was startled to find in a newspaper column a poem he had written, entitled "My Small Wish." It started out like this:

> A mug of hot milk
> and a piece of savory, buttered toast—
> ah, even in my dreams they come to me.
> Wife, do not mock
> the smallness of this wish.
> Children, do not mock
> the humbleness of this wish.

I wrote to him after that, but there was no reply, and then a while later I saw word of his death in the paper.

Mansaku Itami made twenty-one masterpieces of cinema, including *The Unrivalled Hero* (Kokushi Muso, 1932) and *The Frivolous Servant* (Kimagure Kaja, 1935). He died at the youthful age of forty-six.

LISTENING TO MEMORIES

Mansaku Itami entered Matsuyama Middle School in 1912, the first year of the Taisho period. In his essay "Memories of Mansaku Itami," haiku poet Kusatao Nakamura wrote, "Matsuyama Middle School was the setting for Soseki Natsume's novel *Botchan*, but beginning in early Taisho, for about ten years a magazine called *Rakuten* (Optimism) was put out, at roughly four-month intervals, by those among the pupils with artistic aspirations."[2] The genius of Itami was first nurtured in the pages of that magazine.

One of Itami's classmates was a brilliant student named Minoru Noda, whom Itami admired for his intellect as well as his personality. Noda's littlest sister, Kimi, adored her handsome big brother so much that she always insisted one day she'd marry him. But Noda died young of tuberculosis, and it was Itami that Kimi ended up marrying. Recently she shared with me some reminiscences of her late husband.

The Nodas were a wealthy family in Matsuyama. Their home was encircled by a wisteria trellis that produced magnificent blossoms in the spring, hanging a full meter below the eaves. They had a spacious garden with an enormous wire-mesh aviary in one corner. The aviary, as grand as those found in zoos, even housed hawks and peacocks. Even now, Mrs. Itami says, on a moonlit night she remembers wild geese flying high inside the aviary.

Itami lost his mother at an early age and was raised by his grandmother, but because his maternal grandparents lived close to the Noda family, he knew the Nodas well. He first saw Kimi when she was in about the fifth grade, a tomboy who loved to climb trees and run barefoot between rice paddies. For years, he kept that vision of her close to his heart, settling on her as "the girl for me."

Later, determined to establish himself as an artist, Itami went to Tokyo to study painting while producing illustrations for a magazine called *Chugakusei* (Middle-school Student). Also in Tokyo was a former colleague from *Rakuten* named Tsurunosuke Shigematsu, another aspiring painter, who had had a painting selected for a prestigious exhibition. Nicknamed Tsuruman, he was a hot-blooded, zealous young man. Under his influence, Itami wrote the following to Kusatao: "From meeting with Shigematsu and talking to him, I have come to see just how abysmally low my expectations of myself and the art of painting have been. I am thoroughly ashamed. From now on I will work, work, work."[3]

Full of resolve, Itami returned to Matsuyama with Tsuruman—not just to reapply himself to his calling, but to visit Kimi's brother on his sickbed. More than anything, though, I suspect it was the strength of his feelings for Kimi that drew him home. He was then twenty-two years old.

To Kimi's mother, Itami's return was unwelcome; she regarded him as merely a hack painter with no future. For as long as she remained alive, the two were unable to marry.

On top of that disappointment came the death of his friend Noda. Reeling, Itami left Matsuyama and returned to Tokyo, where he and illustrator Shigeru Hatsuyama lived together for awhile, cooking their own meals. Unable to do the illustrating work he had done before, Itami ran out of money and drifted back to Matsuyama, where he and Tsuruman opened an eatery specializing in *oden* hotpot. Tsuruman spent all his time painting, and so the cooking fell largely to Itami.

Kimi was then undergoing outpatient treatment for earache,

and on her way to the hospital and back she would pass in front of the *oden* place. Once, attracted by the savory smell, she looked in and saw Itami and others eating *chameshi*, or rice boiled in tea and soy sauce, with bowls of hot *oden*. Itami called out to her, inviting her to come in and join them, but she shook her head and walked away; back then, such establishments were strictly off-limits for girls. She continued looking in as she passed by, though, and she sometimes saw Itami making soup stock, in the process throwing away a big sheet of kelp after just one use. With such extravagance, she told herself, the business couldn't last.

She was right. The eatery folded in less than a year. Penniless again, Itami went to Kyoto to work with Daisuke Ito, who was already directing films for Nikkatsu, and he wrote his first scenario. This formed the basis for the 1931 film *Fireworks* (Hanabi), which Itami himself directed.

Tsuruman subsequently became involved with leftist activities and was sent to prison. On the last day of his sentence, just when he was scheduled to be released, for some reason he leaped from the prison building to his death.

Eventually Kimi's mother passed away, and Kimi was finally free to wed Itami. This was in 1930. He had told her she needed no dowry but the clothes on her back, and so all she took with her to Kyoto as a bride were some shiitake mushrooms, strips of dried gourd, and the like. To her amazement, the house had a full complement of kimonos, storage chests, and everything else she could have needed, all selected by actress Junko Kinugasa at Itami's request. How he must have looked forward to the day of her coming!

The couple set up housekeeping in Uji, a town south of

Kyoto, in a house surrounded by vast tea fields. Nearby there was nothing but a small train station on the Nara Line, and often she would walk there to meet him on his return from work. On nights bright with silver moonlight, the two would wind their way home through the rice paddies, where the moon's reflection shimmered on the water. As they walked along, Itami would compose poetry based on the surrounding countryside:

> How full and tranquil the clouds
> gently enfolding the moon!
> On such a night as this
> water pours from field to field,
> the black soil swelling until
> water covers it entirely,
> while the lusty cries of frogs
> fill the air all about.

This was surely the happiest time of Mansaku Itami's life. Here are two haiku he wrote during those halcyon years:

> Hazy spring moon—
> the nightingale sleeps
> in a field of tea.

> In the shadow of bamboo
> lies yesterday's snow—
> seed pods of butterbur.

This serenity was not to last: in 1938, Itami's shock from the poor critical reception of his film *The Life of a Giant* (Kyojinden) must have been great. He suffered a relapse of lung disease and never directed another film.

On September 21, 1946, after his lengthy convalescence in Oshima and subsequent return to Kyoto, Itami's condition suddenly worsened. Kimi hastily phoned for his doctor, who had left his bedside only a short while before, but could not reach him. Not knowing what else to do, she asked the local doctor to administer first aid, and sent her son Takehiko to fetch director "Uncle Ito" (Daisuke Ito).

At 6:30 that evening, surrounded by his wife, Kimi, and his children, Takehiko and Yukari, Mansaku Itami breathed his last.

That summer, he had written this haiku:

> Nine years an invalid—
> I'll try to bear just
> one more summer.

The boy who went to fetch Daisuke Ito would go on to become the distinguished film director Juzo Itami.

A FEMALE MUHOMATSU

In 1946, when Itami died, Tokyo was still a city of burned-out ruins as far as the eye could see, with no tall buildings to block one's view. People flocked to the black markets that sprouted around train stations, where enterprising dealers hawked their wares till their voices grew hoarse. Fleas and lice were a widespread problem. When I went to the public bath, I used to poke holes in my bar of soap and wear it on a cord around my neck; otherwise it would have been stolen.

I quit my newspaper job, took the examination for prospective employees at Yakumo Shoten Publishing Company, and was hired. The author and critic Daizo Kusayanagi, then a dashing young man, was hired at the same time as me.

Soon after this, I accompanied writer Taiko Hirabayashi on a fact-finding tour of the famous black market in Shinjuku called Harmonica Alley. The area took its name from the station front, where crude drinking establishments divided by single sheets of plywood were crowded together like harmonica pleats. I followed Ms. Hirabayashi's sturdy back as she plowed through the crowd; I remember my surprise at one point when she suddenly turned around and exclaimed, "You know, Lenin said that what exists is inevitable. And it's true!"

At that time, a devoted fan of Itami's work, Seiichiro Eida, was manager of the Baraza theater company in Tokyo, headed by Minoru Chiaki. The Baraza was known for plays such as *The Abortionist*. Eida later became a film producer and nurtured the careers of many actors.

Eida was also a frequent visitor to the Itami home in Uji, where he made himself useful in all sorts of ways. Food was scarce in those days, and he took it upon himself to see that the family was supplied with its ration of food and other goods. This was necessary because Mrs. Itami was not the sort of person who could make deals on the black market.

Itami's diary contains these poems, written during his last months:

> Carefully holding
> the single onion she bought
> as if it were a gem—
> the sight of my wife
> wrenches my heart.
>
> Even if my illness
> should now grow worse,
> O wife,
> may you increase in power
> to battle on and to endure.

Clearly he was very concerned about how his wife and children would live in the event of his death.

When he died, Kimi was left with thirteen-year-old Takehiko and ten-year-old Yukari to bring up. Around that time, she wrote this about her children in a postcard to Tomoko Hoshino (the actress who had played the small child in Itami's *Life of a Giant*): "Yukari got the highest grade in her class in reading, and that's turned her into a grind who does nothing but slave away at her studies. Takehiko seems to think a person hasn't lived till he's failed a time or three, and the whereabouts of his schoolbooks are unknown. The longer you live, the more there is to worry about."

Despite being such a slacker, Takehiko earned an outstanding scholastic record. Not only that, he displayed early signs of talent and initiative, taking up book-binding while still in junior high.

Back in Tokyo, the kindly and generous Eida gathered together all those who had had any connection with Mansaku Itami, however slight, and formed a society in his memory called

Itaman-kai or "The Itaman Club." He used to take us all out eating and drinking. Apparently he had heard about me through Kimi, and kindly let me join the group as well. Other members included the haiku poet Kusatao Nakamura and scriptwriters Senzo Nada and Shinobu Hashimoto.

I once had occasion to read a scenario of Hashimoto's that he had also shown to Itami. This later became the basis for the searing TV drama and film *I Want to Be a Shellfish* (Watashi wa Kai ni Naritai, 1958), about a conscripted barber in World War Two who is ordered to kill a POW by his superior. He follows orders and winds up condemned to death as a war criminal.

Eida first took me with him to visit the Itamis early in the spring of 1949. Mrs. Itami and the children had vacated the main house in Uji, giving it back to the landlord, and had moved into a cottage out back that had a tiny library and one other small room. I followed Eida through the gate and down the pathway by the side of the main house, until the detached cottage came into view. Kimi Itami was standing in the doorway awaiting us, and as soon as she caught sight of me she called out warmly, "Well, well! I've been waiting for you. You must be Miss Nogami!"

She was like the image of a beautiful woman in a woodblock print by twentieth-century master Shinsui Ito.

"I would always take your letters to my husband and lay them by his pillow," she said, gesturing as if she held a letter in her hand. "I'd tell him, 'It's from Mademoiselle.'"

In less than an hour, I felt like part of the family. "Why on earth didn't you come sooner?" she said to me. I, too, could only regret that I had never had the opportunity of meeting Mansaku Itami in person.

Eida and the others all referred to Mrs. Itami informally as *Kaachan* or "Mom." I can only describe her as a woman of flawless charm, but even that does not do her justice. She was said to be a marvelous cook, but in those days there were no ingredients available with which she could show off her talents; she would blow on her tiny clay stove to stoke its flame, saying gaily, "Today it's plain miso soup for dinner!" She was also skilled at needlecraft, and embroidered constellations on pillow covers; even her cleaning cloths were gay with sprays of embroidered flowers.

"Mom" had another great talent: she knew by heart all sixty-six verses of "Song of the Railroad" (*Tetsudo Shoka*, lyrics by Takeki Owada), a poetic tour of the country from Shinbashi to Kobe published in 1900 to commemorate the tenth anniversary of the opening of the Tokaido Line railway. She would start out singing the famous opening verse ("With a whistle blast / my train pulls out of Shinbashi; / the moon over Mount Atago / will be my travel companion") and would continue on from there. I would listen in amazement to the seemingly never-ending railway journey depicted in the lyrics.

Unable to find work that would allow her to support her family, Kimi Itami ended up moving back to Matsuyama. Her son, however, was dead set against going back. It was Eida's idea that I live with the boy in Kyoto and cook for him while working at a movie studio on the side. Things at the publisher were not looking very promising anyway, and I was interested in working with movies, so I decided to accept the proposal.

Eida was not only a gracious man who enjoyed looking after others, but a master of the hard sell. He took me to see a Mr. Soga, then a board member of Daiei Kyoto Studios, made extravagant claims on my behalf, and got him to hire me as an apprentice "script girl" or script supervisor.

During summer vacation that year, Kimi and Yukari went back to Matsuyama, and I moved into the Itami residence in Kyoto to cook for Takehiko. Or as Eida put it in announcing the move to the members of the Itaman Club: "She'll be a sort of female Muhomatsu"—a reference to the 1943 movie *The Life of Matsu the Untamed* (Muhomatsu no Issho, directed by Hiroshi Inagaki and written by Mansaku Itami) in which the main character, a rough-and-ready rickshaw man, looks after a widow and her son. But while he dies leaving bankbooks in his protégés' names, the accounts filled with money, I had no savings of any kind to offer Takehiko. The best I could manage was to bring home leftovers from the boxed suppers I got when working late.

In 1950, when Akira Kurosawa's production of *Rashomon* came sweeping into town, I was assigned to work on it as script supervisor, a novice with barely one film's experience under my belt.

In this connection, I'd like to note that Mansaku Itami lavished praise on Kurosawa's early script *A German at the Temple Daruma* (Daruma-dera no Doitsujin, 1941) and, upon reading his script *All Is Quiet* (Shizuka Nari, 1939), declared, "This man's future is limitless." He foresaw the immense success of filmmaker Akira Kurosawa long before anyone else.

IMAGES

Once upon a time I would introduce Juzo Itami to people by saying, "You remember the great filmmaker Mansaku Itami, don't you? Well, this is his son." Nowadays the situation has reversed. I find myself saying, "What, you've never heard of Mansaku Itami? Why, he was the father of Juzo Itami."

When I mentioned this the other day to Mrs. Itami (not Nobuko Miyamoto, Juzo's wife, but Mansaku Itami's widow Kimi), she laughed like a little girl and said, "Goodness, when did our Take ever get to be such a big-shot director? If his father heard that, it would surely make him happy."

In 1944, when Itami was recuperating from tuberculosis on the small island of Oshima in Yamaguchi Prefecture, the thought of his family on their own back in Kyoto was so troubling that he pulled up stakes and rejoined them, traveling by way of Matsuyama. Kimi took Takehiko with her to meet him at Kobe Harbor, and along the way they ran into him, riding in a rickshaw. On the train back to Kyoto, the father carefully removed a hardboiled egg from his kimono sleeve and showed it to the boy. On the shell he had sketched the face of a *hina* doll in pretty color.[4] He must really have been determined to please his son, for toward the end of the war, eggs were precious objects, extremely scarce in cities. "But you know what," says Kimi with a laugh, "Takehiro just grabbed that egg, peeled it right there in the train, and gobbled it up!" The story conjures a heartwarming scene of the reunion between father and son.

As a boy, Mansaku Itami was the sort of child who would linger in the classroom after school to draw pictures on the blackboard. When he had nothing else to draw on, he would paint on his fingernails. In 1912, not long after entering Matsuyama Middle School, he produced a magazine called *Rakuten* (Optimism) with Daisuke Ito and other friends. His talent became ever more evident. At eighteen he went to Tokyo to seek his fortune as an artist, and for a time he drew illustrations for a magazine called *Shonen Sekai* (Boy's World), published by Hakubunkan under the name Gumi Ikeuchi.

Not all painters go on to become film directors, but the best directors are often talented painters. It was true of Sergei Eisenstein and Federico Fellini, and of Yasujiro Ozu and Akira Kurosawa as well. Kurosawa once entertained ambitions of being a painter. He used to say, "Now I paint pictures for the cinema." Doing so, he explained, forced him to plan everything down to the smallest details. Drawing a picture helped him to visualize just how the strings on armor were fastened, say, or what sort of design a costume should have.

But in 1922, ashamed of his previously naïve conception of what it took to be an artist and determined to make a fresh start, Itami went back to Matsuyama. Kimi clearly remembers the day he came calling at her home. "Are you back now?" she asked. He grunted in the affirmative. "What for?" Pointing a finger at her, he said simply, "I want to paint you."

From then on he came every day. He would sit Kimi in a rattan chair and paint her portrait, with her mother always hovering nearby. When she fussed over Kimi's kimono, making little adjustments, Mansaku would tell her, "Don't worry, it's not a photograph."

He opened a little eatery in town, but it stayed in business barely a year, leaving him in debt with not a penny to his name. Not knowing what else to do, he went to Kyoto to live with his old friend Daisuke Ito, by then a director for Nikkatsu. Soon he had written his first screenplay. In 1928, for the first motion picture made by Chiezo Productions, at Ito's behest he wrote the script for *Peace on Earth* (Tenka Taiheiki), using the professional name "Mansaku Itami" for the first time. Four months later, he wrote and directed *Wandering Revenge* (Adauchi Ruten) in a brilliant directorial debut.

In 1930 he finally married Kimi. After a brief sojourn in the green Sagano area of Kyoto, the newlyweds moved to a farming village in Uji, south of Kyoto. Kimi told me this story about the time a burglar came to their house.

One summer night as they lay in bed, a man's voice sounded close by, calling, "Mister, hey mister." Kimi was so terrified she froze, and lay scarcely breathing under the covers, her heart pounding so loud she was afraid the intruder would hear it. After a while, her husband got up and went with the man into the room next door. They talked about something, and apparently some money changed hands. By this time the sky was starting to get light, and she heard her husband tell the burglar he might just as well wait and take the first train home. She got up too, then, and found a young man with a dirty face sitting in front of her husband.

Itami told him, "As long as you're here, you might as well have some breakfast while you wait," and the man said, "In that case, I'd like to go get the leather sandals I left behind the manure shed, as I don't want anyone helping himself to them." Itami remarked, "That's a fine way for a burglar to talk."

While the three of them were having breakfast, a farmer from the neighborhood walked by and called out a cheery greeting, under the impression that the couple was entertaining a house guest. Finally, when the trains began running, the burglar took his

Newlyweds Mansaku and Kimi Itami serve breakfast to their burglar.

leave, saying, "Thanks for everything. I'll come by again." Itami told him dryly, "Don't bother."

It sounds like a scene from one of his comic movies.

Just the other day, Kimi Itami told me, "He died when he was forty-six, you know. Goodness, when we meet in the next world I expect he won't know me, I've gotten to be such an old lady!" She is now over ninety years old. Perhaps, having left this world at such a young age himself, her husband is seeing to it that she lives to a ripe old age.

THE LIFE OF A GIANT

The 1938 movie *Life of a Giant*, directed by Mansaku Itami, is now available on video, but one time, through the offices of Juzo Itami, I attended a viewing of the original at the Sagamihara branch of the National Film Center. With us were director Kiyoshi Saeki, screenplay writer Shinobu Hashimoto, and actress Tomoko Hoshino. For both Juzo and me, it was our first time to see the picture.

No sooner was it over than Juzo stood up, turned around and said to me feelingly, "Wow, he did a good job." As one who shared his father's profession, he must have had special empathy for his father's struggles.

The Life of a Giant is based on Mansaku Itami's own adaptation of the 1862 novel *Les Misérables* by Victor Hugo. An avid political activist, Hugo sympathized with those suffering from poverty and starvation and sought to change the system that oppressed them. Translated in 1902 by Ruiko Kuroiwa under the title *Aa Mujo* (Ah, No Mercy), and published serially in the *Manchoho* newspaper, the novel gained many devoted readers in Japan.

In the story, poverty drives main character Jean Valjean to steal a loaf of bread. Later, through the influence of a Catholic bishop, he reforms and goes on to become mayor and perform charitable works. Through it all, the detective Javert pursues him relentlessly, determined to send him back to prison for breaking parole. Valjean, meanwhile, bestows unselfish, unconditional love on the orphan Cosette. His tumultuous life is portrayed in the epic novel.

Movie versions of the novel were made all over the world as early as 1907. In addition to Itami's movie, a surprising number were filmed in Japan, starting in 1910 with *Aa Mujo*, produced by the M Pathe Company, founded by Shokichi Umeya in 1906. Here are the others: in 1923, *Les Misérables*, produced by Shochiku (Part One, directed by Kiyohiko Ushihara, and Part Two, directed by Yoshinobu Ikeda; starring Masao Inoue and Sumiko Kurishima);

in 1929, *Aa Mujo*, produced by Shochiku (directed by Seika Shiba, starring Yonosuke Toba and Yoko Umemura); in 1931, *Jean Valjean*, produced by Nikkatsu (directed by Tomu Uchida, starring Nobuo Asaoka and Takako Irie); in 1950, *Les Misérables*, Part One, produced by Toyoko Film Company Eiga (directed by Daisuke Ito, starring Sesshu Hayakawa and Fujiko Hayakawa). Of all the versions filmed anywhere, the only two that rank as masterpieces are both French, and both are entitled *Les Misérables*; one was made in 1934 starring Harry Baur, and the other in 1958 starring Jean Gabin.

Mansaku Itami started his career with Chiezo Productions, then moved to Nikkatsu, Shinkyo Cinema, and J.O. In 1937, J.O. merged with P.C.L. and was renamed Toho Films, and so early in 1938, Itami left his home in Kyoto to join Toho in Tokyo, setting right to work on *The Life of a Giant*.

Kiyoshi Saeki, Itami's chief assistant director and right arm from the first, also switched to Toho at the same time. Because it was his first experience of Tokyo, and because he plunged right away into a work of such grand scale, Saeki says he remembers nothing but running around distractedly.

One thing Saeki says he will never forget is that when they rehearsed on Stage One of the Toho Studio in Kinuta, Masako Tsutsumi in the part of Okuni had to say the single word *hai* ("yes") but could not do it to Itami's satisfaction. They rehearsed that one word over and over again, all day long and on into the night. In the end, Saeki said, he nodded off, too sleepy to tell anymore which way of saying it was good and which was bad. Later he and Itami shared a laugh over the incident, which Saeki memorialized in a satirical poem:

> In the cold sky
> the single word "yes"
> means no sleep tonight.

I have gone over the film, hunting in vain for that scene—after all their trouble, perhaps it was cut in the end.

The part of Jean Valjean/Sanpei Onuma was played by Denjiro Okochi, and Cosette/Chiyo was played by Setsuko Hara. Chiyo as a little girl was played by Hinako Katagiri, a darling, round-eyed child who grew up to become Tomoko Hoshino—the actress who attended the screening in Sagamihara. It was Itami who gave her her stage name.

Tomoko Hoshino vividly remembers February 8, 1938, when they shot the scene in Inokashira Park where she scoops up water from the pond while crying for her mother to the night sky; Itami said the scene as written was so sad that he wanted to start shooting from there. The scene where she goes to a hot-water spa with Okochi was not in the original script, which might have something to do with the fact that they did so many retakes she ended up getting nearly cooked in the hot water.

The movie incorporates a line Itami heard from the wife of actor Ryosuke Kagawa, who reportedly said after giving birth, "I thought it would be a funny-looking kid with rice all over its face or something, but what do you know, it was a beautiful little baby!" Itami was apparently very taken with the remark, which he also mentioned in an essay.[5]

The role of Setsuko Hara's lover went to Ryo Sayama, a handsome young art school graduate. This was his debut work, but the following year, illness forced him to retire.

On the release date of April 11, 1938, the movie opened at Nihon Theater. Itami and Saeki went together, but the grand theater held a mere scattering of viewers, whose response was so tepid that the two men emerged greatly downcast. As they stepped outdoors, Itami said, "Let's go have a drink." Ordinarily he was no drinker, and Saeki was a teetotaler who (on those rare occasions when he had any) sipped beer from tiny sake cups. Nevertheless, together they entered a nearby pub. Saeki recalls, "We sat and drank in silence, but it didn't taste good." That was the first and last time the two men ever went drinking together. Every time I hear the story, I feel sad yet again.

After that, Itami collapsed with tuberculosis and returned to Kyoto, making this the last movie he would ever direct. Since it marked the end of his career he hoped it would be a box-office hit or earn critical acclaim, but most reviews were harsh, like this one: "Okochi has been in a succession of turkeys, and this one by Itami is another clunker. It tries to be clever but goes too far, and trips on its own cleverness." Without a word in protest or in his own defense, Itami silently retired from the scene.

It seems to me now that, while the movie is set during the Satsuma Rebellion of 1877, Itami's intention was to convey to his contemporaries the difficulty of remaining true to oneself during a time of social upheaval, and the precious nature of love directed toward the poor.

The following year saw the Manchurian Border incident at Nomonhan, ending in a complete rout of Japanese forces by Soviet troops, while at home, the nationalistic Film Law of 1939 amounted to a priori censorship of motion pictures. The sound of tramping boots—Japanese militarism—was close at hand.

FACE TO FACE WITH DEATH

On the night of May 22, 1992, film director Juzo Itami was attacked by thugs.[6]

With great relief, I heard on the TV news that his life was in no danger. I calmed down and telephoned his sister Yukari, and together we rushed to the hospital. Already several live-broadcast vans were parked in front of the building, and clusters of reporters were standing around waiting.

Being the victim's sister, Yukari was naturally granted admission, and I tagged along in her shadow. The waiting room was packed with staff members of the Toho publicity department, all sitting in morose silence. An acquaintance came over and explained in a low voice that Itami was not yet out of the operating room.

Upstairs, in an anteroom next to the ICU on the third floor, Juzo's wife, Nobuko Miyamoto, lay curled on a couch. When we came in, she sat up and greeted us, but her face was gray and haggard. She was so tense that her head ached and she felt sick to her stomach, she said.

We spent hours waiting for the operation to end. In the meantime, investigators hurried in and out, and close friends and relatives came by to offer support. Each time someone came along asking questions or extending sympathy, Nobuko responded with a cold wet towel pressed to her forehead.

It was past midnight when word came that the patient would soon be leaving the OR and entering the ICU. His gurney came toward us surrounded by a team of white-clad attendants, all walking with an air of confidence. As they strode past, I caught a brief glimpse of Itami's face.

In movie parlance, the moment lasted barely two feet.

I had to marvel at the wonders of modern bandaging. Juzo's entire head, except for his face, was swathed in white mesh that was fastened at the top of his head in a point. All I could think was that he looked like a Welsh onion flower head, or maybe a kewpie doll. And so, disrespectful though it may sound, the sight of him evoked no sense of pathos in me.

His face was white, his eyes shut. As I watched the gurney trundle off, surrounded by his team of caregivers, I gave silent thanks that he was alive. I was able to follow his progress through television and newspaper coverage.

On September 8, 1992, the papers all devoted great space to the announcement of his newest film project, *The Last Dance* (Daibyonin, 1993), which treats the theme of death. What makes Juzo Itami productions truly outstanding, I think, is the way the director gives concrete expression to the most universal human problems.

He was quoted in *Sankei Sports* as saying, "I am now of an age when I think a lot about death, so I decided to make a movie about it." Naturally, having suffered such dreadful injuries, he must have contemplated his own death while in the hospital. He displayed presence of mind in taking a calm look at the subject, but it could well be that deep inside, he was struggling with his fear of dying.

For eight years, Juzo Itami's father, Mansaku, waged his own struggle with death. Although confined to a sickbed, he never eased the strict demands he placed on himself. However many times I reread his diary from that era, it never fails to move me.

> (September 9, 1941) This evening I felt a sudden premonition of approaching death, and shivered. My usual resignation was blown away, gone without a trace. Noticing that my legs are wasting away by imperceptible degrees, and recalling how my brother looked at the end, I felt the steady approach of an irresistible power. At the fear, or rather the measureless unease roused in me by this sensation, I felt a tremendous quickening of my heartbeat.[7]

The death of Mansaku Itami came as a huge loss to untold numbers of people. One small thing to be grateful for is that he lived beyond the end of the war, if only for one year. His diary entry for August 21, 1945, reads as follows:

> The moon tonight was clear. Profoundly struck by peace, I lost myself in wondrous thoughts. At night, unable to sleep, I worked on plans for the scenario study group. I turned the lights back on and drew up bylaws.[8]

The lines convey his welling excitement, close to death as he was, at the prospect of finally being able to write scenarios freely. But malnutrition caused by the privations of the immediate postwar era proved too much for his fragile health.

> (April 22, 1946) My temperature this evening went up to 37.8°C [100°F]. These recent fluctuations fill me with dark foreboding. I have spent a long time

sick in bed, struggling to support my family, but when my condition turns worse, I really feel sometimes that I have come to the end of my strength. Knowing this won't do, I try and try again to get ahold of myself. . . .[9]

Itami passed away at home on September 21, 1946. Kimi has shared with me her memories of that day.

Throughout his illness, Itami faithfully charted his pulse rate and temperature. That day, after the doctor had come by as usual to give him an injection, Itami unrolled the chart and made the latest entries, commenting, "My pulse line and my fever line have crossed."

Kimi had already been told that for the lines to cross was a bad sign. She bent down close over her husband to peer at the chart. All of a sudden he let it fall, reached up, and tried to put his arms around her neck, only for his strength to fail. Stunned, Kimi hastily telephoned the doctor, but he was not yet back at the hospital. Not knowing what else to do, she sent urgently for a local doctor, who came and administered first aid. When Itami did not revive, she sent her son off at a run to notify Mansaku's childhood friend, director Daisuke Ito.

In a reminiscence, Daisuke Ito wrote, "I held his wrist and found his pulse sporadic and weak. It gradually grew fainter, and then it ceased in my hand."[10] However, Kimi tells me that she does not think he arrived in time to witness her husband's passing. Time and the inconstancy of memory perhaps account for the discrepancy.

Hometown is
a place for dying—
autumn burnet.[11]

Ah, the chill—
the sound of rain falling
on my grave.

These are the last poems Mansaku Itami ever wrote.

2

Life in Miniature: At the Daiei Kyoto Studios

INSIDE A SMALL ARENA

The writings of Mansaku Itami contain numerous wise sayings that continue to resonate today. He once wrote:

> On your way to work in the morning, when you come to a place where the entire studio can be seen at a glance, stop for a moment and think about this: within that small arena, a whole lot of people are running around making a big fuss. How silly! When you understand the silliness of it all, your spirit can stand still while only your body goes on into the studio. (September 11, 1936).[12]

When I was commuting to Toho, there was a curve in the road just before the studio gate where I would brake and inevitably reflect on those words.

Mansaku Itami died in 1946, and after that a surprising turn of circumstances led to my being hired at Daiei Kyoto Studios as an apprentice script girl, or script supervisor in charge of continuity. This was in 1949. Ever since, I too have been making a silly fuss inside that "small arena." It is an arena of struggles, jealousy, joy, and anguish—a microcosm, to me, of human life itself.

My first day at work, a production staffer introduced me to a senior script supervisor named Emi Kimura. She was tiny, neatly dressed, with an alpine hat on her head—the very image of a pioneering career woman. She kindly showed me all around, explaining which section belonged to which director's unit. This was when I learned that unit names came from the director associated with them.

The great Daisuke Ito was busy filming *The Flower-Hat Flying in the Mountains* (Yama o Tobu Hanagasa). Emi was part of his unit, and she had me stay and watch, telling me it was the best way to get oriented. Although I can't remember anything about the film itself, the title is quintessential Ito, conjuring up the humorous image of a hat sailing through the air, its trajectory followed by a panning camera.

That day the set included a theater, and the camera crew was shooting someone in the upper-level seats from the seating area on the ground floor. Along came the star of the movie, actress Kogiku Hanayagi, all dressed up in a chic kimono even though she was not on call that day. She stood behind the camera, looked up at the actor being filmed, and started to tease him. Putting a hand to her mouth, she called out demurely, "Excuse me, what movie are you filming here?" The entire crew burst out laughing. To me she was dazzlingly beautiful. That one lighthearted scene is printed indelibly on my memory.

Emi supplied me with a stopwatch and pencil, and a folder full of script paper. These were our essential tools. The stopwatch was for timing the length of a take, and the paper for jotting down notes to send to the darkroom and editing room.

In the darkroom, the crew examines the negative while checking the continuity notes to learn that for one shot the third take is a go, for another the first, and so on. The desired takes are then arranged in proper order (of course, films are never shot in sequence according to the script). For obvious reasons of economy, only approved takes are made into work prints. The editing crew takes these and once again examines the notes to check details such as which lines are spoken in which cut, which actors exit after which scene, etc., before proceeding with their work.

This procedure is standard today, but back then in the Daiei Kyoto Studios, one stage was missing: that of making work prints. The negative containing successful takes was sent straight to the editing room without being printed first. Based on the continuity notes, the film editor would run through the reel, snipping away with scissors and splicing the cut ends. Only then was a positive print made.

This procedure was followed in a spirit of frugality. The work prints, also known as rush prints or dailies, were then previewed by the director and the rest of the staff in an edited format differing from the way they were originally shot. The rough edit from the pre-cut negative was even seen as a chance for the editor to show off his talents.

Shintaro Miyamoto, who was well known as a distinguished film editor in those days, would stand, wearing his hat at an angle, and dump the negative into the motorized Moviola Editing Machine while bellowing, "What is this!" It was certainly a rough way of doing things.

In 1950, when Kurosawa came to Daiei to work on *Rashomon*, the first time he saw the dailies made from this negative editing he was taken aback. His first demand at Daiei was that work prints be made with no pre-editing.

Within this pre-modern "small arena," however, some things happened that were so primitive, they were actually endearing. One example took place on a film whose name escapes me, although the cameraman, I remember, was Kazuo Miyagawa. There was a chase scene in which actor Denjiro Okochi was supposed to be galloping down a straight road along a riverbank. Having finished the long shots on location, filmed with a stand-in on horseback, the crew was now ready to shoot close-ups of Okochi's face on the set. Instead of a horse, he sat astride a carton covered with cushions. With nothing behind him but a clear sky, however, the great actor could twist and scowl all he liked—it still didn't look like he was riding a fast steed. To get the proper effect, there had to be movement in the background, as suggested by this line from the schoolchildren's song "Train": "Forests and woods, paddies and fields, one after another fly quickly behind."

At such times, it was the production assistants who were called on to save the day. Each one was handed a small tree, and they were told to run in a row past Okochi to create the needed background, maintaining an appropriate distance from one another. After passing in front of the camera, they would jog on around behind it, and then back into camera range once again. In other words, they would simply be running in circles around the stationary Okochi, but their movement would make it appear that he was indeed galloping along on horseback.

If each tree went by at a different speed, of course, the effect would be spoiled, and so each person had to maintain the same speed as the person in front of him. It wouldn't do for the branches to bounce up and down, either, and needless to say, nobody's head must pop into the frame. Around and around in a circle ran the assistant directors, the picture of solemnity, while I fell on the floor and doubled up, laughing until my sides hurt. Kazuo Miyagawa, looking through the lens, said with a grin, "You gotta love the movie business."

AN APPRENTICE

Old films now available on video include some I worked on around 1949–50 as an apprentice at Daiei Kyoto Studios. Teinosuke Kinugasa's *Koga Mansion* (Koga Yashiki), Daisuke Ito's *I Saw a Phantom Fish* (Ware Maboroshi no Sakana o Mitari), Taizo Fuyushima's *Demon Azami* (Oni Azami), Keigo Kimura's *A Fool's Love* (Chijin no Ai)—for me, familiar titles like these conjure up the aroma of miso soup in the studio cafeteria, the squeaking of boards in the corridor outside the editing room, the feel of the sofa in the production room.

The room where those of us on the continuity crew changed clothes and relaxed contained little more than lockers and often, on a small raised floor fitted with two tatami mats, piles of folded futon bedding. All-nighters were frequent: we were lucky if we could grab even a little sleep. I can even remember working around the clock for a week.

"You gotta love the movie business."

Daiei released 49 movies in 1949 and another 51 the following year. If movies by other Japanese companies are included, the totals are an amazing 156 for 1949 and 216 for 1950.[13] To meet the deadline for release, it was often necessary to create B and C units to divide the work of shooting the film.

Kinugasa's *Koga Mansion* had to be out by year's end, and so from the start it was shot with actor Kazuo Hasegawa in one unit and actor Yataro Kurokawa in another. Originally the picture was supposed to be made by Shin Engiza productions, home of stars Hasegawa and Isuzu Yamada, in a tie-up with Toho. But financial troubles at Toho and its sister company Shin-Toho had left Shin Engiza saddled with a debt of over one hundred million yen (approximately $300,000). The picture was being done with Daiei in exchange for their shouldering part of that debt.

According to Miyoko Akiyama, who worked as a script girl in the B unit, when production got underway on *Koga Mansion* the entire crew was assembled in the lecture hall to hear Kinugasa make a tear-laden plea. The gist of it was that because Toho had ceased production, Shin Engiza was at a crisis point; we were to welcome its members warmly and do all we could to support them.

Sometimes during lunch hour I would catch sight of Kazuo Hasegawa walking around the studio dressed as a mendicant Zen priest, complete with bamboo *shakuhachi* flute and wicker hat. I remember being surprised at how short he seemed in person.

Emi Kimura, my friend and mentor, had worked with him before, and one day she told me, "When I saw him again, he laughed and said it was weird to work with someone from the same company that had once hired someone to slash his face." In 1937, while still working under his early stage name Chojiro Hayashi, Hasegawa, though under contract to one major studio, left for their competitor, as did Kinugasa, and he was later attacked by a razor-wielding assailant. Besides scarring his face, the incident doubtless had a disturbing effect on his state of mind.

In any case, matinee idol Kazuo Hasegawa surely had the greatest sex appeal of any star of the day. A suggestive, sidelong glance from him had a powerful effect on women.

One time as Emi and I were heading back to our room for lunch, we ran into Hasegawa dressed as a beautiful young woman, with a train of attendants. He might have been in costume for *Travels of the Snake Princess* (Hebihime Dochu, 1950): he was wearing a bright red *uchikake* over-kimono with trailing skirts, holding the front up with one hand as he slowly made his way along, weighed down by the heavy garment. Impulsively, Emi cried out, "Hasegawa-san, how lovely!" He tilted his head coquettishly to one side, aimed one of those killer sidelong looks her way, and said, "What is, sweetheart? The kimono?"

In 1950, when I was working as a full-fledged script supervisor on the Taizo Fuyushima film *Demon Azami*, we went to a fishing village whose name I have now forgotten to shoot scenes aboard a boat. There was a festive mood there as the fisher folk turned out from early in the morning to watch the filming, letting their work slide. Fishing boats large and small, filled to overflowing with local families, trailed the location crew's boat. They made as much noise as a crowd of Hong Kong boat dwellers, calling out in shrill voices. Our boat, being bigger, picked up speed in an attempt to get away from them, but they followed along tenaciously.

Even at such a time, Hasegawa obligingly stood on the deck and bestowed flirtatious glances on the fishermen's wives, to their delight. When he swept the starboard boats with his gaze, rapturous cries rose up from that side, and when he did the same on the port side, identical cries could be heard from there. The scene was mesmerizing.

When he had finished treating the crowds on both sides of the boat, he said to us nonchalantly, "Well, whichever way I face, I guess I can't pee here!" I'm sure he wasn't seriously contemplating doing any such thing from the boat, but it was a good line.

To get back to my story, when I was a mere trainee I wasn't allowed to go along on location shots in outlying areas; I could merely see the bus off as it left. Even so, I was so busy in the editing room, helping to roll up film, carry it from one place to another, and so on, that I had no time to go home. It was all I could do to stretch out on the linoleum floor of the editing room with nothing but a flat cushion for pillow.

"Anybody want an injection? Philopon here!" When work went on around the clock for days at a time, production department staff distributed the then-legal methamphetamine philopon. A true story.

In the long, narrow editing room, various film crews worked crowded together around the editing desk, just like medics in a field hospital. One crew member, Taizo Kinugasa, had a special gift for working through the night. He would always sit crouched in front of the editing desk with one knee raised, turning film with his right hand; later, looking back, I used to think he resembled the witch played by Chieko Naniwa in *The Throne of Blood* (Kumonosu-jo, directed by Akira Kurosawa, 1957).

A lowly temporary worker like me made 120 yen (33 cents) a day, with nothing extra for overtime, as I recall. However, anyone who worked overtime got a boxed meal, and I was glad of that. Even when I wasn't working late, Emi would often bring a meal from one of the other units for me to take home, urging, "Go on, take it! No one cares."

When Emi came back to our room on lunch break, she would toss the script down with a tired sigh, swiftly roll up her sleeve and inject herself with philopon (a synthetic drug similar to "speed" or methamphetamine). I will never forget the look of sheer pleasure that came over her face as she injected herself. At the time, philopon was not yet banned, so people used it quite openly. When we worked through the night on successive nights, the production crew would walk around with trays of capsules and syringes, inviting us to help ourselves, or offering to administer the injection if we preferred. That is the absolute truth.

During the war years and immediately thereafter food was scarce, and yet the habit of working hard for a goal was deeply ingrained in us, which is perhaps why we lived the way we did.

EYES ON THE GOAL

The other day I had dinner with an old friend, actor Keiju Kobayashi. I felt a sudden surge of nostalgia when I saw him, and the feeling was apparently mutual.

Once, quite a while ago, I ran into him by chance in the Toho building where dubbing, or the final work on a picture's dialogue, is done. The corridor outside the mixing theater (where post-synch dialogue, or dialogue needing to be redone, is recorded after filming to synchronize with the picture) was filled to overflowing with actors awaiting their turns. As I pushed my way through them, with some other task at hand, I bumped into Kobayashi. We hailed each other with surprise and delight. He said, "This is like meeting a war buddy on board the repatriation ship." The expression could not have been more apt; he and I are true war buddies.

My promotion from apprentice to full-fledged script supervisor came in 1950, on the film *Resurrection* (Fukkatsu), written by Yoshitaka Yoda and directed by Akira Nobuchi, and based on the novel by none other than Leo Tolstoy. Katyusha was played by Machiko Kyo, then a budding actress with Daiei, while for the part of Prince Nekhludoff they called on Keiju Kobayashi, bringing him to Kyoto from the Daiei Tamagawa Studios. All I can remember of the film are certain images, like Miss Kyo's profile as she leaned against the iron bars of her cell dressed in soiled prisoner's garb, or how dashing Keiju Kobayashi looked in the uniform of a naval officer—nothing else. I do remember, however, his comment, "The only reason I was chosen for this part is that there are so few male actors around. They all went off as soldiers, and a lot of them aren't back yet." He always had a gift for making people laugh by telling the truth.

Director Akira Nobuchi, a trailblazer in the Western-influenced "new drama" (*shingeki*) movement in the Kansai region encompassing Kyoto, Osaka and Kobe, was well known for his work in the theater. He was also a former professor at Doshisha Higher Commercial School in Kyoto. He was always dressed neatly in a suit and fedora, looking something like a taller version of writer Kafu Nagai. I can close my eyes and see him slouching along pigeon-toed, a cigarette in his mouth.

In those days, Daiei Kyoto Studios still boasted not only the great Daisuke Ito, but an assortment of other directors, including Issei Mori, Taizo Fuyushima, Keigo Kimura, Kimiyoshi Yasuda, Bin Kado, Nobuaki Adachi, and, from the Shin Engiza troupe, Teinosuke Kinugasa. As noted above, the studio produced roughly fifty motion pictures a year, which worked out to four every month, or one a week. We might as well have been putting out a weekly magazine.

The studio was run with all the urgency of wartime munitions factories, where production was spurred under the motto "Better today's one airplane than tomorrow's two." Working through the night for successive nights happened all the time. Anyone who stayed up all night to work got a meal ticket for breakfast. Often I would go to the cafeteria in the morning and see the assistant directors sitting at the sink area off to one side with towels on their laps, washing their faces, brushing their teeth, and grousing about how many days this made away from home.

Breakfast was a simple affair, little more than a bowl of miso soup, but when standing in line and being served my steaming bowlful, I was always overjoyed at getting a free meal. At home was young Juzo Itami, his future still unknown; while I was working away through the night, what could he have been feeding himself, I wonder now. (Not that worrying about it at this late date will do any good. . . .) I can remember scraping together the remnants of boxed suppers and carrying them home like a mother fox for her kit, so I must have gotten food for him sometimes.

It wasn't only food shortages that we had to cope with. There was also a shortage of film stock due to a lack of raw materials: in 1947, production of negative film fell to a mere 2.5 million feet, and companies made up the shortfall by buying it on the black market. The following year, an increase in prices sent the cost soaring to 10.455 yen (29 cents) per foot; ironically, production was also increased and ended up outpacing consumption.[14] Even so, negative film remained a scarce commodity, so precious at Daiei that directors hardly dared call for retakes.

Motion pictures are of course made of images and sound, first recorded separately using different equipment and later printed together on one film. The key to synchronizing the two is the clapperboard: If the frame on the work print of the two pieces of wood hitting together is matched with the "clap" on the audio tape, dialogue and sound effects for the scene fall smoothly into place. But when things got really tight, producers begrudged even the two or three feet of film needed to record the clapperboard signal. Don't bother with it, they would say, we don't need it. Then the editors had to go to enormous pains to synchronize the actors' lip movements with the recorded dialogue.

As release dates were nonnegotiable, the primary burden of getting a film ready in a short time fell to those involved in editing and dubbing. If things looked hopeless, work would be divided among as many as three units. While the director in unit A worked on dubbing, other units would often be busy filming. When things got really hectic, it sometimes happened that music for a scene was recorded *before* the scene had actually been shot. When that happened, the length of the scene would be estimated, and white leader tape would then be spliced in as spacer. We called such inserts "ghosts." The composer would be told, "This passage has a couple of ghosts in it, one here and another here."

But when the "ghost" went on for a very long time, as much as several minutes, the composer needed help to visualize the scene, so we would draw in red or blue lines on the white leader tape and explain what they meant: "Where the red line is, there'll be a close-up of the two people. Starting from the blue line, there'll be a long shot of them starting to walk off." Composers back then worked under exclusive contracts with production companies, so

Explaining a still-unfilmed cut to the composer.

they were used to this sort of thing, but I have to say they did a marvelous job.

In 1950, MacArthur's "red purge" hit the motion picture industry and the Korean War broke out, with both events sending out great shock waves throughout society. Through it all, I worked doggedly in my small arena, struggling to get films into theaters on time, running around in circles with my eyes set on the goal.

BLACK-MARKET CIGARETTES

In his work *A Record of Two Sen (Nisen Ki)*, writer Hyakken Uchida (1889–1971) tells about a time during his boyhood when he was at a loss at finding himself two sen short of the train fare home from Kyoto to Okayama. After turning the problem over and over in his mind, he finally used what little money he did have to ride as far as Himeji. When he got off the train there he had a sudden brainstorm, and sold the books he was carrying to raise money for the rest of the trip. He lamented, now why couldn't I have thought of that in Kyoto in the first place?

In those days, as this story shows, if you lacked even one sen of the money for a train ticket, you were out of luck. To commute from the house where I cooked for young Juzo Itami to Daiei Kyoto Studios, I took the streetcar from Karasuma to Kitano Hakubaicho, changed there to the Kitano Line, got off at Katabiranotsuji Station, and walked the rest of the way.

One time, I dashed out of the house early in the morning to go to where a film was being shot on location in the city. Running to the streetcar stop, I felt around in my pocket for money and realized I was short, but leaped aboard anyway. I managed somehow to purchase the streetcar ticket (was it eight yen?), only to discover with dismay that I had nothing left over. When I got off at Hakubaicho, I had no idea what I was going to do next.

It was almost time to leave for the location site. By now the line producer would be poking his head inside the bus and muttering, "Where's that new kid? What the devil is the matter with her, can't she get to work on time?" I knew very well that he wouldn't hold up departure on my account, and the thought that the bus would leave on time without me was strangely reassuring. I decided to walk the rest of the way.

Casting a regretful, sidelong glance at the station beside me, I set off on foot. I had taken only a few steps when the red light of a corner police box came into my sight, like a lighthouse beacon on a dark night. Alone inside was a young officer, the very picture of a trusty public servant, seated writing at his desk. I rushed inside and told him I'd lost my wallet. On hearing of my predicament, he stood up with a genial smile and lent me ten yen from his own wallet. (Needless to say, I paid him back later.)

In such a tough world, I still have no idea how young Juzo managed to survive, left to his own devices as he was. Eventually the landlord requested that we move out, and we found new quarters in front of Katabiranotsuji Station. From there it was only a five-minute walk to the studio, so I had no more worries about train fare. We rented two second-floor rooms, so close to the station that if we poked our heads out the window we could make out the passengers' faces.

Rent was 900 yen ($2.50) per month. It was nice to live so close to the studio, but now I often invited people over after work to eat and drink, so my finances were perpetually strained. I soon became well acquainted with the neighborhood pawnbroker, taking almost all of my clothes there and forfeiting them in the end.

One day after the weather started to turn colder, I was sitting around at work with nothing to do for once, when a telephone call came for me on an outside line—a rare event.

"Surprised? It's me, Sachiko Ichida [not her real name]! You remember, from grade school? I'm here in Kyoto."

Satchan, as we always called her, had formerly lived near my house. Her father had worked for the national railway and her mother had taught at a well-known vocational college, so the family was well off; in contrast, my father had been imprisoned in line with the Peace Preservation Law of 1925–45, and my mother had barely managed to support us by teaching at a primary school.

After fourteen years, Satchan's voice sounded as cheerful as ever. She explained that her husband was a person of some influence with the occupying forces and that they had come to Kyoto to lay in supplies, their three children in tow. She laughed merrily as she told me all this, adding, "I've supplied all sorts of people with Western cigarettes. If you know anyone who wants Lucky Strikes, just say the word."

Listening to her chatter on about selling cigarettes on the black market, I couldn't help remembering a visit I had paid to her house years before: It was wartime then, and yet her family's shelves had been fully stocked with bags of sugar and boxes of soap. Even now, amid the general privation of the postwar era, she was evidently continuing to prosper. *If I'm nice to her, there might be something in it for me.* I cannot say that this base thought did not cross my mind. I told her I'd ask around to find people interested in cigarettes, and I invited her and her family to come over to my place.

In autumn 1950, a box of Peace cigarettes cost 50 yen (14 cents), and Hikari 40 yen (11 cents), but I cannot remember how much Lucky Strikes fetched on the black market. Still, plenty of my colleagues were interested, including my friend Emi, the directors, the cameramen, and others. We had to pay in advance, and so Emi took charge of collecting the money. In no time, we had amassed the sizable sum of 15,000 yen ($42).

Satchan showed up with two little boys and a baby. The four of them were accompanied by a man in a windbreaker—her husband, she said. He was dour and taciturn, but she made up for it by prattling and laughing gaily. She accepted the money and left, with instructions for me to meet her at one end of Shijo Bridge the next day at four in the afternoon, when she would personally hand me the cigarettes.

The next day, I arrived early at the agreed-upon spot. The

wind off the river was cold, and I soon regretted having come ahead of time. Four-thirty came and went, and still no Satchan. Thinking I might be at the wrong end of the bridge, I walked back and forth from one end to the other. Perhaps one of the children came down sick, I thought, and I stood waiting until after six, but there was no sign of her. Night fell, and the lights of the city winked on. Knowing Emi was waiting for me, I dragged myself back to the studio with a heavy heart. Emi heard me out and commented, "Hmm. Sounds to me like she pulled a fast one on you."

At that, my blood ran cold. I had entrusted that woman with a fortune in money from my coworkers and friends. All I could think was, *I have to get it back*. Borrowing train fare from Emi, I took off for the lodgings in nearby Otsu where Satchan had told me she was staying.

By the time I arrived, it was late at night. I walked around making inquiries to find the right place. When I finally tracked it down, I still half expected her to come rushing out with tearful apologies, but the man at the desk informed me that the guest by that name had checked out early in the morning. Hopefully I asked if she had left anything for me, but it was no use. How I made my way back to Kyoto I do not remember. In the end I had no choice but to travel to Tokyo and get my aunt to advance me the necessary money to pay everyone back.

While there, I went to Asagaya, hunting down the address for Sachiko Ichida that I'd been given at the lodging-house. When I finally found it, I opened the front door ready to explode with anger at my erstwhile friend, my mouth full of bile.

To my surprise, inside there was hardly a stick of furniture. The place looked abandoned. It was already dark out, but no lights were on. From the back of the house there emerged an old woman in a plain kimono. I could just make out her face in the dim interior: it was indeed Sachiko's mother.

After hearing me out, she said quietly, "Go ahead and report it to the police. My daughter was arrested in Numazu on a charge of absconding from a restaurant without paying her bill, and ever since, she's been running around to all her father's friends and acquaintances, using name-cards she took from his pocket, deceiving them into giving her money. As you can see, I have nothing left to offer you in amends."

Some years later, I spotted an article in a newspaper headlined "Woman Swindler Arrested," with a picture of Satchan.

3

Smiled on by Lady Luck: Rashomon

AKIRA KUROSAWA ARRIVES

In 1946, the year that Mansaku Itami died, producer Seiichiro Eida arranged for everyone in Tokyo with some connection to the man to get together in a pub and drink to his memory. Together we formed a society called "The Itaman Club." Members included haiku poet Kusatao Nakamura, whom Itami had called "Basho reincarnate"; Kiyoshi Saeki, Itami's chief assistant director; fledgling scriptwriter Shinobu Hashimoto; and many others.

A strange series of circumstances led Hashimoto, who was born in 1918 in Hyogo Prefecture, to embark on the career of scriptwriter under Itami's tutelage. As a young man, he had such radiant good looks that Mrs. Itami tells me his nickname was "shining prince Genji," after the title character of the Heian-era novel. Nonetheless, he had been sickly from childhood. Having suffered from pulmonary tuberculosis, intestinal blockage, diseases of the kidney, pancreas, and liver, and even bone fractures, he had been through major surgery time and again. Virtually no part of his body was left untouched—yet after each bout of sickness he made a full recovery, with all the resilience of a Rasputin.

Had he never come down with tuberculosis, however, Hashimoto might never have become the great scriptwriter that he is today. Indeed, the motion picture *Rashomon* might never have existed, either.

Among Itami's unfinished scenarios was one entitled *If*. In it, a samurai on a journey rushes to a ferry crossing but arrives a second too late, so the ferry leaves without him. The story develops from there, showing what would have happened if he had caught it in time. As that storyline showed, sometimes luck truly plays havoc with people's lives.

Hashimoto was drafted into the Tottori Fortieth Regiment during the war, but he soon came down with TB and was sent to the Disabled Veterans Sanatorium in Okayama, where tubercular members of the military were housed. He was put in a middle bed in a six-man ward. One day the soldier next to him handed him a magazine, saying, "If you're bored, try reading this." The magazine was *Nihon Eiga* (Japanese Movies), published by the Great Japan Motion Picture Association. In the back was a scenario. Hashimoto read it through and said to himself, "I could write one of these." Turning back to his neighbor, he asked who the top scriptwriter in Japan was, and was told, "Mansaku Itami." His roommate must have been an avid movie fan.

Transferred to a new ward, Hashimoto decided to write a scenario, but he had no idea what to write or how to begin. He went ahead and bought some writing paper, and at the top of the first page he wrote in bold letters, "Scene 1," followed by the name of the sanatorium, which was known informally as the "mountain sanatorium." He decided to do a portrait of the soldiers who came there, calling it *Mountain Soldiers*.

When he had finished, he sent it off to Itami in Tokyo. The reply he received came from Kyoto, however, to where Itami had retired after leaving Toho upon contracting TB himself. This was in 1941.

In his letter, Itami wrote frankly, "Your style is immature, and I see no sign of a gift for writing." But he added, "Yet there is something beyond these flaws." Hashimoto says he suspected that Itami's interest lay less in the scenario itself than in the new treatment for tuberculosis it described. Still, he was thrilled to have heard from Itami at all. He went to show the letter to his former roommate, only to find that he had already been released and sent home to Matsue. When he telephoned his home, he was told that the soldier had died three months before. The man who opened a door that fatefully changed Hashimoto's life never lived to see the outcome of his chance remark.

Hashimoto kept on writing scenarios and sending them to Itami for advice. His health gradually improved, and after the war he got a job working as an accountant for a bicycle company in Himeji. One day, having injured his back, he stayed home from his job and read works of the brilliant short-story writer Ryunosuke Akutagawa. Realizing that none of them had ever been made into a film, he decided to try adapting "In a Grove" (*Yabu no Naka*) for the screen.

He put his desk out on the veranda and began writing with such absorption that he never even noticed when it began to snow. In three days he was finished. He titled his script *Male and Female* (Shiyu). It was very short, only ninety-three pages of half-size writing paper.

Unfortunately, by this time Itami too had passed away. When Hashimoto went to Kyoto to attend a memorial service for his mentor, Mrs. Itami introduced him to Kiyoshi Saeki and told him that from now on, this was the person to whom he should send his scripts. Accordingly, he later sent a packet of them, including *Male and Female*, to Saeki in Tokyo.

Born in 1914 in Matsuyama, Kiyoshi Saeki attended Matsuyama Middle School, as did Daisuke Ito and Mansaku Itami. This connection led to his becoming Itami's assistant director. After Itami's retirement, Saeki stayed on at Toho as chief assistant director for Hisatora Kumagai and Yasujiro Shimazu. He also became friends with Akira Kurosawa, who was then chief assistant for Kajiro Yamamoto.

In 1941, Saeki was dispatched to Borneo as a member of the navy press corps, and he remained away from Japan until April 1945. In the interim, Kurosawa achieved great success with his directorial debut, *Sanshiro Sugata* (Sugata Sanshiro, 1943), a film whose reputation reached even Saeki overseas. When Saeki came back to Toho just before the end of the war, Kurosawa wrote a script for him called *Bravo! Tasuke Isshin* (Appare Isshin Tasuke) to demonstrate support for his friend's debut as director. But Saeki left Toho, which was beset by postwar labor strife, to join the breakaway Shin Toho company, and Kurosawa made *The Quiet Duel* (Shizukanaru Ketto, 1949) at Daiei.

After the two men went their different ways, in another trick of fate, they suddenly met again one day in front of the fountain at Toho Studios. Kurosawa mentioned to his old friend that there was talk at Daiei of doing a period piece, and asked if he knew of any likely stories. When Saeki mentioned the Hashimoto script, Kurosawa expressed immediate interest. The two men set off right away, walking over to Saeki's house. Kurosawa skimmed the script and asked if he could borrow it for a while. It was a tad short, he said, but it might have possibilities. Saeki agreed, and said that if the script seemed usable to let him know and he would have the author came up from Himeji.

In the course of time, Hashimoto received a postcard from producer Sojiro Motoki and made the trip to Tokyo. He stayed in Saeki's house and traveled to and from Kurosawa's house in Komae to work on the scenario. This is how Kurosawa met the man who would go on to write the scripts for masterpieces like *Ikiru* and *Seven Samurai*.

To lengthen his script, Hashimoto tried combining the story with another Akutagawa work called *Rashomon*, but the result was too long and less interesting than before. On top of that, Hashimoto's back pain returned, rendering him immobile, so in the end Kurosawa did the rewriting himself.

In 1950, the Daiei Kyoto Studios were abuzz with the news: Akira Kurosawa was coming. *Stray Dog* (Nora Inu, 1949) had just been released. With his regular entourage in tow, including producer Sojiro Motoki and actors Toshiro Mifune, Takashi Shimura, and others, Kurosawa swept into the studios with all the grandeur of the rising sun.

In our excitement, we rushed to the window, making comments like, "Look, it's really Akira Kurosawa!" and "I can't believe how tall he is!" as we watched him stroll around the lot with Mifune and the rest. Just walking around, he and the others exuded a kind of overawing vitality.

DANCING ON MOUNT WAKAKUSA

I wrote earlier about being cheated out of good money we paid for Lucky Strike cigarettes—an episode that underscores how popular Western cigarettes were back then. Here is director Yoshitaro Nomura talking in 1974 about the filming of *Scandal* (Sukyandaru), 1950):

> I was quite impressed that while our maestros [at Shochiku] all smoked Western cigarettes, director Kurosawa puffed away on a Japanese brand. [*laughter*] Then, after a while, Kurosawa turned to me and said he had run out of smokes, and did I know of any place nearby that sold Western cigarettes? [*laughter*][15]

I have a personal recollection in the same vein from the shooting of *Rashomon*. For location shots in Nara, we stayed in an inn at the foot of Mount Wakakusa. Directly above the assistant directors' room was the banquet room where the crew and actors all ate dinner. I was in the assistant directors' room for a meeting, and heard waves of laughter from overhead. Then we saw a cigarette come tumbling down; clearly, someone upstairs had stubbed it out and pitched it out the window. The misshapen butt landed on a stone in the garden, where it continued to emit a steady stream of thin smoke. Tokuzo Tanaka, the third assistant, looked at it and commented wryly, "Looks like upstairs they're smoking Western cigarettes. See, it doesn't go out."

The chief assistant then was Tai Kato, and second assistant was Mitsuo Wakasugi, who later joined the theater group Mingei.

Later, each of the three men would go on to become a film director with a unique style of his own. Kato, then thirty-three years old, was the nephew of the famous director Sadao Yamanaka. He joined the Toho Studios in Kinuta through his uncle's good offices and would go on to direct many superb yakuza movies; despite his undeniable talent, however, for some reason he and Kurosawa did not get along.

Before shooting began, the three of them called on Kurosawa, told him they found the script impenetrable, and asked him to explain it. Kurosawa answered by telling them that the script was about the very impenetrability of the human heart. From that point on, Kato began to drag his feet. He would show up late for a shoot or stand looking from a distance, a pipe in his mouth and a critical look in his eye. Still, it was he who affectionately bestowed on me my nickname, "Non-chan." It happened like this.

One day before shooting began, Kurosawa was playing a game of catch with Takashi Shimura. As I walked by, the ball came rolling right up to my feet. Wearing a piqué hat, a white T-shirt and jeans, his hand encased in a baseball mitt, Kurosawa waved at me to get my attention. "That's our ball," he called, and to Kato, beside him, he said, "What do you people call her?" I was still a newcomer with no nickname, so Kato was at a loss for a reply. On the spur of the moment, he mumbled, "Er, Non-chan. That's Non-chan." Lacking the strength to throw the ball from a distance, I picked it up, went over close to Kurosawa and then tossed it to him a bit shyly. He smiled at me in that charming way of his and said, "Thanks, Non-chan."

And from that moment on, Non-chan is what Kurosawa always called me. Peering through the viewfinder, he would call,

"Non-chan, bring me some water," or "Non-chan, haven't you got any ice?" My heart beating fast with excitement, I would run to do his bidding. (Later, of course, as my bloom wore off, he was more likely to yell, "Non! What do you think you're doing!")

Anyway, the Nara shots were in midsummer, and when I took Kurosawa his glass of water, the pungent smells of sweat and garlic would assail my nostrils. The garlicky smell was a leftover from the banquet the night before. Night after night, he ate a dish they called *sanzoku-yaki*, ("mountain bandit broil"), consisting of beef sautéed with garlic.

At that infant stage of my career, naturally I was not present at the banquets, but most of the rest of the crew, even teetotalers like cameraman Kazuo Miyagawa and lighting man Ken'ichi Okamoto, would join Kurosawa for a festive dinner. The practice became a hallowed tradition, partly because for Kurosawa, a banquet was a key venue for directing. Sometimes right in the middle of boisterous merrymaking he would make an important announcement of some kind, so you always had to be ready.

Miyagawa was a very scrupulous person. When he got back to his room after a banquet like this, he would carefully write down all sorts of data and notes on filming:

> Amid the forest blackness, I opened the lens as
> much as possible to gauge the brightness on-screen.
> Then I used eight mirrors (four feet square) to send
> extra light over the trees and over the cliffs, so that
> I could clearly capture the figures and the acting in
> black-and-white contrast.[16]

Rashomon was filmed in the virgin forest of Nara. The movie opens with a shot of Shimura as the woodcutter, proceeding deeper and deeper into the mountains with a hatchet over his shoulder.

Kurosawa loved using mirrors to reflect sunlight. But because the sun is in constant motion across the sky, the lighting crew had to scout out places where the sun was still shining and lug the heavy mirrors there across the sloping forest terrain. One late afternoon, Okamoto called up, "Kameoka, could you turn that mirror a hair more to the west?" The answer came down, "Yeah, I could . . . but the sun won't hit it." The soft drawl of the Kyoto dialect is pleasant on the ear, but to anyone from Tokyo it sounds slow and happy-go-lucky. With sunset fast approaching, the director bellowed in irritation, "Then for God's sake move it someplace where the sun WILL hit it!" His angry words echoed off the hills. Such incidents help explain why the Kyoto crew complained that Tokyo speech sounds too harsh.

The site where we were shooting had mountain leeches, we were told. They were not only underfoot, but could plop down on you from branches overhead to suck your blood; upon hearing this, we were literally shaking in our shoes. Every morning before setting out we smeared our necks and ankles with salt. Okamoto, however, said cheerfully that he would rather deal with mountain leeches than with snakes. One day as we were preparing to shoot a scene, all of a sudden he stared, pointed, and leaped up like a monkey. His face was ashen. He thought he had seen a snake, but it turned out that a cord dropped by the lighting crew had come sliding down the path. He got teased for being afraid of an electric cord, but there was no doubting that his phobia was real.

At night, when the reveling reached its peak, oftentimes

We were all young: dancing to "The Coal Miner's Song," far into the night.

Kurosawa and the rest would dash outside and race each other up Mount Wakakusa. At such times I would join in, puffing along behind them. Mitsuo Wakasugi wrote, "There was one time Tokuzo Tanaka and I raced in nothing but our underwear. Yelling 'Return to the wild!' or some such thing, he stripped down, and I rashly followed suit."[17]

When we had all reached the top of the mountain, we'd get in a circle to sing the folk song "Tankobushi" (Coal Miner's Song) and do the accompanying dance in the moonlight.

Tsuki ga deta deta	The moon is out
Tsuki ga deta	The moon is out
Miike tanko no ue ni deta	Over Miike coal mine
Anmari entotsu ga takai no de	The chimney is so tall that
Sazoya otsukisan kemutakaro	The moon must be smoky

That far, we danced in the style of the summer Bon dance, but from that point on we shifted to an energetic digging motion, like coal miners.

Everyone was young. Kurosawa himself was barely forty.

THE CAMERA WORK IS 100+

At the Kyoto studios, it was customary to address the director respectfully as "Sensei." It might be his first picture, he might be only twenty years old—it didn't matter. As soon as someone became a director, he was automatically given this title of respect. One day, however, Kurosawa banned the use of the word, insisting that he be called by his name. Conventions die hard in Kyoto, and at first people found it awkward to address him as "Kurosawa-san," but in time they got used to it and even felt closer to him because of it. This was only the first of many revolutionary changes he brought about at Daiei in Kyoto during the filming of *Rashomon*.

One such change I have touched on already: the editing of the work print. In those days it was customary not only at Daiei but at most companies to pre-edit the negative. The daily rushes were rough cut, but even so, "extra" material had been snipped away, and what we saw was in close to final form. I assumed that this was the proper way to edit a film. Undoubtedly, the main reason for doing it that way was to save money on work prints, and also to get a sense of the overall length of the film.

After filming on location in Nara, the crew of *Rashomon* all trooped back to the studios in Kyoto. The first dailies after a location shoot are always awaited with a special mixture of anticipation and trepidation. Cameraman Kazuo Miyagawa, who would be seeing the dailies alongside Kurosawa for the first time, must have really been on tenterhooks, as if awaiting judgment. But all of us were feeling nervous as we showed up in the preview room.

As it turned out, that day's viewing ended unlike any other. No sooner were the lights back on than Kurosawa tore outside and began lambasting producer Sojiro Motoki. Editor Shigeo Nishida, a good-natured elderly man, stood off at a little distance, listening with an air of anxiety. The rest of us filed outside, looking uncertain. Kurosawa was walking along, still giving Motoki a piece of his mind. Perplexed, I caught up with them, and heard the director say, "I never shot the scenes that way!" He was clearly upset. Turning around, he told me, "Print up the whole thing again, just the way we shot it."

The editor had simply trimmed the shots and assembled them in order as usual, but in so doing he had apparently altered them somehow. Kurosawa fumed, "Showing me something like that throws me all off!" He formally notified the company that from then on the dailies should be made without any changes and the editing be left entirely to him.

The location shots in Nara were the important scene where Takashi Shimura's woodman proceeds deeper and deeper into the forest, a sequence of shots whose rhythm was particularly difficult to establish. Subsequently Kurosawa re-edited the scene and finally pronounced himself satisfied. Today, editing the work print, rather than the negative, is universal standard practice.

Amid all this hoopla Miyagawa never got to ask what Kurosawa thought of his camera work. Kurosawa for his part had meant to praise the cinematography, but forgot to do so. Hearing from Shimura that Miyagawa was worried about it, he hastily declared, "One hundred percent. The camera work is one hundred! One hundred plus!"[18]

Another change he brought about had to do with sound recording on location. In those days, location shots were always silent, with no recorded sound. Even the camera they used on location was a primitive, hand-wound contraption; you could almost hear the cameraman protesting, "Who wants to lug a heavy battery so far? I'll just crank the darn thing myself." An assistant cameraman would attach a measure and crank to the motor, and then keep an eye on the gauge while turning the crank at the rate of twenty-four frames per second. If the shot lasted ten or twelve seconds that was one thing, but if it went over three minutes the assistant would be pouring sweat, his body bent double from exertion as he cranked along.

This crank-style camera was used on location for *Rashomon*, too—until Kurosawa banned it, saying he found it disagreeable. Of course, he had personal experience operating such a camera. In the dream sequence of *Drunken Angel* (Yoidore Tenshi, 1948), at one point Toshiro Mifune is given chase by his own ghost. While Kurosawa was shooting the open sea in the background, some good waves appeared, and with no assistant cameraman around, he took it upon himself to turn the crank—only to find it was extremely difficult to maintain a constant speed. Fluctuations in his feelings were conveyed straight to his hand, creating unevenness in the speed of the film. At the time, he declared himself pleased with the irregularity, but whether those shots made the final cut, I never knew.

To record sound on location, far from a hand-cranked camera, we needed a crystal motor to synchronize the image and sound. Even if the two were recorded simultaneously, little of the original sound was ultimately usable, and generally much of the dialogue would be replaced later. This procedure is still followed today, and it is quite practical. Until it was adopted, the recording crew was never taken on location. It created a stir when we first did it, but the company allowed it because the request came from Kurosawa.

The third technical revolution also had to do with sound recording. Back then the lowliest recording technician of them all was Ken'ichi Benitani. Today he is a superlative master of his craft, but then he was just a kid in a sweaty T-shirt, lugging a heavy battery. I always called him "Beniyan." Whenever he and I get together, we share endless memories of *Rashomon*, and one of the most notable has to do with the outdoor post-recording of additional dialogue.

Generally, any sound recording done after filming takes place in a recording studio, while the edited film is being projected. But Kurosawa declared that for voices heard from a distance, or loud shouts, you couldn't convey the proper sense of distance in a studio, and so we would have to do it outdoors. It sounded reasonable, but no one had ever done such a thing before. Confronted with this challenge, recording technician Iwao Otani wailed, "This is cruel!" Beniyan has vivid memories of the experience.

They erected a sort of screen in an empty lot out in back of the recording studio, and reflected the image from the projector on it using two mirrors. The mirrors were big ones we had used frequently during filming. One was fastened to the right side of the projector, and the other was set in the doorway of the projector room so that the image flashed from mirror to mirror and onto the outdoor screen.

"That was a real first," says Beniyan. "I'll never forget it. But in the daytime it was so noisy outside we couldn't do it. The trains on the Arashiyama Line made a lot of noise. So we had to wait till the middle of the night, after the trains stopped running, to get started."

That's right. His words brought it all back—the sight of Mifune and Shimura standing outside in the middle of the night, watching that screen and whooping back and forth.

Of the original *Rashomon* crew, few of us are left now. Beniyan suggested the other day that we all get together someday with Kurosawa to share our memories. Now that would truly be a gathering of war veterans.

SHOOTING THE SUN

It should surprise no one if I say that Akira Kurosawa knew all about movie cameras. He would consult with his cameraman and decide the structure of every shot himself, peering through the viewfinder and even selecting the proper lens. As a result, he always knew the precise limits of the frame, and had no trouble telling what was in the picture and what was not.

If we were shooting on a snowy day, for example, the rest of us would tiptoe around, careful not to make footprints in pristine snow, but he would stride fearlessly in front of the camera. Seeing the horrified looks on our faces as we gaped at the big footprints he had made, he would reassure us confidently, "Don't worry, this is all outside the frame." You had to marvel at the accuracy of his eye.

Perhaps because he had this reputation, people assumed that he loved cameras in general, and often—particularly when he traveled overseas—he would be presented with first-rate still cameras. But he had no interest in them. Kurosawa was something of an anomaly in that way, a modern man who never in his life clicked a shutter.

Later in his career, from *Seven Samurai* on, he became famous for shooting with multiple cameras, but in the beginning he used only one. *Rashomon* was shot with a single camera.

Cameraman Kazuo Miyagawa was another one who stayed glued to the finder from the time his camera was set up. Kurosawa would come and sit down alongside him, and from then on one or the other of them was always looking through it. Hei-san (Heizo Kondo), an assistant cameraman, used to complain, "When do I ever get a turn?"

To the end, Kurosawa would insist that his assistants look through the camera. "Come see!" he would yell. "Why put passers-by over there when they won't be in the frame? It's a waste!" Certainly the assistants did look through the camera, but it was no easy matter to develop an eye as unerring as Kurosawa's.

All of this is meant as prologue to a discussion of *Rashomon*. I think the beauty of *Rashomon* stems from the simplicity of its compositions and the exquisite sense of light and shadow it maintains. In an early scene the bandit, played by Toshiro Mifune, lies asleep under a large tree and awakens—when a gust of wind shifts the shadows of the overhead foliage—to see a woman passing by on horseback. (If only it had not arisen, none of the rest of the action would have occurred.) The shadows play across his chest as he pursues her with his eyes. The scene is beautiful, and ominous.

There is also the beauty of the scene where a beam of light falls on the woman as she rests her white horse in a ravine, waiting alone by the stream for the return of her husband. That scene was shot early in the morning, after Kurosawa happened to notice the ravine when we passed by.

Then the bandit returns, tells her that her husband has been bitten by a snake, takes her hand, and pulls her along as they hurry through the forest. On they rush, through the shadow and light of the surrounding trees. Usually this kind of shot is done with a dolly, the camera on wheels, all of us scurrying along trying to keep up. But Kurosawa rejected that approach because it wasn't fast enough. He insisted that the scene would work only as a panning shot. So he set up the camera, drew a circle around it, and had the actors tear around while the camera panned a full 360 degrees.

The completed scene shows the pair running at full tilt through the forest. Since Miss Kyo's feet did not show, he had her wear sneakers. The combination of sneakers with that ancient costume of hers was hilarious.

Akira Kurosawa loved the sun, and in his autobiography he discusses the role of the sun in *Rashomon*:

> One of my major concerns in filming *Rashomon* was how to capture the sun itself. This was necessary because the light and shadows of the forest would form the keynote of the entire film. I decided to resolve the problem by photographing the sun directly.[19]

At that time, cameramen were still afraid to film the sun straight on, fearing that the sun's rays might destroy the film in the camera. Miyagawa, however, boldly turned his camera up toward the sun, capturing wonderful images of sunlight filtering through the treetops.

The famous scene where the bandit grabs the lady and kisses her against her will was shot from many angles, including one from below showing the sun through the treetops in the background. To do the scene, the actors had to get up on something called an *intore-dai*. This is an easily assembled raised platform named after D.W. Griffith's 1916 film *Intolerance*, where it was first used.

The first Japanese film with a kissing scene was the Daiei production *One Night's Kiss* (Aru Yoru no Seppun), directed by Yasuki Chiba in 1946. Back then, that one scene was enough to pull in huge crowds, but since then the novelty of simple kissing scenes had worn off. Even so, Mifune appeared quite tense. He refrained from eating garlic the night before, gargled before the shooting began, and generally tried to be as considerate as possible. When the time came for him to plant his lips on hers, he first said, "Please forgive me," with an air of embarrassment.

When it was time to record her reactions, the camera had to be mounted on the *intore-dai* in order to capture her facial expressions from above. I remember Kurosawa standing up there and saying over and over, "Kyo-chan, open your eyes, keep them open wide!"

As the pair embraced, dappled shadows of leaves played on the sweaty shoulders of the bandit. So that the shadows would stand out clearly, members of the lighting crew stood with tree branches in their hands, waving them in front of the lights. For larger shadows they spread a net overhead, piled it with branches,

The epoch-making kiss scene from Rashomon, *with the camera tilted toward the sun.*

and then swayed it gently. Mifune's sweat was the work of the make-up crew, who scooped up water in their hands and splashed it on him.

The thicket where all of this took place—i.e., the scene of the rape-murder—was behind the temple Komyo-ji, near the Katsura Detached Palace in Kyoto. It started out as a small clearing surrounded by woods, but as the crew moved in with camera and lights, it was slowly transformed into a movie set. At first the crew would hesitantly ask permission every time they needed to lop off a branch or cut down a tree, but they soon went about their work in a matter-of-fact way, and eventually the clearing became a usable set. The temple's abbot was taken aback; he'd never before realized how much effort went into making a movie, he said. He gave the director a fan on which he had written the words "Benefit all living beings."

Shooting went remarkably fast, lasting from July 7 to August 17, 1950, or just forty-two days. When the weather was sunny we went to Komyo-ji, and when it was overcast we worked at the open set of the Rashomon gate at the Daei studios. Records indicate the reconstructed gate was some 33 meters (98 feet) wide, 22 meters (72 feet) in depth, and 20 meters (65 feet) high, and covered 1,980 square meters (2,368 square yards) on the ground. I can vouch that it was really huge—so big that if we had built the whole roof, the pillars could not have borne the weight. And so we destroyed half of the roof, which also helped bring about the desired effect of ruination. Standing under that gate, you could always get a cool breeze, even on a hot midsummer's day. During lunch breaks the carpenters used to nap under it in a row, like a fisherman's catch laid out on the beach.

For the scenes with Rashomon gate, Kurosawa wanted to create a downpour through which the gate would loom dimly in the mist, so three fire engines were kept stationed nearby to douse it with spray. No one foresaw how providential this would be.

THE NEGATIVE, GET THE NEGATIVE!

Looking back, it seems unbelievable: despite experiencing two major fires during production, we managed by some miracle to finish *Rashomon* on time. The official history of Daei describes it this way:

> Moreover, on the evening of August 21, just before completion of the film, unfortunately a fire broke out on the second stage of the Kyoto Studios, cast-

ing doubt on the scheduled release, but the crew members came together and worked so hard that the picture came out as planned. It premiered on August 25 at the Imperial Theater, sponsored by the *Yomiuri Shinbun* as a benefit for the Yukawa Foundation, and went on to be shown at Daiei theaters nationwide from the next day with overwhelming box office results. The fighting spirit shown by all concerned is a source of pride at Daiei.[20]

As noted here, the premiere took place only days after a major fire. Not only that, the picture premiered at the most glamorous venue in Tokyo. During the intervening three days, although it is not mentioned in this account, there was in fact another, smaller fire as well. Despite this spate of bad luck, we were able to scramble to meet the deadline. Perhaps our never-say-die determination harked back somehow to the spirit of the final days of the war, when everyone was supposed to be ready to drive the enemy from our shores. In any case, we somehow did the impossible.

A short circuit, we were told, caused the fire on the second stage where director Kimiyoshi Yasuda had been shooting *The Mendicant Monk Mansion* (Komuso Yashiki). Filming of *Rashomon* had wrapped the week before, and we were busy with the editing and synchronization of the music, sound effects and dialogue. I have no memory of just when or how I heard the cry of "Fire!" but I do remember the editing room quickly turning into a madhouse.

The reason is plain: people were editing the negative, with piles of it lying everywhere. In those days, we used nitrate film stock, which was flammable, so the whole room was a virtual tinder-

Rashomon *being saved from the fire. Its loss would have changed history.*

box waiting to explode. And the tenement-style wooden structure we were in, with a series of long, narrow rooms connected by a squeaky wooden corridor, was itself just so much kindling.

The spirit of cooperation was strong in the motion picture industry of those days, and as news of the fire spread, people from the nearby Toyoko Film Company (later Toei) came running. They dashed into the chaos of the editing room and swiftly helped carry out the precious film. In the midst of all this confusion, as people ran around like chickens with their heads cut off, I can remember Kurosawa himself towering over everyone else and bellowing, "The negative! Get the negative!"

Fire engines tore to the studios along the same route they had traveled so often before, this time with sirens wailing. The water tank on the open set was still full, and soon jets of water from the hoses were crisscrossing over the roof at full blast, just as they had during shooting. Once the film had all been carried out, we sat around at a safe distance and watched as the billowing white smoke and leaping red flames gradually subsided. Some girl assistants were crying hysterically.

Later, Kurosawa told me that at the height of the confusion he spotted a bit of negative on the floor, rolled it up and stuck it in his pocket. Then a security guard came along with the news that cameraman Miyagawa had collapsed at the gate. Kurosawa barked, "What do you mean, he's collapsed? Don't leave him there, get him to the infirmary!" When he reached the gate, Miyagawa was going on distractedly about a missing segment of negative. Kurosawa produced the rolled-up bit from his pocket, and Miyagawa exclaimed with delight, "That's it!"

Tokuzo Tanaka, then assistant director, has another story to tell. As he was running around in the aftermath of the fire he bumped into director Kurosawa, who abruptly said, with a strangely satisfied look on his face, "Well, there's no way we'll make the release date now." Having come from the Toho studios, he underestimated the determination of Daiei not to let a little snag like this interfere with a deadline. Soon he had to eat his words.

Rashomon was safe. Second assistant Mitsuo Wakasugi told me that he loaded the cans of negative on the back of his bicycle, went out to an empty field in front of the set, and watched the firefighting efforts. Kurosawa soon came walking along, looking glum. Wakasugi reached over wordlessly and tapped the cans behind his bicycle to indicate that all was well. Understanding, Kurosawa gave him a delighted smile of relief.

"The next step was harder," Wakasugi remembers. "Straightening it all out again." All the different batches of film in the room had been grabbed up and thrown in together, so everything had to be sorted out. "Mixed up with *Rashomon* was part of a movie called *Raccoon Dog Palace* (Tanuki Goten)," he recalls with a chuckle.

I was put to work alongside the assistant editors in the hunt for a missing piece of sound negative containing a bit of Toshiro Mifune's dialogue. It was the part where his character, the bandit Tajomaru, says, "I've never met such a tough woman." The search was complicated because unlike camera negative, sound negative gives you no visual clue—nothing but a pattern of stripes, like a bar code, so there's no way to tell what you may have without putting it into the Moviola Editing Machine and listening. Anyway, there we were with the premiere breathing down our necks, and we just couldn't find it. In the end, we had to have Mifune make a special trip back from Tokyo just to dub that one line.

Several years ago I spoke over the phone with Iwao Ohashi, the recording engineer for *Rashomon*. His voice sounding exactly the same, he marveled that "our" filming had been so many decades ago. The recording room had been just off the second stage, the source of the fire, he told me, so when the fire started he got flustered and threw the recording equipment out the door, smashing it in pieces. As a result, for dubbing he was stuck with an older model that was usually reserved for working outdoors. He lamented that the process didn't work very well. "No use whining," he told me, "but I wish it had come out better."

Whatever he may say, in my opinion the dubbing came out beautifully, a testament to hard work and dedication. Ken'ichi Benitani, a recording assistant at the time, recalls that the night before the dubbing they had an expert from Toyoko Film Company come over and work with them all night as they tried to put the smashed machine back together, to no avail.

With no time to catch our breaths, the day after the big fire we were back at work, rushing to get the film dubbed, when yet another fire broke out. Suddenly the picture on the screen froze; evidently the film was stuck in the projector. The next thing we knew, the center of the projected film frame began to turn black, a hole opened in it, and then it was in flames. All of this showed on the projection screen. "Another fire!" we shouted, and scrambled outside. Smoke billowed from the projection room.

As before, everyone scurried around, carrying bits of the film to safety. Benitani and some others, feeling like old pros, formed a bucket brigade to throw water inside the burning room, but this turned out to be a mistake: the nitrate film stock then released a poisonous gas, filling the room instantly with clouds of noxious smoke. Otani and Benitani both had tears streaming from their eyes and saliva drooling from their mouths, and suddenly they fell down, unconscious. When they came to, they were lying on straw mats outside the infirmary, along with many others.

There was nothing to do but start the dubbing all over again. Back then there was no tape, so all the music was recorded live as the picture was projected. If anything went wrong, it meant starting again from the top. The famous segment reminiscent of "Bolero" went on for a whole ten minutes. I can remember looking at the backs of director Kurosawa and composer Fumio Hayasaka as they sat and listened without stirring. When it was finally done, Kurosawa looked at Hayasaka with apparent satisfaction. By then, it was already morning.

After an all-night recording session, I accost composer Fumio Hayasaka.

LADY LUCK

Today's youngsters will unfortunately never know the thrills we experienced dubbing movies in the era of *Rashomon*. Time spent recording the music was filled with special intensity: a mistake by one person meant starting all over again from the top, or just gritting your teeth and letting it go. Today you can say, "Okay, we'll take it from a few bars back. Connect it where the drum comes in," but not back then. Nowadays editors use tape with abandon, cutting and splicing all they please. Do they have any idea how lucky they are, I wonder? The difference between having and not having tape is about as dramatic as the difference between before and after the light bulb.

Nowadays a two-inch tape has twenty-four tracks, divided by instrument, so with a flick of the finger you can adjust the sound any way you want, increasing the volume of the chorus, say, or eliminating the piano. All of the orchestra members don't even have to show up at the same time. If people's schedules don't match, there's no reason different parts can't do their recordings on different days.

Back in the old days, all of the musicians had to show up at once. As the scene requiring music was shown on a big screen, the conductor kept watch, synchronizing the movements of his baton with what was unfolding before him. Since the musicians had their eyes on the conductor, naturally they were sitting with their backs to the picture. When a love scene came on, those with nothing to do at that moment would twist around in their chairs to watch.

Bear in mind, this was an age when each company put out four motion pictures a month. The musicians worked for different companies simultaneously, wandering from place to place with their instruments in hand, and often working nights at a cabaret to boot. Many were old foxes who gambled on cards and horses when no one was looking.

They held Hayasaka in awe, however. Once, during the recording, one musician asked him, "Isn't there something wrong with this part?" Hayasaka retorted, "No, there's something wrong with your head."

Once the recording for *Rashomon* was done, everyone stepped out of the room, rubbing their bleary eyes and saying "Look, it's morning." I went outside and found Hayasaka sitting in the coolness of the summer dawn, smoking a cigarette with evident enjoyment. Going over to him, I had the boldness to say, "Listening to that Bolero music, it sounds as if the woman is being held in contempt"—as if I knew what I was talking about. He listened and said only, "Is that so," with what actually seemed to be a contented smile.

At the time, I was immensely drawn to Hayasaka, which is probably what led me to say such a thing. "Is that so" was a pet expression of his, and even when some busybody went and told him I had a crush on him, that was all he said. Unfortunately, I was quite beneath his notice.

As I mentioned earlier, one segment of dialogue by the bandit Tajomaru was mislaid in the confusion caused by the fire, and actor Toshiro Mifune had to make an emergency trip back to Kyoto. His whiskers now gone, he showed up at the dubbing room looking dapper, and said sympathetically, "Well, you've had quite a time of it, haven't you?" According to recording engineer Iwao Otani, his line, "I've never met such a tough woman," was added during the recording of the music, using a separate microphone. That's how desperate a state we were in.

Although the August 25 premiere at Tokyo's Imperial Theater loomed dead ahead, the fire on August 21 paralyzed the studio. Then on August 22 we experienced the smaller fire in the projection room in which Otani and his assistant Ken'ichi Benitani were knocked senseless by poison fumes. It really seemed as if God was testing our endurance.

Today I wonder: How on earth could we have made the release deadline? Did we force Otani and Benitani to revive, and then start dubbing that very night? Even assuming we set to work on the morning of August 23 and worked straight through the night, it would have taken at least until noon of the following day to record all the music. A car must have been parked idling outside the recording room, ready to take off at an instant's notice for the processing room. As soon as the shout went up, "Here it is!" the courier must have grabbed it, yelled, "Okay, I'm off!" and torn off posthaste for the darkroom.

The first print was ready at around seven that night, I believe, but for the life of me, I cannot remember sitting down to preview it with the director and staff. After working around the clock for the better part of a week, I must have been pretty woozy. In any case, there was nothing for it but to send that print off to Tokyo overnight. The job fell to assistant director Tokuzo Tanaka, who boarded the last night train and headed for Tokyo with a fresh print in his lap. If it had been a movie, music would have swelled up, overlapping with the train whistle as he departed.

Early on the morning of the twenty-fifth, Tanaka arrived in Tokyo and went straight to Daiei Studios, where President Masaichi Nagata and other executives were waiting. An immediate pre-screening was held. Later, Tanaka described the scene this way:

> After the pre-screening, the lights came back on, and nobody said a word. Usually this was when somebody would say, "This picture'll do well," or "It'll be a hard sell," or that sort of thing. Not this time. The room was hushed, all of the executives trying anxiously to read the boss's face. After a while, he opined, "Well, I don't get it . . . but it certainly is a high-toned picture." Just like that, the screening room filled with its normal buzz and chatter.[21]

And so, one hour after its preview at the home studio, having been completed as if by a miracle, *Rashomon* premiered at the

Imperial Theater in Tokyo and was released nationwide the following day.

Reviews were not favorable, however, and it looked as if the movie was destined to create only a brief stir before fading into oblivion. That might well have happened had not the Japan representative of Italiafilm, Giuliana Stramigioli, chanced to see it. Thanks to her enthusiastic endorsement, in September 1951 *Rashomon* was entered in the Twelfth Venice Film Festival, where it won the Grand Prix. This electrifying news provided inestimable encouragement and inspiration to Japanese in the postwar era.

It is well-known that Daiei president Nagata, on being informed of the picture's success, said wonderingly, "What's a Grand Prix?" He wasn't alone; nobody knew. Kurosawa himself never even knew that his film was in competition until it won. His next picture, *The Idiot* (Hakuchi, 1951), shot at Shochiku, had been so badly received that Daiei rescinded permission for him to shoot his next picture with them. Kurosawa, full of bitter disappointment, decided to go fishing, but the first time he tried to cast his line it caught on something and snapped. Feeling like the whole world was against him, he went home in a dark mood. When he opened the door, his wife said, "Congratulations!" and told him the news about the Grand Prix.

He commented, "Thanks to that award, I was spared from having to eat cold rice [i.e., be shunted aside]."

Not everyone connected with the picture basked in its glory. Some, like assistant director Mitsuo Wakasugi, went into limbo. Just after the release of *Rashomon*, Wakasugi was forced out of the film company in a "red purge," and expelled from the labor union as well. Just as colleagues were distancing themselves from him and he found himself suffering in isolation, he received a postcard from Kurosawa:

> It said, "This is the perfect chance, so write a scenario. Don't be afraid of failure." I was so happy, I broke down and cried like a baby. I thought, I'm still in the movie business. In that trying time, he was the only one in the movie business who gave me any encouragement.[22]

Wakasugi's "purge" must have struck a chord of sympathy with Kurosawa, himself a survivor of the labor strife at Toho.

After winning the Grand Prix, Kurosawa was in demand from all sides. The following year, in 1952, he went back to Toho for the first time in four years to make *Ikiru*.

FAREWELL TO KYOTO

The year 1950 was a tumultuous one in the Japanese movie industry. It was also, of course, the year of the outbreak of the Korean War.

In May, Toho dismissed 1,300 people from its payroll. General MacArthur's official notice of a purge of Communist elements quickly took effect nationwide, and in September, Daiei also sent out pink slips to thirty people. Meanwhile, another twenty-nine members of the film industry previously purged as war criminals were now happily "de-purged," and they returned to work one after another. It was interesting to see the two groups switch places.

The official history of Daiei contains the following description:

> Our company quickly published the names on the twenty-fifth, and except for those involved in filming, from that day on their access to the studio was denied. From then on Daiei faithfully kept its pledge, not allowing the invasion of any destructive elements, and cooperating internally as well.[23]

I'll never forget a scene I saw then, exactly like something from a movie. On either side of the tightly closed main gate, people who had been work colleagues the day before stood with their arms reaching out, grasping and thrusting, jostling and tussling with each other. I walked by at a distance, pretending not to see, but deep down the sight left a lasting sense of shame.

After *Rashomon*, the next movie I worked on that year was Taizo Fuyushima's *Demon Azami*. This was the seventh picture made at Daiei by actor Kazuo Hasegawa, who had joined Daiei the previous year on the picture *Koga Mansion*, with the rest of the Shin Engiza people.

Fuyushima started out as a scriptwriter, and he apparently wrote a lot of scripts for Hasegawa when he was still a budding actor known as Chojiro Hayashi. He knew a lot about Kabuki theater. He could only have been fifty or so, but to me he seemed like an old man. He walked with a shuffle, and his voice was weak. With skin as fair as a Caucasian's, thick hair, and lustrous black eyes, he was handsome, but there was something gloomy about him. Cameraman Kohei Sugiyama, on the other hand, was stylish and cheerful. While testing his panning shots on location, he would say, "After all their practicing, suppose they do the scene and finally get an OK on it, and then I tell them, 'Oops, forgot to turn the camera!' That would be just great, wouldn't it?"

In those days, shooting with a Mitchell camera was tricky. After looking through the viewfinder lens you had to slide the camera body laterally back in front of the shooting lens, or nothing would be filmed.

From the first of the following year, 1951, I began working on Issei Mori's *Ashura Hangan*. Mori was from Matsuyama, and so sometimes when we happened to meet in the studio we'd chat about Mansaku Itami and one thing or another. Mori was a big bear of a man; I remember fondly how he used to come lumbering down the corridor. Though you'd never have guessed it from the size of him, he was actually quite shy. Whenever we talked he had a habit of blinking and pursing his lips.

"When I got accepted into Kyoto University, I came in number two. Number two, you got that?" he would say, and then add with that shy laugh of his, "Of course, that year there were just two of us in aesthetics."

When it came to making a movie, though, he was a different man, quick-thinking and decisive. He had a knack for shooting a movie quickly. To save time, he would do all the shots with the same background at once, so he easily managed fifty shots a day.

"Ready, action. OK. Skip the next scene. Ready, action. OK. What? It's all right, it's all right. Skip the next two. Ready, action. OK. Now a long shot. Next. Ready, action. OK." He kept up such a fast pace, there was barely time to change the numbers on the clapperboard. Since I was from Tokyo, sometimes he would tease me by deliberately adding a little Tokyo flavor to his speech as he went along.

Ashura Hangan, based on Eiji Yoshikawa's novel *Ooka Echizen,* about a famous judge, featured three major stars: Denjiro Okochi in the title role, Kazuo Hasegawa as the shogun Yoshimune, and Takako Irie. In the course of the movie, there was a love scene between Denjiro Okochi and Takako Irie. Some love scene—it consisted of no more than Okochi lying down beside Miss Irie. Even so, Okochi was hugely embarrassed. As soon as the director called, "Cut," he jumped up and gasped, "What took so long!" The entire crew burst out laughing.

Not long after that, Daiei was shaken awake by a huge piece of news. On September 12, 1951, every newspaper in Japan carried the flash that *Rashomon* had been awarded the Grand Prix overseas. Here is an excerpt from the write-up in the evening edition of the *Mainichi Shinbun*:

> (Venice, Sep. 10, UP) The Japanese film *Rashomon* (a Daiei film directed by Akira Kurosawa), which was entered in an international film festival currently being held in Venice, received the Grand Prix (the highest award) on the tenth.... *Rashomon* was released on August 23. Former British prime minister Winston Churchill put in an appearance at this event while on vacation, and is said to have praised *Rashomon* lavishly.

Famous directors from Daiei Kyoto Studios. All of them are now gone. Clockwise from top left: Daisuke Ito, Kenji Mizoguchi, Akira Nobuchi, Taizo Fuyushima, Issei Mori.

The studio was in an uproar. Even a nobody like me was showered with congratulations by everyone I met: "Good for you!" "What a terrific prize!" "How wonderful!"

Orders for *Rashomon* came pouring in to Daiei from far and wide, and soon it became necessary to do a special dubbing for an overseas edition. We were set to re-record the music at the Daiei Tamagawa Studio, and for that I would have to go to Tokyo.

One other factor contributed to my decision to go back to Tokyo. Around that time my colleagues had been cautioning me against crossing any forbidden boundaries with Issei Mori, whose wife was a former script girl and our senior. Never do anything to upset her, they stressed.

When I told Mori that I would be returning to Tokyo, he stared at me and said he was going there, too. He would be shooting *Vendetta of Samurai* (Ketto Kagiya no Tsuji, 1952), with screenplay by Akira Kurosawa, for Toho. "It's all settled," he told me.

Later I, too, joined Toho, but I never worked with Mori again.

In 1951, young master Juzo had gone home to Matsuyama, entering Matsuyama East High School. His fellow alumnus, writer and Nobel laureate Kenzaburo Oe, once gave me this description of his friend during his schooldays: "He always wore a short cloak, and looked like [French actor] Gerard Philipe." It gives me pleasure to imagine what a dashing figure he must have cut.

Just before New Year's 1952, I left Kyoto.

And so I bade farewell to Uzumasa, the neighborhood of the Daiei Kyoto Studios. Looking back now, I feel warm nostalgia for all the people I worked with there.

4

Toho Paradise

THE FOUNTAIN

I left Kyoto. Walked away from it all—the kimonos in the pawnshop and the annoying gossip alike. But my time there, just over a year and a half, had a decisive impact on the rest of my life. Raw beginner though I was, thanks to Mansaku Itami I was able to participate in the making of *Rashomon*. That led to my switching to Toho. Then from *Ikiru* (1952) through *Madadayo* (1993), I remained a constant member of Akira Kurosawa's group. Life really can surprise you.

Having said that, in defense of Kurosawa's honor let me quickly add that I did not go to Toho to work on *Ikiru* at his beckoning, having bowled him over with my contribution on *Rashomon*. It wasn't like that at all. Instead, while I was helping at the Daiei Tamagawa Studios with the re-dubbing of *Rashomon* for overseas distribution, composer Fumio Hayasaka showed up for the music recording and said, "I hear Kurosawa is making a movie with Toho next. If you want, I'll put in a word for you with them."

Soon after the *Rashomon* dubbing was completed, I paid a call on production manager Kazuo Nishino at the Toho studios in

Kinuta, a neighborhood in Tokyo's Setagaya Ward. The studios are rich in history, having been used to produce one fine movie after another ever since 1933 (when they belonged to Toho's forerunner, PCL), and also having been involved in the postwar labor disputes.

Kurosawa wrote in his autobiography, "From seeing a picture of a white building with palm trees in front of it, somehow I thought the studios were in Chiba on the coast." Indeed there were several palm trees on the lot, giving it a rather tropical air. It humbled me to think that Kurosawa must have taken his examination for entering Toho at this same location.

In the center of a plaza in front of the stage there was a fountain. Well, we called it a fountain, but I have no memory of ever having seen it spurt any water. There was a pool of water in it, though, and its circular stone edge was a fine place to sit down. With grass around, it was a pleasant place to sit and bask in the sun.

There is a photograph from the early days of Toho showing Toshiro Mifune, Yoshiko Kuga, and other young actors of the day grouped around the fountain, eyes sparkling and arms extended skyward. There is also a photograph of Kurosawa seated there alongside his mentor, Kajiro Yamamoto. Still an assistant director, I think, Kurosawa is wearing his favorite alpine hat and overcoat, looking down with a smile at a book spread open on Yamamoto's lap.

Kurosawa later told me that in the old days, prominent artists like Yasujiro Shimazu, Mikio Naruse, Sadao Yamanaka, and Mansaku Itami used to gather at the fountain to chat. "No wonder they made good movies back then," he reminisced.

Kazuo Nishino rarely smiled, and when I passed him in the

"How about forty thousand a picture?" Jumping at the chance to work at Toho.

studio his way of greeting me was to stick out his chin and grunt. I always thought him rather frightening, although in time I came to realize that he was surprisingly sweet. The first time I ever met him he grunted, motioned for me to follow him outside, and then sat down by the fountain. After inquiring about my personal situation and so forth, he said, "What do you say to forty thousand yen ($111) a picture?" He was from Kyushu, but like many people in motion pictures back then he often spoke in Kyoto dialect. Of course, I jumped at the offer. After all, at Daiei my monthly salary had been only one-tenth as much.

I sat there by the fountain where doubtless Director Itami had also sat in his day, and looked up at the sky. Toho seemed like paradise. This was the winter of 1951.

In March of that year, Toho worked out a revised labor agreement with Zen'eien (National Film and Theater Labor Union).

Soon afterward, directors, actors and cameramen from the splinter company Shin Toho began returning in rapid succession.

Producer Masazumi Fujimoto, who had been blacklisted and was working independently, was de-purged and quickly brought back to Toho on the condition that Kon Ichikawa of Shin Toho be brought over to direct a New Year's movie. Although he had started his career at Toho, Ichikawa had later transferred to Shin Toho, becoming an overnight success with the smash hit film *Three Hundred Sixty-five Nights* (Sanbyaku-rokujugoya). Ichikawa's New Year's release for 1952 was a comedy called *Wedding March* (Kekkon Koshinkyoku), produced by Fujimoto, written by Toshiro Ide and Natto Wada (Ichikawa's wife), and starring Ken Uehara, Hisako Yamane, and Fubuki Koshiji—an all-star blitz for the New Year.

My first official work with Toho was on *Wedding March*. Script girls usually work steadily with the same director, but when Ichikawa came over to do this film he had no regular script girl, and so I, the newcomer, got assigned to do the job.

This was not my first encounter with Ichikawa, who had served as third assistant director or so on Itami's *Gonza and Sukeju* (Gonza to Sukeju) in 1937. Once when I asked him to describe what Itami was like back then, he said, "He scared me silly." Kiyoshi Saeki, Itami's chief assistant, scratched his head and said he could never understand why Kon Ichikawa had found Itami so intimidating.

Once Ichikawa got an actor's costumes mixed up. Fearfully, he went up to Itami to apologize, and was told, "No need to say anything. That was the director's responsibility." Hearing of this episode, I was deeply impressed at Itami's kindness, but Ichikawa wouldn't back down, insisting, "He was a scary man."

Actually, in the course of shooting *Wedding March* I made a similar gaffe. It was a scene where Fubuki Koshiji enters a party from another room. Unfortunately, I had her showing up at the party wearing a different outfit from the one she'd been wearing in the other room. When I saw the discrepancy on the dailies, I was shocked. The blood drained from my face. Re-shooting the party scene would be horrendously expensive. Still, Ichikawa had to be told—so I hurried out of the projection room to find him, feeling crushed.

He was smoking a cigarette, huddled with his cinematographers. They were going over the party scene, I realized; something about it bothered Ichikawa, and they were intensely debating whether or not to do it over. Finally they decided to shoot it again.

I gave an inward shout of joy. The wardrobe supervisor and I held hands and thanked our lucky stars that that dumb mistake would never see the light of day. Not long ago, I told Ichikawa about this episode and asked him if the statute of limitations had run out on my offense; he replied that he'd never noticed a thing. Later, I realized that Ichikawa would often shoot a scene many times over, but that was one time I can never forget.

His movies always had a certain flair, which he unfailingly attributed to his wife: "That's because Natto has such an ear for dialogue." In *Wedding March*, he sought to have everyone speak their lines quickly. "Faster, faster!" he would shout, as if cheering them on at a sporting event. I seem to recall spending all my time with a stopwatch, ticking off seconds. Never before had there been a Japanese film of such swift tempo, and it took critics by surprise.

SCRIPT SUPERVISOR

My blunder with costumes in *Wedding March* was fortunately kept quiet. Had word of it gotten out so soon after my hiring, I would have lost all credibility. It was a close call.

While mistakes with props and wardrobe are the responsibility of whoever is in charge, in the end it all rests on the shoulders of the script girl, or script supervisor, who does a final check before shooting begins. For her, continuity is a life-and-death issue.

Many readers, I am sure, will already have a very good idea of how movies are filmed, but for the benefit of those who may not, let me explain what continuity means and why it is so crucial. I'll start by describing the work of the script supervisor or script girl. (The latter job title, incidentally, is a misnomer, as most of those who do the job have long since left girlhood behind.)

In the old days, shooting on location meant that whoever was in charge had to tussle with crowds of onlookers, struggling to keep them behind ropes while shouting, "Visitors, please stay behind the line!" (They were never addressed as mere "sightseers" but always as "visitors," with the implication that they were perhaps there on some sort of a study tour, which was ridiculous.) These studious visitors of ours would always ask the same questions: "What actors are in this?" "What's the name of the movie?" Sometimes a title could sound embarrassingly risqué, but whoever was in charge would be stuck repeating it over and over again, blushing all the while.

Finally it would be time for shooting to begin: The director's voice rings out: "Ready!" An assistant director holds up the clapperboard in front of the camera, and the recording technician recites numbers into a microphone: "Scene 10, Cut 5, Take 1."

The director calls, "Action!" and the camera rolls. The assistant director brings down the hinged stick on top of the clapperboard with a loud bang, and makes himself scarce. The actors go into motion and say their lines—perhaps something like this:

> WOMAN: Call me when you get there, okay?
> MAN: Yeah.

The director then says either "Cut, print" or "Cut, let's do it again."

Even for a scene as short as ten seconds, if things don't go just right the actors can end up repeating their lines dozens of times. Onlookers grow restless. "They're just doing the same thing over and over, how boring," they complain, and start to drift away.

This is what it's really like to make a movie. No matter what the script says, it is impossible to shoot scenes in the order they're written. Each scene is divided into a certain number of cuts; in all, a movie may contain anywhere from three hundred to eight hundred cuts. The shooting order depends on factors like the angle of the sun, the condition of the lighting equipment, the actors' schedules, and so on. Basically, the goal is to make the movie in the most cost-effective way possible.

The exposed film is developed into a negative in the processing room, outtakes are deleted, and only then are the accepted ("OK") takes assembled in correct order, now becoming the work print. Outtakes we call "NG," for "no good." The only way to tell which takes are NG and which are OK is to check the dispatch from the script girl, which contains the identifying number and length in seconds of each take, and the notation "NG" or

"OK." Sound for the OK scenes only, recorded on 1/4-inch magnetic audio tape, is transferred to 35mm film and taken to the editing room, where the sound and picture are synchronized and the rushes are thus readied for viewing.

The clapperboard plays an essential role in synchronization. The bottom of it is a slate on which the numbers of the scene, cut, and take being filmed are written in chalk to serve as visual identification. The device gets its name from the hinged wooden clapper on top which the assistant director brings down smartly at the start of the take. Matching that action with the corresponding sound ensures that the rest of the scene will fall automatically into synch as well. It doesn't have to be the clapperboard, of course; in principle, slapping your forehead would work just as well.

The rushes are the raw footage; the skill with which each shot is connected to the next depends on the art of the editor. Here again the continuity dispatch comes into play, as it is the job of the script supervisor to report the content of each take so that the editor, who knows nothing of the shooting conditions, can understand it. Detailed information is included, such as who says what dialogue, who leaves the frame at the end of the shot, and so on. Sometimes there will be a direct message from the director, telling which shot to use.

Akira Kurosawa's editing was exceptional, the inimitable work of a genius. He never looked at any dispatch, but remembered everything himself. No one was a match for him. It sometimes happened that he filmed each shot in a scene in a completely different place. For example, a shot of someone walking toward a window could be filmed on location in Gotenba, Tokyo, a shot of the same person looking down out of the window could be shot in the southern island of Kyushu, and a shot of him turning around again could be done back in the studio. A sequence of shots could be separated by time as well as space: The Kyushu shot could be summer, the studio shot, midwinter. When the shots were finally assembled, if the character was wearing glasses while at the window but not when he turned around, the effect would be ludicrous. This is why continuity work is so important.

Over the years I have committed many sins of this nature, but one I will never forget took place on the set of the 1958 Kurosawa film *The Hidden Fortress* (Kakushi Toride no San Akunin). In the opening scene, Tahei (played by Minoru Chiaki) and Matashichi (Kamatari Fujiwara) are walking along on an oppressively hot day, bickering, when suddenly a defeated samurai on the run bursts on the scene, chased by a crowd of samurai on horseback who attack and kill him before riding off. The two men cower in fear, Matashichi declares his intention to go home, and they part, still quarreling. This entire scene was shot in one three-and-a-half-minute cut.

The shooting was not only long but difficult, and it took all day to finish. As a result, some planned close-ups of Tahei and Matashichi were shunted off to the next day. That's when I made a grave error: the cloth bundle that Fujiwara wore crosswise over his right shoulder in the long take was, in the close-ups, on his left. I did not realize my mistake until several days later, when looking at still photos. My shock was great. There was nothing to do but re-shoot the cuts; with a heavy heart, I realized I would have to go to Kurosawa and confess.

I told Fujiwara about it first, wishing bitterly in my heart that *he* had noticed. His only reaction was to brush it off with a laugh:

The penalty for my "crime" should have been ten years in the pen, but all charges were dropped.

"Really? If I paid attention to things like that, I wouldn't be an actor!"

The weather was bad that day, and filming had been canceled. Kurosawa was back in his lodgings, I was informed, playing mah-jongg. I went there despondently and knelt on the wooden floor in the corridor outside his room. The door was open. He glanced over at my somber face and asked, "What is it?" while continuing to play. "I'm sorry," I said, and then, both hands flat on the floor, head down, I told him what had happened. Never taking his eyes off the tiles, he said, "Well, that's no good, we'll have to do it over.... Wait! That makes *pong*! ... We'll do a retake." He remained absorbed in his mah-jongg game, so the moment felt anticlimactic.

Wondering if that was really all, I stayed put until Kurosawa, rattling the tiles, told me, "There's really nothing to it."

And so, thanks to mah-jongg, I escaped a tongue-lashing from the director. I do remember distributing beers to the camera and lighting crews in apology.

Ensuring continuity in a movie is a very complex task, much more so than I have indicated here. Toward the end of shooting, a tsunami of details must be handled. The one in charge must time musical segments down to the second, oversee any substitution of dialogue, and so on. The weight of responsibility can be crushing.

CINEMATOGRAPHY

The traditional word for the person running the camera is cameraman, or cinematographer. Nowadays you sometimes hear "director of cinematography," which sounds even more important. Whatever you call him, to the extent that he determines the on-screen images that give "motion pictures" their name, his skill can make or break the movie. No director can simultaneously run the camera and give direction, however much he may wish he could. A director faced with unsatisfactory results has only two choices: fire the cameraman, or leave the offending bits on the cutting room floor.

Here is what my mentor, Mansaku Itami, had to say about cameramen:

> Probably due in part to my own lack of talent, I have never had the courage to say straight out who among Japanese cameramen uses a soft tone and

whose work is contrasty. You could say I have no idea what it means for one cameraman to be more skillful than another. I only know that I like a man who will do what I tell him to.[24]

Probably most directors would agree with this in their hearts. Kurosawa himself once told me, "No director can stand it when a cameraman who thinks he's great comes in and starts taking pictures artistically, without the least regard for content."

There were many famous cameramen during Kurosawa's time as assistant director, including Hiromitsu Karasawa, master of panning, and Yoshio Miyajima, a brilliant theorist who apparently told Kurosawa, "If I'd been a little less smart, I might have been a director."

Kazuo Miyagawa, the one whose work on *Rashomon* earned a rating of 100+ from Kurosawa, wrote, "The director and the cameraman are like husband and wife. I may be old-fashioned, but that is the approach that I have always taken."[25] As a cameraman, he was the model of a devoted wife who does all she can for her husband. He loved his job more than anything in this world.

Of all the "wifely" cameramen with whom Kurosawa worked, Kazuo Yamasaki, who photographed *The Lower Depths* (Donzoko, 1957) and *The Hidden Fortress* (Kakushi Toride no San Akunin, 1958), was in a category all his own. A tall man of forbidding appearance, he had long limbs and an extremely long face. Contrary to the stern impression he gave, he was actually cheerful and kindhearted.

It is generally acknowledged that Yamasaki was poor at panning shots, an opinion in which he himself concurred. My jaw dropped when he told me the following story with an easy laugh: "Doing a panning shot of an airplane is hard. I was never good at it, and hated to even try. But one time, I succeeded with an Eymo (a small camera). When I looked through the finder, there the plane was, smack in the middle, and it stayed right there for as long as I kept panning—a black dot right in the middle of the lens finder. I was pretty proud of myself until I realized there was a piece of dirt on the finder. I should have known it was too easy!"

Takao Saito worked on Kurosawa's films over a long period of time as assistant to these great cinematographers. His role too was wifely, being crucial, yet inconspicuous. He was proficient at both panning shots and dolly shots, using a telephoto lens of 500 or 800mm so that the picture had speed and the rough, protruding quality that Kurosawa liked.

From *Seven Samurai* (Shichinin no Samurai, 1954) on, Kurosawa used multiple cameras, and the B camera was always given to Saito for him to use as he pleased. Whenever Kurosawa looked at the dailies, he would murmur, "Interesting," and linger with pleasure over what the B camera had turned out. Today, Saito is the last cameraman to enjoy Kurosawa's full confidence.

Saito's own mentor, Asakazu Nakai, worked on more Kurosawa films than any other cameraman. Starting in 1946 with *No Regrets for Our Youth* (Waga Seishun ni Kui Nashi), he shared pleasure and pain with director Kurosawa for over forty years, till the end of his life. The monochrome beauty of *Seven Samurai* is, I think, Nakai's greatest achievement. I know nothing about the technical details, but I have no doubt that finding the exposure to produce that subtle shading was a task of phenomenal difficulty.

One scene is set just at dusk, as the farmer Rikichi returns to the village with the samurai, who have finally agreed to his request, in tow.

> Scene 58. At the pass. Kanbei and the rest are approaching. Rikichi runs ahead and gazes down. The others stand alongside him and look down. Rikichi points in silence. Setting sun—the village is sunk in the shadows of the mountain.

Far from coming out to greet their champions, the village farmers are tucked away in total silence.

Shooting for this scene was set to take place on June 9, 1953, in Shimo Tanna on the Izu Peninsula. Preparations would take all day, so we were only going to shoot this one evening scene. The location crew ate an early lunch and set off. The location site was in the mountains where you could look down on the village as a whole. The farmhouses scattered below were the creations of the art department, constructed just for this event.

The cameras were set up and the lighting equipment was readied. The actors rehearsed their movements and made sure of their positions. This was important because with eight actors arriving and standing in front of the camera, it was likely that some would overlap so that they wouldn't be seen. Also, the entire village had to be visible from over the samurai's shoulders. When all the arrangements were done, the sun was still high in the sky. We all sat down on tree stumps or whatever was handy and chatted.

At some point, the camera crew began taking readings with their light meter, and Nakai frequently went over to peer through

Gauging the light at sundown is tricky. A costly miscalculation, off by mere seconds.

the camera and look up at the sun. Kurosawa came over and asked him, "How's it coming? Are we about ready now?" Nakai replied, "A little bit more."

"The person in front has got to be in focus."

"He will be."

"Will the whole village show up clearly?"

"Yes," Nakai said, and then, hesitating for a second, added, "although it is an evening shot."

"Doesn't matter," the director fired back. "This shot is crucial."

The actors began to gather around. The air was now charged with tension, unlike a few minutes ago. Meanwhile, as the two men talked, the sun edged closer and closer to the horizon. None of us was Taira no Kiyomori, the medieval leader who once pointed his fan at the sun and ordered it to stand still so a temple could be finished before dark; nor was there any way to call back the sinking sun.

This was a sixteen-second shot, and for that small space of time Nakai no doubt had a certain hue in mind. But he hesitated. And all the while, the clock kept ticking. The director and the cameraman continued taking turns looking through the viewfinder, more and more urgently, until finally Kurosawa looked over at Nakai and growled, "Now it's too dark! You can't shoot in this light, can you?"

Nakai shook his head and answered weakly, "No, I'm afraid it's too late now."

"We're leaving! Let's pack up and get out of here." The director's voice rang out over the dusky location site.

Nakai took off his hat and bowed his head. "I'm sorry," he said.

The production manager held up his arms crossed in a big X to signal to everyone that the day's shoot had been canceled. Silently, in a strained atmosphere, we began packing up to leave.

When we got back to the inn, I saw Nakai sitting slumped over just inside the doorway, his shoes still on. One after another, people filed past him, mumbling the standard greeting at the end of a day's work: "*Otsukare-san*" (Thanks for all your hard work). I wanted to say something too, but the words stuck in my throat. I thought I saw him crying.

After we'd hauled actors and crew members to the top of a mountain, taken all day to set up and rehearse, and then made everyone sit around waiting for the sun to set, he wasn't able to shoot the scene. I could imagine how terrible he felt. The light had to be just so, but capturing those few precious rays was extremely difficult.

On February 28, 1988, cameraman Asakazu Nakai passed away.

ART DIRECTION

Production designer Yoshiro Muraki is one of Kurosawa's oldest soldiers, having worked with him ever since the 1948 *Drunken Angel* (Yoidore Tenshi), where he assisted art director Takashi Matsuyama. The sets Muraki makes are grand and spectacular: nothing little and fussy about them. Their strong presence must be what Kurosawa liked so much.

The sight of Kurosawa and Muraki face to face with the set plan spread out flat between them was like watching two grandmasters at a game of chess. I was always impressed by the ease with which Kurosawa read those blueprints, which looked like something from a construction site, but that is a necessary skill for any director. With budget considerations involved, unless a director has a firm grasp of his plan, he might have trouble answering questions like "Are we supposed to see what's outside the window?" or "Do you want to be able to take down this wall?" If a young director hasn't learned his job as an assistant director, he may find himself stymied by the finished set.

Someone told me that when director Mikio Naruse had background scenery made that he ended up not liking, he would arrange in the course of the scene for an actor to go over and close the window.

No one could be better than Muraki at making castles. The black castle he made on the skirt of Mount Fuji for *The Throne of Blood* (Kumonosu-jo, 1957) was outstanding. And in *Ran* (1985), the castle going down in flames was beautiful. That one was modeled after Maruoka Castle in Fukui Prefecture.

Apparently the hardest part of building a castle is making the stone walls. For the third castle in *Ran*, the walls were some 6.4 meters (21 feet) high, while the top of the keep was all of 15.5 meters (51 feet) above the ground. The curving line of the wall itself was made with boards, but for the stones, they enlarged photographs of the wall of an actual celebrated castle, cut out Styrofoam in the shape of each individual stone, and glued the fake stones to the boards. It took months, because they applied them using a technique called "rough-stone piling" (*noishi-zumi*), requiring each stone to press up against those around it.

The biggest challenge was the scene of the burning castle. Styrofoam does not hold up well under heat, but if the fire caused the castle walls to melt or burst into flames, the art department would be disgraced. To prevent such a thing from happening, the surface of the Styrofoam was coated and recoated with cement, four times in all, and then painted the color of ancient rocks. It was a massive undertaking.

Fires are usually made using thin plywood, but since that burns up quickly it isn't realistic, according to Kurosawa. For a burning castle, where the fire must last a long time, it would be even less appropriate.

The third castle looks impressive on screen, but it consisted only of the front and side walls; around back it was empty, with nothing but scaffolding. To make the fire last longer, Muraki packed the keep with lumber, and set up wire netting to catch falling pieces of burning wood and keep them from hitting the inside of the walls. If the walls had caught fire on the inside, all that trouble of spreading cement on the outside would have been for nothing.

Shoot day was December 15, 1984. It was cloudy and windless—ideal conditions for a fire. The shoot was a go. Kurosawa left his villa in Gotenba, relishing the prospect of the day's work.

The yellow-flagged Taro army and red-flagged Jiro army, some four hundred men who had been undergoing preparations since early morning, gathered on location. Tatsuya Nakadai, having finished the three-hour process of being made up for the role of protagonist Hidetora, arrived dressed all in white. Producers Serge Silberman and Masato Hara, who had been eagerly awaiting this day, were there, along with a team of excited press photographers from France.

The remote control fire squad took their places. The Gotenba fire brigade was there, too, keeping watch just in case. On everyone's mind was the awareness that once this 300-million-yen ($1.17 million) castle went up in flames, that would be it—no second chances. The air crackled with tension, as we would have to do the scene without rehearsal.

First, from Position One the cameras would capture Hidetora as he staggered out from the burning castle, focusing on him from the front until he reached the bottom of the stone stairs.

Next, the cameras at Position Two would back out the front gate, with five different cameras filming Hidetora as he walked off, Jiro (Jinpachi Nezu) and Kurogane (Hisashi Igawa) watching him go, and the castle in flames behind them.

First, Kurosawa called to the cameramen poised at Position One: "Ready?" "Ready!" came the reply. All was hushed as Kurosawa's voice rang out over the megaphone "This will be a take."

The cry was taken up by each of the assistant directors in turn. Next Kurosawa called, "Ignite!" The remote control squad flicked a switch, and inside the castle four hundred liters of kerosene ignited. Flames leaped through the windows of the keep.

Then came the signal for dry ice. To keep Nakadai from choking on smoke, the area from where he would emerge was to be swathed not in smoke but in the vapor from dry ice. Bags of dry ice were hanging everywhere like persimmons hung up to dry, and at the signal, they would be dropped into containers of hot water.

Nakadai, who had been standing by, now entered the castle, disappearing from view.

"Ready!" shouted Kurosawa, in an unusually high voice. The cameras all started rolling at once.

"Smoke!"

Clouds of white and gray smoke billowed from the castle windows. Cries of "The smoke is rolling! Smoke is ready!" rebounded from the castle.

"Action!" thundered the director. The bar on the clapperboard snapped down.

"Nakadai!" This was the actor's cue. All eyes turned to the castle entrance. We were breathless with suspense. Kurosawa gripped the megaphone tightly in apparent concern. Pure white clouds of dry ice swirled and billowed, but no Hidetora came out. His eye pressed to the camera, Takao Saito said to his assistant, "No sign of him?" Kurosawa muttered worriedly, "What's he doing?"

Then all at once a clatter arose inside the castle, and through the smoke Hidetora finally appeared, carrying his sword scabbard. Some twenty-five seconds had gone by, but to us it seemed like an eternity. Staring out into space, Nakadai descended the steep stone steps one by one. For the mad Hidetora to have looked down and made sure of his footing would have been incongruous, and yet, fearing he might slip and fall, I watched anxiously until he reached the bottom.

"Form a path!" Kurosawa ordered, and the soldiers parted right and left. "Cut! Print! Position Two!" went out the call. So far, one minute and thirty-two seconds had gone by.

The assistant cameramen scurried outside the gate, carrying the cameras and dragging electric cords behind them, and everyone else shifted to their second positions. At the end of this cut, Jiro and the rest disappeared off the frame to the left as they saw Hidetora off, and Kurosawa announced, "Cut! Print! Douse the fire!"

A huge cheer went up, and everyone burst into applause. The fire brigade sprang into action, turning their hoses on the burning set. The tension gone, gay laughter and whoops echoed back and forth: "That went great!" "Man, when it started off, I tell you. . . ."

As Nakadai came over, looking pleased with himself, Kurosawa burst out, "You took so long coming out, I was worried. Was everything okay?" Nakadai laughed. "I took my time because I thought it wouldn't do to rush."

Later I asked Nakadai how it felt to have that much pressure, if he'd felt any fear. "Not at all," he answered. "It was rather pleasurable, that sense of sacrificing all for the picture." Of course those were the words of a true professional, but I had to admire his nerve. The sentiment was echoed by Muraki, who said of his destroyed set, "People say it's a waste, but after all, the thing was

A take! Fire erupts from the castle tower windows.

made in order to be burned. As art director, I can't ask for anything more than a good picture."

Kurosawa turned toward the crew with an air of satisfaction. "I'm going home," he said. "This calls for a toast, doesn't it. Turn out the lights when you leave. *Otsukare!*" He got in his car and drove off, leaving behind the glow of a million-dollar smile.

Shooting had begun at 10:20 A.M. and ended at 12:50. It had used up 2,800 feet of film (approximately 32 minutes in length). On screen, that day's work would amount to two minutes and five seconds.

THE ASSISTANT DIRECTOR AND THE ANTS

Akira Kurosawa has the reputation of being a fearsome director. It is actually his assistant directors who come under concentrated fire, while the rest of the crew may suffer light casualties from occasional stray bullets. Indeed, assistant directors are like soldiers crawling over a minefield under heavy artillery fire.

Why? Because a movie director is like a military commander who controls an entire arena. Assistant directors are there literally to assist in maintaining this control, and therefore they bear responsibility for every aspect of the operation. The responsibility for props is particularly heavy and demanding—especially when the props happen to be alive. Story after story comes to mind, episodes over which one scarcely knows whether to laugh or to cry, but one that must be told has to do with the performing ants in *Rhapsody in August* (Hachigatsu no Rapusodi, 1991).

Toru Tanaka applied to be an assistant director for *Ran* in 1984. He was one of only three people to pass the scenario-writing examination and, as the name "Toru" (completion) implies, he turned out to be thorough in all he did. For the van Gogh section of the 1990 movie *Dreams* (Yume), he succeeded brilliantly in getting a huge flock of crows to fly up out of a wheat field. From then on, he was Kurosawa's go-to guy when scenes with birds or animals came up.

Rhapsody in August contains a sequence where old folks gather to commemorate the Nagasaki atom bomb attack by chanting the Heart Sutra. They are joined by Clark, a Japanese-American played by Richard Gere. Here is what the script called for:

> Shinjiro is watching a long line of ants go over the ground by his feet. Clark also watches to see where they will go. As the voices chanting the sutra rise, the ants climb up a rose bush.

Not even Kurosawa could have foreseen that these few innocent-sounding lines would give rise to such endless trouble.

Tanaka first approached the challenge scientifically, studying books on ants and telephoning every expert and scientific institution he could find. Everywhere he turned, he got the same answer: the scene couldn't be done. Finally a ray of hope came his way, as someone suggested that Ryohei Yamaoka, an assistant professor at the Kyoto Institute of Technology, might be interested in the problem. Tanaka set off for Kyoto immediately and managed to persuade Professor Yamaoka to come aboard. However, on August 11, the day of the shoot, he had to attend a conference in India and could not be around, while our schedule was fixed because of our contract with Richard Gere.

Professor Yamaoka kindly offered us the use of his assistants, and pronounced himself optimistic of success: "Ants have chemical signposts called pheromones, so if you get them to work for you, it should be doable." He tells the full story himself in a chapter titled "Why the Ants Paraded in a Line" in his book *Mysteries of Co-Evolution*.[26] His account is so fascinating I would like to quote it all, but here is the gist.

> First off, we had to settle on what species of ant to use. In line with Kurosawa's request for typical-looking ants, we chose the glossy black *Lasius nipponensis*. (We couldn't help noticing that the insect's Japanese name, *kurokusa ari*, sounded vaguely like "Kurosawa Akira.")
>
> It turned out that ants from different nests, even if they are the same species, are so belligerent

that cooperation is impossible, on or off camera. Consequently, we had to gather ants from the same nest. With at least two thousand ants needed for one scene, collecting ten thousand ants would allow us to do only five takes. Picking them up with tweezers one by one was out of the question. In the end, we purchased ten small vacuum cleaners and in about two hours managed to capture several thousand ants.

Poor things—they were to be crushed to manufacture the pheromone fluid, thinned with ethyl alcohol, which would lure the rest of the ants. These advance troops were mercilessly pulverized, but their remains would be key to our success—the secret map to our own treasure island, as it were.

On August 6, in the face of an oncoming typhoon, three research assistants at Professor Yamaoka's research institute—Junji Akino, Yasuhiro Nakatani, and Nobuko Shibayama—piled in a small van and headed for Gotenba, the shooting site, some five hundred kilometers (three hundred miles) away. With them were thirty thousand ants.

Due to heavy rain, their arrival was much delayed. Their three meals laid out on the dining room table grew cold. It was after midnight when Tanaka led them in, cheerily saying, "They've just now arrived." The trio sat down in wet clothes and ate their suppers in tired silence.

The next day, while the rest of us shot another

scene the ant team worked hard in preparation, but Tanaka wore a glum look all day. When anyone asked him how it was coming, he would just look at his feet and say, "We're not there yet." He had fatigue written all over him.

To make matters worse, the ants staged a great escape—a genuine exodus. The walls of their container were supposed to be coated inside with talc so that if they climbed up they would only slide harmlessly back down, but Akino had mistakenly used a plaster powder that was for ant nests. He woke up in the middle of the night to find all thirty thousand ants crawling up the wall in one great, black band. At first he couldn't believe his eyes. He thought it must be a nightmare, or a hallucination. The clever ants had apparently sensed danger and planned a mass getaway. Despite their valiant efforts, however, a vacuum cleaner was brought out and in short order they had all been retrieved.

Replacements were needed for the exhausted ants, and Miss Shibayama gallantly stepped in, driving back to Kyoto that very night and returning to Gotenba with another twenty thousand.

Soon came the big day, August 11. The camera was to pan down as Richard Gere glanced at his feet and saw the procession of ants. Kurosawa wanted to do the scene in one take to show man and ants in the same frame. Just out of camera range was the ant team, gripping the container. At a signal Toru Tanaka, using something like an eye-dropper, made a pheromone line on the ground leading straight to Gere's feet. Then came Kurosawa's voice: "Ready. Action!" Gere started acting, the ant team tapped the container, and as the camera panned down we all held our breath, waiting to see what the ants would do.

Alas, there was no procession. Instead, the liberated ants fanned out in every direction. We only needed to capture five seconds or so of them marching, and we tried again and again, but not once did they show any interest in the pheromone trail.

Kurosawa's voice gradually became testy: "That's no good! What's the matter?"

With every take the ants were sucked up in the vacuum cleaner, returned to their container, and then sent off again, only to repeat the cycle. Soon they were clearly fagged. In the end we had to give in and call it a day.

Worn to a frazzle, Tanaka stayed on with the ant team to discuss the problem. Finally they decided that the reason the pheromone had no effect was that the lot had originally been a wet paddy field. The soil was soft, they theorized, and so it absorbed the fluid too quickly.

The stagehands set out to replace the faulty soil by morning. They mixed it with cement to firm it up, dried it with burners, and matched it to the original color. The next day, the ants still did not march in strict order but they did much better, managing to pass muster.

The remaining scenes were of ants alone, and so they could be shot anywhere. Sounds easy, but it meant another major investment of time and personnel as a phalanx of twenty people made a special trip to Kyoto. This time, under the direct supervision of

Two thousand ants run every which way.

Professor Yamaoka, Tanaka and the rest spent three days persuading the ants to climb up a rose bush and onto a rose. They succeeded in the end.

In all, the ants appear in seven shots amounting to one minute and six seconds. That short sequence took an unimaginable amount of energy. Today computer graphics make it possible to create any image on the screen, and stories of gargantuan efforts like this one are just something to laugh about while sitting around waiting on the weather.

5

The Past Won't Return: Remembering *Dersu Uzala*

OFF TO SIBERIA

Kurosawa was feeling extremely lonely and despondent. I often heard him lament, "When they think you won't make them any money, friends drift away. They never even phone." When he bothered to show up at our office in Akasaka, he would sit staring moodily into space and jiggle his leg nervously, something he rarely did.

It was spring 1973. Barely a year before, he had injured himself in a suicide attempt from which the scars were still visible. Undoubtedly, people were avoiding calling out of consideration, meaning to give him some space.

He was just back from Moscow, where he and producer Yoichi Matsue had signed a production agreement with Mosfilm—the largest film and TV production and post-production facility in Russia—and the All-Soviet Union of Filmmakers to make *Dersu Uzala*.

The agreement stipulated, "*Dersu Uzala* is a Soviet film.

127

However, the creative opinions of director Akira Kurosawa will be respected one hundred percent."

The rugged mountain road ahead was strewn high with problems, and Kurosawa was standing at the foot of the mountain, staring up at them.

His first-draft scenario had already been sent off to the Soviets, and the Japanese translation of a second draft by their scenario writer, Yuri Nagibin, had just been returned to us. Nagibin would be arriving in Japan in October for discussions.

Nagibin's version had increased the action scenes in a blatant attempt to dramatize the film; it simply would not do. Kurosawa read it through once and tossed it on the table, exclaiming, "I can't make the movie with a script like this!"

The October conference with Nagibin went on for days on end. We crew members took to calling it the "Russo-Japanese War." In the end, the Soviets decided to go ahead with Kurosawa's scenario after all, in line with the original agreement.

The Soviets laid down stiff requirements regarding Japanese crew members. After much wrangling and ado, it was settled that Kurosawa would be accompanied to the site only by producer Yoichi Matsue and four others—director of photography Asakazu Nakai, and assistant directors Tamotsu Kawasaki, Norio Minoshima, and myself.

Kawasaki was mainly a stage director, and he also had acting experience. As he was fluent in Russian, the Soviets put in a strong request for him. But in winter 1974, past the midway point of the shooting, he left the production. It was surely not the outcome he could have wished, but evidently there were complex issues involved affecting the Soviet and Japanese crews.

In any case, with our hearts full of anxiety and high hopes, we set off for the Soviet Union on December 11, 1973. At 1:00 that afternoon, our party of six, Kurosawa included, took off from Haneda Airport in a USSR Aeroflot plane. Incredible though it might seem today, Kurosawa traveled economy class with the rest of us—eleven long hours in a cramped seat. He never spoke a word of complaint, but spent the whole trip silently reading magazines in the seat beside me. He gave off an air of firm resolution, as if determined never to turn back, no matter what the cost.

Due to a delay, we arrived at Moscow's Sheremetyevo Airport at ten at night. Cars were waiting for us, and we piled in and headed for the Hotel Russia. Out the car windows we could see a birch forest covered in snow, with more snow silently falling. It looked like a Christmas card.

When we entered town, the driver turned to me and exclaimed "Ginza! Ginza!" with an air of pride, as if to say this was the equivalent of Japan's most exclusive and expensive shopping area. The most I could see, however, was a couple of neon signs.

On December 12, we entered Mosfilm studios for the first time. To set foot inside we needed a pass called a *propusk*, but the basic procedure is the same in studios everywhere.

What was utterly different from Japan was the spaciousness of the premises.

The staff room for *Dersu Uzala* was a third-floor office. Hanging on the door was a sign with "Kurosawa" written out in Japanese, a thoughtful touch that made us feel how eagerly the Soviet crew had awaited our arrival. When we walked in the room, everyone stood up and applauded, all smiles.

Kurosawa and Matsue had been there before, so they already knew many of those in attendance, but we first-timers had to shake hands and trade names with everybody, one by one.

The walls were covered with sketches of each scene in the movie, drawn by art director Yuri Raksha; it was like being at a one-man art exhibition. There were also photographs of location shots, helpfully captioned in Japanese.

Next, we were invited to look at screen tests of candidates for the leading role of Arseniev, filmed by chief associate director Vladimir Vasiliev, so we filed into the screening room. For Vasiliev, this was clearly a chance to strut his stuff. We were treated to fairly elaborate shots of the set and of outdoor snow, including not only exchanges of dialogue but birdsong; the actors, however, were less than impressive.

Until we cast the two lead roles of expedition leader Captain Vladimir Arseniev and his guide in the Siberian forests, Dersu Uzala, auditions for expedition members could not get underway. Kurosawa explained, "A cast is like a symphony orchestra; balance is vital." Just then Vasiliev came up and announced, "The first violinist has arrived." It was Yuri Solomin, of the venerable Maly Theater in Moscow.

The role of Dersu, meanwhile, was virtually set to go to Maxim Maximovitch Munzuk, leader of a theatrical troupe in the Socialist Republic of Tuva, in southern Siberia. Screen tests of the two men were conducted over and over; not until February 1 of the following year were the roles officially theirs.

In the interim, Vasiliev and I went over the film schedule time and time again. It turned out that in the USSR, moviemakers were required to shoot a certain number of meters of film each day. The quota was 55 meters for filming on sets, 35 meters for summer location shots, 25 for winter location shots, and 17–20 meters for scenes involving animals. Dividing the total length of the film by this daily quota automatically gave you the number of days needed for shooting.

Except that, of course, there was no reason to expect that filming would proceed according to this timetable. I asked what would happen if we fell behind schedule, and was informed that the difference would come out of staff salaries. "Lenin told us to plan production. We must struggle to achieve the best conditions."

"Don't be ridiculous," I said indignantly. "Mr. Kurosawa is never going to shoot this movie according to a predetermined quota. I'll come up with my own schedule, and after that we can compare the two and see what's what." My show of righteous anger was unfortunately lost in translation.

There were no copy machines in the Soviet Union, and so I was forced to use sheet after sheet of carbon paper, pressing down with all my might as I painstakingly wrote out my version of the schedule. After all that trouble, when we finally sat down and compared our two schedules, reached by two completely different systems, we laughed to find that they were almost identical anyway.

The biggest problem after that was finding an interpreter. We had been using a woman of mixed Russian and Japanese ancestry named Maria Dorya, who was also knowledgeable about films, but she was unavailable to accompany us to Siberia. Since we would require the services of an interpreter for all of eight months, we had trouble finding anyone who was willing and able to go, even among male interpreters, but we finally settled on a man named Lev Korshikov from the Asian Institute. He turned out to be extremely professional, and so good at reading Japanese that he could take a hastily scribbled memo from Kurosawa, look it over, and start issuing directions on the spot. Without him, the shooting would have been vastly more difficult.

The Soviet side included a team of seventy, as well as a platoon of some thirty soldiers on work detail; in contrast to this huge entourage, we Japanese crew numbered only five.

In May, the hundred or so of us divided into smaller groups and began migrating to the city of Arseniev in the Primorsky district of Ussuri, in eastern Siberia. The city is of course named after the hunter and expedition leader Vladimir Arseniev, the main character of the movie; the Ussuri railway, which opened in 1903, also has a station by that name.

Here, in 1906, Captain Arseniev met a member of the Gold tribe named Dersu Uzala. The setting for the movie was chosen to be faithful to the historical record.

We were off to a flying start.

TICKS, MOSQUITOES, AND OUTDOOR TOILETS

Kurosawa left Moscow May 8 with me and the rest of our unit on a domestic flight for Khabarovsk. There was an airport in Arseniev, but it was off limits to foreigners, who were expressly forbidden to take off or land in aircraft there. This was to protect military secrets, we were told, but we joked among ourselves that none of us could have made heads or tails of any of it, whether we gazed down from the sky or received a guided tour on land. Korshikov accompanied the Japanese contingent as our guide.

From the airplane, we saw below us the Siberian taiga, an

endless sea of dark green. Nothing showed in it but a silver band of river, winding snakelike through the green forest. Looking out of his window, Kurosawa exclaimed, "Look at that! You know, Chekhov said the beauty of the taiga lies in its vastness." Then he sighed. "But how do you show that in a film?"

In 1890, before the construction of the Trans-Siberian Railway, Chekhov went through Siberia by boat and on horseback, traveling widely over 40,000 kilometers (25,000 miles) of territory between Moscow and Sakhalin—a feat we all admired.

Along the way, our airplane developed engine trouble and had to land for refueling in Omsk; we arrived in Khabarovsk at eight in the morning, May 10. From there it was over six hours traveling south on the Ussuri railway. We boarded the train at 11 at night, took a little nap, and arrived at 5 A.M. in the station of Spassk Dalni. From there we climbed in a pair of waiting cars and headed for Arseniev.

Having traveled 9,000 kilometers (6,000 miles) from Moscow, we were now a stone's throw from Japan. The driver hospitably turned the radio to a Japanese broadcast, grinning as if to say, "How's that?" A voice began announcing the weather for Japan, and then a Japanese popular song filled the air, loud and clear. On the street, every light truck we passed was a Nissan or a Komatsu. We rode, swaying, for another three and a half hours before reaching our destination.

The city of Arseniev was brand new, having been built only twenty years earlier amid a local economic boom, we were told. It resembled a village on land just reclaimed from the wild. Our accommodations were in the Hotel Taiga, overlooking a plaza of red clay. From the outside, the hotel looked like an emergency shelter of some kind, but it was big enough for our entire crew with room to spare.

None of us had any inkling then of the nine months of tortuous shooting that lay ahead.

At night, sounds of a lively rock band came drifting out of nowhere. It appeared that local young people gathered every night at a nearby park. Kurosawa said he was tired and wanted to turn in early; the rest of us, accompanied by Korshikov, went over for a look. The park was chock-a-block with young people, swaying and dancing to loud go-go music. Off in a corner, we imitated their dance movements, but the locals began murmuring together and staring at us as if we were strange animals, and so we beat a hasty retreat. Since the area was off-limits to foreigners, we were the first ones ever to go there, by special permission.

The next day Korshikov told us with a twinkle, "The local folks said they'd never laid eyes on Japanese before, and even the crew from Moscow was a novelty; then when they heard we were making a movie, they really got excited. We were a hit!"

That day we piled into a microbus and drove through thirty kilometers (twenty miles) of taiga so that Yuri Raksha, the art director, could show Kurosawa the location he had picked out. The road had only recently been cut through the forest, and it was in terrible condition. We bounced till our heads hit the roof. Occasionally someone in the back seat would be thrown forward with such force that he came perilously close to landing in the driver's seat.

The taiga thereabouts had no majestic trees, but only ordinary oak and Japanese larch. Kurosawa was unhappy, complaining, "This looks no different from Hakone!"

Though it was still May, the midday sun was warm. Everyone's image of Siberia is that of a remote and frozen place, but the summers there are quite hot. Inside the taiga the heat grew oppressive. Where the ground was swampy, at every step a swarm of mosquitoes flew up, filling the air like smoke.

When shooting got underway, we were all given special headgear as protection from the mosquitoes, with netting that wound completely around the head and neck so that we looked like beekeepers, or duchesses. Of course that only made the heat worse.

But that wasn't the worst of it. We were also beset by blood-sucking ticks. So tiny they were practically invisible, the ticks were as swift as baby spiders, and where they sucked your blood the skin swelled ominously, turning a bright red. Once embedded, a tick had to be removed by a physician or other healthcare worker; it was no task for a layman. The treatment was simple enough: it entailed winding silk thread tightly around the little pest's mouth, and hauling it out. We knew that these ticks could cause brain fever, and so we had all been inoculated in advance in Moscow as a precaution.

The ticks were as likely to fall from a tree branch overhead as they were to come crawling up one's leg. We walked along nervously, preoccupied by these parasites, hardly able to focus on the task at hand. Finally Asakazu Nakai, the cinematographer, had had enough. "The hell with this!" he spluttered. "Look, if we get bit, we get bit. I say worry about that later. Spend the whole time thinking about ticks and we'll never get any work done!"

Raksha, who had arrived a month before the rest of us, was already acclimated. He alone was able to go around shirtless and carefree.

Getting inspected for ticks. The scene looked like a roadside inspection under martial law.

Assistant Director Brodsky, a barrel-shaped man, did not come with us into the taiga as walking was difficult for him; he agreed to wait by the bus to hear our decision. When we emerged back onto the road, we came out with our hands in the air like surrendering rebels, went up to Brodsky, and had him inspect us for ticks. We made quite a spectacle; the scene looked like nothing so much as a roadside checkpoint under martial law.

Most of us did get infested with ticks. Kurosawa had them on his side, so the production manager and Korshikov hastily bundled him into the microbus and rushed him to the hospital. When they came back a while later, they were still laughing: the hospital they dashed into turned out to be a maternity clinic, to everyone's consternation.

We went in the microbus as far as Olga, on the Bay of Olga in the Sea of Japan, looking for a river. In the movie, as Arseniev and his men cross the river Takema by raft, Arseniev slips into the waters and is nearly engulfed by them, but Dersu's quick-wittedness saves him. We needed a suitable river for the scene but had a hard time finding one.

We had left our hotel in Arseniev at nine in the morning, and by the time we arrived in Olga, it was after five. Naturally we had to stay the night there.

On the way to Olga in the bus, production assistant Kilshon had stood up and announced, "Folks, Olga is way out in the country, so there's no big hotel there like the one in Arseniev. You'll have to sleep two to a room. The biggest problem is the toilets. They're not inside the hotel. They're not flushing, either, but that can't be helped."

When we got there, it was just as he had said. The hotel looked more like workers' barracks, and the ground floor was a market. It had what you might call a folksy air. We made our way up the creaking wooden stairs to find a number of rooms on the second floor. Kurosawa roomed with Nakai and I shared a room with the sound technician, Olga Burkova.

Straight off I went out to check out the worrisome toilets while it was still light out. Going down the stairs and out through a field behind the hotel, I came upon a wooden public lavatory. While there were separate cubicles for men and woman, the stench and filth were overpowering. I reported my findings in some alarm, and Kawasaki suggested we arm ourselves with flashlights.

With Kawasaki in the lead, the Japanese contingent lost no time in trooping to the market to purchase flashlights. We were in for another surprise: the gadgets were powered not by battery, but by tiny manually-operated generators. I had never seen such a thing before, but Nakai grew nostalgic and said they reminded him of his childhood. The end of the flashlight was shaped something like the end of a bicycle handlebar, or the top of a stapler, and to make the flashlight light up, you had to generate electricity by continually squeezing it, good and hard. Kurosawa took one up curiously and declared with a wry smile that he didn't have a strong enough grip to make it work. Regardless, it was essential that we have light, and so we each purchased one. Nakai said delightedly that he would take his back to Tokyo as a souvenir.

After dark, we all went down to the water's edge. The beauty of the starry skies over Siberia is something no one could believe who hasn't seen it. A mass of innumerable stars covers every inch of sky, so many that they give an illusion of heaviness. The sky is packed with stars all the way down to the horizon.

Only Korshikov had thought to bring his bathing suit. Joking that he might swim straight across to Japan, he plunged into the water.

Later that night I set out for the outdoor toilet, my manually operated flashlight at the ready. As I walked down the hallway squeezing it in my hand, it sounded a steady *skritch, skritch*. I could hear the identical noise coming up from the bottom of the stairs, accompanied by a tiny light. It was Kawasaki, on his way back. We couldn't help giggling as we said good-night and passed each other. Those gadgets were pretty hard on the hand muscles.

In the morning, Kurosawa grinned and said with a shrug, "Last night it was too much trouble to go all the way out back, so Nakai and I just peed out the window!"

The morning air was clear and crisp. Chickens were cackling to each other as if trying to see who could raise the most racket.

And with not a soul in sight, a solitary horse was walking down the road.

FEELING LIKE NAPOLEON

Shooting finally got underway on May 27, 1974.

Kurosawa called me early that morning to ask, "You suppose this weather will do?" That was his routine whenever we were shooting; the question did duty for "good morning." Then there was a knock at the door, and in came Vladimir Vasiliev, the chief director. He announced, "Today the weather is good. Let's go."

Day one. I set off in good spirits to tell Kurosawa it was time to go. We headed for Mt. Haraza, which was visible from the hotel windows. *Scene 55. Young leaves blowing in the taiga. Arseniev and his men make their way along.* This was the scene to be shot. In the scenario it amounted to a mere line of type, but that didn't make the shooting any easier. Either the sky clouded over, or the line of men didn't show up well, or some other problem arose, so that it was 3:30 in the afternoon before we had a cut.

The soldiers assigned to mess duty had prepared lunch for us in a clearing. We ate in shifts at a long, hastily set up table covered with rolls of black bread, each one deeply scored till it resembled an accordion. The Russians would tear off a section of this bread, rub it with garlic, and eat it. The slightly sour taste was exceptionally good. There was always soup at lunch, too. It tasted pretty much like borscht, but in the kettle it was topped by a layer of fat a few centimeters thick. Meat was usually grilled mutton. What surprised me was the time I saw a tick drop from Yuri Raksha's forelock into his soup.

"Oh for some cold tofu . . . sigh." At lunch, the art director discards a tick that had fallen in his soup.

Without batting an eyelash, he scooped the wriggling thing up in his spoon and calmly tossed it behind him.

Nakai, who was from Kyoto, where the cooking features light, delicate flavors, lost his appetite at the merest whiff of sunflower oil. He used to say, "Just some cold tofu or pickled cabbage, that's all I want."

At the hotel, a room was reserved for the Japanese crew's supper, with dishes brought in by a plump woman. A lot of it consisted of tough meat and what seemed like lumps of suet.

Kurosawa would usually down a bottle of vodka unassisted. For a man of sixty-four he showed great capacity; his explanation was that he needed it to sleep.

One time when the interpreter Korshikov joined us for supper, Kurosawa ordered another bottle of vodka. It never did any good to tell him he'd had enough; that only made him drink all the more. Instead, Minoshima and I bought a bottle of vodka in the restaurant, poured out one-third of the contents in the sink, and replaced it with water; since vodka looks exactly like water anyway, you couldn't tell the difference. But when I started to fill Kurosawa's glass, Korshikov's eyes popped. Afterward he told me, "You may have fooled Mr. Kurosawa, but I caught on right away. The bottles of vodka they sell here are never that full!" We had a good laugh.

In summertime, they held an outdoor farmers' market near the hotel. Most of the vendors were Asian in appearance, with years of patience chiseled on their faces. I still remember one who squatted motionless behind three home-grown cucumbers, waiting for a buyer.

I loved to get up early and go to this farmers' market. It always relaxed me. One Sunday morning I bought some eggs, took them back to the hotel, and asked the cooks to make rice for supper. (The girls who did the cooking were about fifteen or sixteen and only too happy to meet our requests, perhaps because they found waiting on Japanese a novelty.) When suppertime came round, even the dry, long-grain foreign rice tasted delicious when we ate it Japanese-breakfast style, with a mixture of beaten raw egg and soy sauce on top. Nakai was moved almost to tears by this unexpected taste of home. Kurosawa had been teasing him steadily about being the kind of fellow who goes abroad and eats Japanese food, but even Kurosawa had to admit it tasted good.

Little by little my room turned into a Japanese food short-order cookhouse. Kurosawa's phone calls didn't end with the weather now. He would put in special requests like, "Could you make us some rice gruel?" or "We're starving. Bring us some garlic rice."

Nakai's troubles weren't all about food: he suffered from the poor quality of the camera equipment and film stock he was forced to work with. The 70mm cameras were so heavy it took three male assistants to move one of them; as there were always two cameras, changing locations was a major job. Nakai didn't speak a word of Russian, nor had he brought along any Japanese assistants. When he needed to communicate with the Russians, he simply rattled on at them in Japanese. Regardless, they became very attached to him.

Fyodor Dobronravov, or "Fedya," a fat, good-natured fellow in charge of camera B during the first half of filming, used to follow around after Nakai with one eye on Japanese phrases he had scribbled in his notebook:

"Mr. Nakai, constipation? Are you in trouble?"

"Yes, I'm in trouble. Fedya, no constipation?"

"No, no."

The two of them were always laughing about something or other.

The Soviets replaced him during the latter half of filming with a Communist party member named Yuri Gantman.

We were told that the camera film given to us was equivalent to Agfa; in fact, when they occupied Germany the Soviets had apparently seized the Agfa facilities, carted them home, and proceeded to manufacture domestic film. The sensitivity of Japanese film at the time was ASA 100-120, but this was ASA 40 and very poor quality. We had no end of trouble with it.

Line producer Karen Agadjanov said, "The film swells when

it gets humid, so don't put more than 50 meters in the magazine." What's more, every time the temperature fell below minus 40° Centigrade, the cameras stopped rolling.

"Dailies" or "rushes" are unedited prints straight from the negative of the previous day's shoot; they are processed overnight and shipped back for the director to screen on location. Whenever the negatives had processing streaks on the emulsion or other flaws, they came back callously punched full of holes, seemingly to indicate that the film was unusable due to *blok* (an accident). The very center of the scene would be ruthlessly punched out, so you could hardly blame Kurosawa for going into a rage.

The scene when Dersu first appears at Arseniev's camp was shot on location at night over a three-day period in early October, but the dailies all had holes punched in them. The shoot would have to be done over.

Kurosawa called me to his room and said, "Who's responsible for this? Who the hell do they think they are, doing that to a scene we went to all that trouble to shoot late at night? They can't go around punching holes in my film! Without the holes in it, maybe it could even be used. It's *my* decision whether or not to use it! They have to leave that to me!" He wiped away tears of frustration with the back of his great hand. Kurosawa was weeping. I completely understood what he was saying.

After the first snowfall on October 20, even though we had lots of autumn scenes left to shoot, the season changed rapidly to winter. The farmers' market disappeared. On the leftover stands, snow piled up and was tossed in the wind.

Kurosawa gazed out of his hotel window at the thickly falling snow and sighed, "I feel just like Napoleon."

Producer Yoichi Matsue and assistant director Tamotsu Kawasaki went back to Japan. In their place came Kazuo Marui from Moscow, where, as a researcher at Moscow Cinema University, he had been assisting with preparations for this film. This was the young man whom Nakai had been pressing the Soviets to provide as assistant director-cum-technical interpreter. With his arrival, things finally eased up a little for Nakai.

BONE-FREEZING NIGHT SHOOTS

The Russian winter fully lived up to its fierce reputation. The same wintry force that previously drove back Napoleon's army and wiped out the German army seemed to laugh aloud at human frailty.

Every time someone passed through the double doors of the hotel, so much steam swirled in the air that it was impossible to see who had come in. That's how great the difference in temperature was between inside and outside.

The filming was not going as planned.

On the night of December 27, we were scheduled to shoot a scene at the campsite: *Arseniev lies sleeping in his tent while outside, next to the campfire, Dersu expresses fear.* The script called for a night that was "strange and mysterious," and Kurosawa insisted that we had to produce a magical atmosphere. He came up with the idea of hanging empty bottles and cans from the branches of fir trees by the tent, like Christmas trees, so that the objects would bump into each other and create a beautiful tinkling sound. Then if the trees were hosed down with water, icicles would form, adding another dimension of crystalline sound. Kurosawa had a wonderful gift for coming up with ideas like this; he was constantly thinking about pictures and sound.

We Japanese and Russian crew members went out to the location by daylight and enjoyed socializing as we hung the trees with empty cans, spoons, and the like. Sometimes I slipped off my gloves to arrange something more dexterously, but I couldn't keep them off more than a minute, as the pain quickly grew unbearable. The cold was so intense it felt like your insides were being frozen solid.

It being winter, the sun set around four. The temperature swiftly plummeted to about thirty below zero. Kurosawa arrived, gave his approval for the decorations, and called for a test of the icicle-making. A fire truck and a fan were both in place, standing by.

The young man in charge of operating the hose, Gondolabula, had the massive build of a sumo wrestler and the innocent, red-cheeked face of a boy. He had volunteered for the job of manning the fire-pump hose. Singlehandedly carrying out a job that would normally have required the strength of three, he bellowed the signal to start the water. The instant a jet of water burst from the end of the hose, he made it into a fine mist, moving the hose up and down to spray the Christmas trees.

Before our eyes, the trees were magically transformed, becoming instantly wrapped in ice. Drops at the ends of twigs froze where they hung, and every ice-encased tree looked like glasswork. As the spraying was repeated again and again, water falling on the frozen drops froze in turn, creating numberless icicles. The sight was breathtakingly beautiful.

Kurosawa was very pleased, and gave orders to keep on,

At minus 40°C, the water in the hose froze solid.

using the same technique on other trees nearby, so Gondola (as we called him) waxed even more enthusiastic, running around with the hose in his arms, waving people aside and shouting, "Out of the way!"

But then the hose itself froze solid, as stiff and straight as a stick, and water pressure started building up inside. The soldiers hastily ran over and started loosening the hose joints and banging on them with sticks. Gondola was shouting something at the top of his lungs; his jacket, covered with ice, was as stiff as a board.

"What's going on?" "Where's the water?" "Over there!" Russian cries flew back and forth through the forest until all of a sudden, water exploded from the mouth of the hose in Gondola's hand. Everyone around him screamed and ran for cover.

We had to provide a blizzard, too. The local snow was light and fine-grained, so we piled it in huge mounds before a fan; when the time came, the soldiers scooped it up in shovels and tossed it high in the air, so that it blew in the wind. The arrangement was fairly primitive, and executing it was hard work. On top of that, the men were hit by the full force of gale winds from the fan, so working conditions were truly ghastly.

When it was wind we wanted, we turned to an airplane engine and propeller transported all the way from Moscow for this purpose. It didn't actually amount to much, consisting only of an engine frame with cockpit and propeller attached. You almost suspected it was a relic from World War I. The man in charge of operating it must have once been a pilot; seated in position, he looked as happy as can be. First his assistant would call out "*Raz, dva, tri* [one, two, three]" and give the propeller a mighty spin by hand. Then the man in the pilot's seat would intently rotate a small crank. Once the engine caught, that was it. "*Otoidite!* [Stand back!]," he would cry, and the assistant would spring away. Generally the engine would go "vroom, vroom" a couple of times and then give up. Then the whole process would start over again.

They spent eight months on location with us just to do that one job, but now when we needed them, that's how it went. Even the Soviet crew was appalled, and stood around looking on from a distance, monitoring their progress. It went on for some two hours, over and over again: "*Raz, dva, tri!*" Spin, spin. "*Otoidite!*" Vroom, vroom, sputter, thud.

The trees were properly frozen, the actors were in their make-up, the lights were in place—and the fan wouldn't go. Kurosawa sat warming his hands by the fire, listening to all the noise and muttering impatiently, "What's going on?"

Then Gondola came over, bringing with him the interpreter Lev Korshikov. Apparently it was too cold for the engine to catch, and because they'd tried to make it go anyway, it had caught fire. End of story. That would be it for today. Gondola bit his lip in evident chagrin.

Kurosawa said, "I see. Well, if the machinery won't go, that's that." He stood up and announced we were canceling the shoot. Canceling for a reason like that didn't place much of a burden on him, because it wasn't our fault. The rest of us had been wondering anxiously how much longer we might have to stay out in the cold that night, so upon hearing that the shoot was canceled, we all cheered up, running around with our arms crossed in a big X to signal it was over and yelling, "That's it, clear out!"

The lights were killed, plunging the forest into instant darkness. With only firelight to illuminate the scene, staff members' shadows crisscrossed the ice as we went about cleaning up. We trundled over the snow, heading back toward the lights of the minibus off in the distance.

Nakai came up behind me and said jokingly, "When we get back to the hotel, let's have a sukiyaki dinner with some hot sake, okay?"

"Sounds great," I responded. "How about some boiled tofu to go along with it?"

"Yes, or *oden* stew would be good."

Trading light witticisms, we piled into the bus and went back to the hotel.

The original schedule called for us to finish shooting on location in Arseniev before the end of the year, and then go back to Moscow. All of us were on tenterhooks, wondering where we would be spending the all-important New Year's holiday; we talked of little else. But progress on filming was slow. As we had pretty much figured, we ended up spending New Year's in Arseniev after all.

Karen Agadjanov, the line producer, would frequently call me in and blast, "What is Mr. Kurosawa thinking! Does he intend to shoot this picture or not?"

On December 31, while people back in Japan were eating seasonal bowls of noodles and watching the gala year-end song show on TV, we were climbing up snowy Mt. Halaza to shoot the scene where Dersu just misses shooting a wild boar. The boar was not cooperating; it showed little interest in running where we wanted it to. Arseniev and Dersu posed in front of the camera with guns aimed, but the animal never came in camera range. Or if it did, it stood stock still and wouldn't run.

Freezing cold, and running out of patience, Kurosawa yelled, "Every time, the same damn thing happens! Do something!" As a compromise, I suggested combining several of the previous shots to somehow get by. He was adamant: "If it's no good, it's no good!"

Eventually the sun began to go down. It was New Year's Eve, after all, so finally Kurosawa called it a day. In the end, the scene was edited so that only the good parts were used.

And so the year came to an end.

DOSVIDANYA, SAYONARA

The hotel's New Year's decorations were festive. All the windows were adorned with lace braid of silver and gold, and frosted with red, white, and green lettering that read *"S Novim Godom"* (Happy New Year). In the entrance stood a great fir tree with a shiny star on top and hung with figures of Father Frost, the Russian approximation of Santa Claus.

In the restaurant, the girls laid out decorations on the tables, chatting happily together with thread and glue in hand as they made their preparations. When I walked by, they called out to me and asked if I was homesick for Japan. "*Nyet, nyet.* I don't want to go home," I said, but they only laughed and accused me of lying.

That night was a most auspicious occasion: we celebrated New Year's 1975 three times in one night.

First was the Siberian New Year's. The mayor of Arseniev and his staff gathered with us in the restaurant, all eyes on the clock. Kurosawa came in as if to say, "Not yet?" All together, we started the countdown of the final seconds. Twelve o'clock. Instantly champagne bottles popped open and cries of "*S Novim Godom*" and toasts to the New Year erupted around the room.

"Here's to Mr. Kurosawa!"

"Here's to the success of the movie!"

Yuri Solomin, the actor playing Arseniev, put his arms around Kurosawa and declared, "I am so happy!"

One A.M. The start of the New Year in Japan. Again champagne corks popped, again toasts were drunk. The band played with great ardor and the restaurant was filled to overflowing with people dancing.

Five hours later, it would be New Year's in Moscow. The drinking and celebrating would go on till then. And yet, there was still plenty of filming to be done.

It was decided to shoot only the scenes that absolutely had to be done in Siberia, and manage the rest somehow after going back to Moscow. We also had to redo the shoots that had been ruled *blok* or unusable.

Feeling the pressure, Kurosawa passed many a sleepless night.

His vodka consumption doubled, from one bottle to two. On location, he yelled at Nakai. The Russians didn't understand Japanese so they had no idea what all the shouting was about.

Kurosawa would bellow, "There's no light on the trees in back! Do it, on the double!"

Nakai gave back as good as he got: "I *am* doing it! It's not as easy as lighting a match, you know!"

It was a good thing he showed so much spirit. If Nakai had been chicken-hearted, he would never have lasted so long in the first place, and besides, Kurosawa was able to release a lot of stress by calling him every name in the book.

January 14 was our worst day.

We set out at nine A.M. and drove up Mt. Halaza. The road was impossible to make out in the deep snow. Then the bus engine gave out. We got out and carried our things up to the location on foot, or set up relays, passing them up hand to hand.

We were to film the scene where Arseniev's men haul a packed sleigh up from the bottom of a cliff and trudge on exhausted through the snow, pulling the sleigh behind them.

The cut began with the men off-camera, and then showed them crawling up with the sleigh behind them; a difficult shoot. We did it four times, and it never went right. Each time we did it over, the surface of the snow had to be smoothed out again and all the footsteps erased, while the actors and Korshikov huddled in painful positions, keeping out of sight at the bottom of the cliff.

Kurosawa had been working on this one scene all day, and by now he was frantic: "Lyova!" (This was Korshikov's nickname.) "Hurry up! We're losing the light! Hurry, hurry!"

Korshikov stood up and answered calmly, "Yes, but Mr. Kurosawa, the sleigh is heavy and the footing here is very bad. Wait a minute, please."

We hadn't eaten all day, and by the time we finally finished shooting the scene, it was six in the evening. We went back to the hotel utterly worn out.

When we got there, we found producers Matsue and Agadjanov chatting over cups of tea. Kurosawa went over to join them, and I went up to my room. Soon Minoshima and Marui came by, one after another, to say that Kurosawa was waiting impatiently for something to eat. I threw on a change of clothes, made some hot rice gruel, and took it to his room.

Kurosawa had already started in on his vodka, and he was in an extremely foul temper. Who the hell did those two think they were, he demanded, sitting around drinking tea and staying warm all day while we were out freezing half to death, working hard without anything to eat? Any producer worth anything ought to show up on location. He went on like that, spitting mad.

"Today I was kept waiting all day, and never once did I get the conditions I wanted!"

"Well, after all, the bus did break down in the snow," I started to say, but he cut me off impatiently, as if to say he was in no mood for excuses. He thrust a drawing under my nose. "*This* is the scene I really wanted to shoot!" He waved it around in the air and pushed aside the gruel I'd set out on the table. Maybe he doesn't feel like eating, I thought.

Then all at once he said despairingly, "Not one time have I been able to shoot a scene the way I wanted!" He ripped the drawing into pieces and threw them on the floor. When I bent down to

"What is this crap!" Kurosawa was exhausted from anxiety and loneliness.

pick them up, he suddenly yelled, "What is this crap!" and flung the bowl of gruel at me.

I had been yelled at often enough, but never before had he thrown anything at me. Naturally, I became angry. "How can you do a thing like that, Kurosawa-san! I've had enough!" I fled the room, slamming the door behind me.

Brimming with indignation, I went downstairs and knocked on the door to Nakai's room. Nakai had just had his identification picture taken to go back to Japan, and was wearing a suit and tie. When I had poured out my tale of woe he responded, "Non-chan, how could he treat you, of all people, that way!"—and burst into unabashed tears.

Nakai's soft heart touched me, and I ended up comforting him. On my way back to my room, I ran into Korshikov in the corridor. He was fairly drunk, his Japanese sounding a bit the worse for wear:

"What's going on? Mr. Kurosawa came alone to our restaurant. He was mad. He said, 'Where is the Japanese staff? I'm angry!' He was very upset. He said all the Japanese should report to his room."

Then Marui came along too, and said Kurosawa was asking for me, but I informed them I wouldn't be going, and went back to my room. Later, Korshikov knocked on my door and came in. He took me by the shoulders and said, "What is it, Teruko?" (This was his nickname for me.) "What happened?" Suddenly overcome, I, like Nakai, burst into tears.

In the morning, Kurosawa phoned me and asked me to come to his room so he could apologize for what had happened the day before. I did, and we made up.

Looking back, I see now that Kurosawa was full of anxiety and loneliness, in a desperate position with his back to the wall. I only wish I had been able to empathize more at the time.

January 17 came, and we left the city of Arseniev at last. We took the bus back to Spassk Dalni and then, following the same route as when we'd come, went by train to Khabarovsk. There was a blizzard in Khabarovsk.

I will never go back to Siberia. The girls in the restaurant saw us off, but I doubt if I will ever see them again.

We arrived in Moscow on January 18. Many difficulties still lay ahead. We had a Japanese maker of artificial flowers send branches of autumn foliage and yellow leaves, and set about filming autumn scenes on the outskirts of Moscow. For a scene that needed to be reshot, we built a ravine in a Mosfilm studio.

What helped more than anything was the presence in the Ukraine Hotel, where we were staying, of Mr. and Mrs. Kazunao

Matsuzawa of Nihonkai Films. I will never forget the flavor of the Japanese-style croquettes, pickles, and other foods they treated us to the day after we arrived.

In Moscow, Kurosawa was more irritable than ever. His yelling went on from morning till night. While in Siberia he had injured both eyes, his legs had weakened considerably, and he had acquired a gaunt, haggard appearance. He was on the edge of total exhaustion.

Shooting finally wrapped on April 28. After that came the editing and music. I can only marvel that Kurosawa had the strength to finish the film.

He returned to Japan on June 18. I stayed on by myself a bit longer, partly to attend a staff farewell party and partly because I had purchased a Russian cat at a bazaar and had to go through the necessary paperwork to take it home with me. I flew back to Japan on June 25.

The day I left the USSR, Korshikov came to my hotel along with the wardrobe and editing staff. They did many little favors for me, including fashioning a cardboard box to hold my cat. Korshikov and the producer Kilshon took me to the airport. At the boarding gate Korshikov said, "From here on it's a foreign country, so this is as far as we go. *Dosvidanya*, Teruko." He hugged me and planted a kiss on my forehead.

"Thank you. *Dosvidanya!*" Wiping away tears, I picked up the box with my cat inside and climbed the stairs.

Dersu Uzala opened in Japan on August 2, 1975. It was released in the USSR in September, taking first prize at the 1975 Moscow Film Festival. In 1976, it won the Academy Award for Best Foreign Language Film.

One night about five years later, I received a telephone call from Mrs. Matsuzawa in Moscow. "Nogami-san, this will come as a shock, but Lyova [Korshikov] is dead. Somebody killed him." After hanging up, unable to believe my ears, I phoned his house. In halting Russian, I asked if it was true. It was.

Later I heard that he had been severely beaten in the head and was taken to a hospital, where he lay unattended for three days. He wasn't wearing the Sony watch I'd given him when he was hospitalized, so perhaps he was mugged. But then, even during filming, we'd been under KGB surveillance, and the other Russians had deliberately kept their distance from us Japanese, so perhaps there was more to it than that. He died at the young age of forty-two, never to know the era of *perestroika*. His son Dmitri, who played the part of Arseniev's son, went into the army and later committed suicide.

Line producer Karen Agadjanov, sound technician Olga Burkova, and art director Yuri Raksha have all passed on as well. When I met Yuri Solomin in Moscow in 1995, I heard from him that Maxim Munzuk, who played Dersu, had been dead for two years. In his later years his eyesight failed, just like Dersu's, Solomin told me.

Nakai passed away in 1988.

Never again will I see Kurosawa, either. Knowing how alone he was, I wonder now—why couldn't I have reached out to him with greater warmth?

Memories from a quarter-century ago, of days that will never return, fill me with keen regret.

6

Kurosawa and Animals

TIGERS

In *Dersu Uzala*, the tiger is an important character. He is feared above all else by Dersu, the expedition's guide to the taiga, who calls the tiger "Amba"—a supernatural creature summoned by Kaniga, the spirit of the forest. Despite his awe, one day, Dersu fires his weapon at the tiger. From then on he lives in fear that Kaniga's wrath will send the tiger after him, and eventually his life takes a tragic turn.

We celebrated New Year's 1974 in Moscow, awash in vodka. As the month of January drew to a close, the casting of the main character, expedition leader Captain Arseniev, remained up in the air. Camera tests of the two contenders for the role went on.

On January 30, producer Galikovsky came into the room, beaming as if to say, "This will cheer the director up!" In his hand was a telegram. "Good news!" he exclaimed.

Kurosawa had never liked this Galikovsky fellow from the start, and was always making complaints about one thing or another. Galikovsky must have seen this as his chance to turn things around.

157

"Kurosawa-san, be happy. We have news that on location in Siberia they have captured a tiger!"

Contrary to expectations, Kurosawa did not rejoice. Gloomily he asked the interpreter, "Is it a proper tiger?"

"Oh, yes," came the answer. "It's still a cub, but by the time shooting starts, it will be fully grown."

"You're joking. It couldn't possibly get big that fast." Kurosawa was more disgruntled than ever.

In the end, however, Galikovsky's prediction proved to be on target. By the time shooting began on October 13, the tiger cub had grown into a strapping young adult. Dubbed "Anchom," the poor thing was confined in a hastily built shelter in the forest, where the cost of feeding it ran to dozens of rubles per day. We had to laugh, as the total per day worked out to slightly more than what Kurosawa was being paid.

It all started when Galikovsky said if it was tigers we wanted, we would find any number of splendid ones in the Russian circus, the nation's pride. He brought out circus magazines, which was a mistake.

As Kurosawa saw it, circus tigers were so used to performing for food that they lacked the sharpness of tigers in the wild; their bellies were full, he said, and their eyes dull.

And that's how we ended up with Anchom.

But by October, Galikovsky was gone, given the axe. His replacement as line producer was Karen Agadjanov. An Italian-Georgian of the stout build often seen in U.S. detective films, Agadjanov was an epicure and a dandy. Since he spoke Italian, he could often be seen talking with our producer Yoichi Matsue, both of them waving their hands in the air. While we were shooting the tiger scenes, he would strut around with a pistol at his waist, which gave us all a laugh.

The shoot called for only two cuts with three cameras, but our wild tiger Anchom proved totally incapable of comprehending any instructions. From up on the platform beside the mounted camera, Kurosawa yelled vigorously: "What's the problem? Listen here! When Arseniev and Dersu come in front of the camera, the tiger walks out of the trees over there, stops and looks this way, then walks on by, okay? That's all there is to it. Why can't you get it right? Once we have that down, Dersu will fire the blanks and the tiger can just run off. That's it. All right, one more time. Got it now?"

Anchom no doubt didn't get it, but the idea was that as soon as the actors were in the frame, the assistant directors would wave sticks in their hands to chase him out. Naturally, the tiger's territory was fenced in to prevent him from escaping—all except for the camera side, where they couldn't put a fence. Instead, on the assumption that any tiger would have a typical cat's aversion to getting wet, they had dug a ditch in the ground and filled it with water.

"Is the tiger ready?" asked Kurosawa. The interpreter said, "*Horosho* (OK)"; the tiger was hidden behind a tree.

The director's voice rang out: "*Prigotovilis* (ready), *motor* (camera), *nachali* (action)!" Arseniev and Dersu came out, holding their guns, and scanned the forest depths for a tiger. Anchom should have showed up then and there, but he didn't. Dersu had no choice but to go ahead and say his line anyway: "Amba! Listen well! Amba!"

Looking over, we saw "Amba" lying flopped in the shade of the trees, utterly relaxed. No motivation whatsoever.

"What the *hell* is going on!" the director roared in a fury. "You've got to scare that tiger, get it up and moving!"

How many times had we been through the same routine? We'd spent all morning getting ready for this scene; this made the seventh take. Looking back, it seems likely that before transporting the tiger for the shoot, they gave him a tranquilizer just to be safe. In any case, script or no script, this tiger was no danger to anyone. He just lay there, sprawled out as if to say, "Go ahead and kill me." There was no way to film him in the shape he was in.

"Find some way we can do the scene. That's all for today!" snapped Kurosawa, and jumped down from the platform.

For the rest of the day, Agadjanov and his crew sat down with the assistant directors, and we batted the problem around in heated debate. It was a classic case of too many cooks spoiling the broth; the discussion got nowhere. In the end, we agreed to try again three days later.

The day came. All morning long, dogs had been barking noisily around the location. Agadjanov had brought them along, having come up with the plan of stationing hunting dogs outside the fence in order to provoke the tiger. He'd also made the alarming suggestion that we shoot around the tiger with live ammunition, but had apparently switched plans, instead preparing long spearlike rods with which anybody whose hands were free could jab the animal from behind the fence.

Even then, Anchom wouldn't cooperate. The hounds bayed and the beaters shouted out while threatening the animal with their sticks. The uproar was so great that Anchom cowered in among the trees, hiding, and wouldn't come out. And then, finally, he darted along the fence toward the ditch and did the unbe-

The Siberian tiger, unable to grasp what was wanted of it, collapsed.

lievable, diving into the water with an enormous KERSPLASH. Everyone was caught off guard. Shouting and clamoring, people poked him with sticks and spears and drove him back inside the fence.

Anchom, who had barely made it out of the water in one piece, was completely done in: he took a few tottering steps and collapsed, foaming at the mouth.

The interpreter came up to Kurosawa and told him that Solomin, the actor playing Arseniev, was so upset at the way the tiger was being tormented that he couldn't bear to go on. Kurosawa bridled at the suggestion that he himself was responsible for any tormenting of the animal. "I don't want to shoot the scene this way, either!" he said, and turned to cameraman Asakazu Nakai. "Just now, the tiger went through the trees for a few seconds, and that's on film, right?"

Nakai hemmed and hawed. "Er . . . yes, I guess so . . .

although it was just for a second or two, as you said." An honest man, he tried to give an honest answer.

Kurosawa snarled, "Damn it all, I saw it for myself! The camera was rolling, so it's got to be on film. It *is* on film, isn't it? It had damn well better be!"

There was no point in snapping the man's head off. Kurosawa was probably intent on the idea that he might yet salvage the scene in the editing room, working with whatever bits there were. As if to say he'd had enough of this charade, he went on, "Shooting's impossible now. I'm calling the shoot off. After all, the actors can't possibly get in character under these circumstances. Tell Solomin I'm sorry," he added, in an attempt to mollify his lead actor.

We did ten takes that day, but all our efforts went for nothing.

I have to say, though, poor Anchom was certainly born under an unlucky star. After being captured in January, he spent a lonely ten months locked up in a cage, only to be hooted at and chased around until he collapsed. In the film, the scenes where he can be seen moving among the trees amount to some four seconds in all.

Early in the new year of 1975, we went back to Moscow after an absence of some eight months and finished filming the tiger scenes there. We recreated the Siberian taiga on a big Mosfilm stage, and signed on a veteran circus tiger named "Tycoon" as well as his handlers, a husband-and-wife team. On February 21, the day of the shoot, we were joined by so many TV crews and foreign journalists that the studio was as bustling and excited as a circus.

The area in which the tiger would move around was enclosed in wire netting, with the director, crew, and three cameras stationed outside. Only Tycoon and his handlers were inside the netting, where they rehearsed the scene. The wife would hold the tiger down in a corner, off-camera, while from the opposite corner her husband called, "Tycoon! Tycoon!" Tycoon would then stride across the studio. Once he had gotten the hang of that, they practiced having him stop midway and look at the camera. After calling, "Tycoon!" the handler would halt the approaching beast in its tracks. It tickled me to hear him say "*Stoppun!*" instead of "Stop," but it worked like a charm: the animal came to a dead halt.

When the tiger paused and looked at Dersu, Dersu was to fire, and then the tiger would flee into the forest. That was the plan.

When everything was ready, it was time for Solomin and Dersu to go inside the netting. Now the reporters jostled to see what would happen, some enterprising cameramen even perching up among the ceiling lights just to get an unobstructed shot. The spectator seats were filled to overflowing.

We felt like Nero throwing Christians to the lions. It was too bad for the two men, but there was no help for it. They had to go into the mesh cage.

Afterward, Solomin told me half-jokingly, "It scared me to think this might be the end. My kids were still little, after all. Dersu looked nonchalant, so I pretended not to be afraid. But he had the advantage of me, because he'd already lived over sixty years."

Tycoon proved to be every bit the veteran. We were done after only two takes.

The roomful of people burst into applause. The reporters then scrambled closer, and began clamoring requests for photos: "Kurosawa-san, one with you and the tiger!" "Kurosawa-san, now pat the tiger on the head!" The handlers were holding Tycoon down, so there was little enough danger, and yet in every picture of Solomin, Dersu, the tiger, and Kurosawa, the men all seem focused nervously on the tiger. Their expressions are stiff, as if to say, "Let's hurry and get this over with!"

Tycoon also appears in other scenes in the film, as the tiger walking through the taiga and the tiger who attacks the campsite.

At one point, Arseniev awakens in the middle of the night and sees a leaping tiger silhouetted on the tent. That silhouette is very beautiful; it is one of my favorite cuts in the entire movie.

The script contains this voice-over by Arseniev: "What Dersu calls 'Amba' . . . could it be the fear of unbearable solitude in the taiga . . . and fear of the decrepitude of old age?"

HORSES

The slightest presence of horses in a movie increases the movie's scale, and makes it seem big-budget. Horses do, in fact, require a huge outlay.

Suppose that on top of horses, you are dealing with a period film containing battle scenes. Most producers will quickly throw in the towel, it being a huge task for which they are eminently unsuited. Nor are there any directors today who could set hundreds of horses galloping to convincingly recreate a battle from the medieval Age of the Warring States. But there was one, once, in Japan: Akira Kurosawa.

In 1979, talks between Toho and Kurosawa Productions concerning *Kagemusha* wrapped up, and preparations for filming got underway right after New Year's. One of the biggest problems was where to find all the horses that would be needed. The answer to that question would affect both the place of filming and the schedule.

Kurosawa said that he wanted about 150 horses for the final scene, in which the Takeda army is wiped out. The location he settled on was in the far northern island of Hokkaido, a land of wide open spaces where he hoped to round up that many horses. The task was not to be an easy one, however.

Back in 1954, when Kurosawa filmed *Seven Samurai*, all we had to do was mention how many horses were wanted and a man named Mago, who had also scouted the Gotenba location where the movie was shot, would provide them, anytime—complete with riders. These were the villagers whom we called *magosakku*, a play on Mago and Cossack. At the time, many farm households had at least one horse. (This was back in an age when few Japanese owned automobiles or telephones.) Mago would ride around on horseback from door to door, telling people where and when to show up the next day. Before dawn, men dressed in full armor would emerge from the houses, mount their horses, and ride to the set over the paths between paddy fields; along the way, the sun would rise, lighting up this remarkable spectacle.

Even so, in *Seven Samurai* the most horses ever used at one time was about fifty, for the scene in which the bandits come galloping down to attack the village. Now Kurosawa was talking about three times that many.

In Hokkaido he obtained an introduction to Minpei Shirai of the famous Shirai Ranch. Shirai had the typical horseman's slight build, but he was enormously bighearted and spoke in a resounding voice. He said he knew just the person for us, and persuaded his friend Toshi Hasegawa to join our group. A fine fellow who now manages his own ranch in Hidaka, Hasegawa was then filming a documentary at the Shirai Ranch.

Years later, Hasegawa told me that when he and Shirai first met with Kurosawa, he had half-decided to turn down the job, afraid he couldn't live up to the high expectations that went with such an important task. But, he went on, "Kurosawa-san was a man of such charm, I was completely bowled over. I made up my mind that if there was anything I could do to help him out, I'd do it. Sounds like a scene right out of *Kagemusha*, doesn't it?"

So he, too, was drawn in by Kurosawa's great magnetism. Without his and Shirai's help, the scenes involving so many horses could not have been filmed successfully.

There were six months before filming would start at the Shirai Ranch in October; during the interim, 150 horses had to be assembled and trained. Most of the horses in Hokkaido are thoroughbreds destined for the racetrack. Alas, those with poor racing prospects, bone fractures, or the like, are auctioned off to go under the butcher's knife. The auctions took place once a week, every Tuesday, involving some 100 horses. Shirai and Hasegawa would go out every week scouting for horses we could use, bringing back five or ten at a time. At first, they cost about 150,000 yen ($700) apiece, but as talk spread about the movie, word got out that Shirai was looking for horses to film, and the price went up accordingly. By the end, one horse would cost nearly half a million yen ($2,300). This may seem expensive, but renting horses would have cost far more: At 80,000 yen per day, renting 100 horses for a single day would have set us back eight million yen ($37,000). With months of filming in the offing, that was prohibitively expensive. Even at half a million a head, it was cheaper to buy.

Once ransomed, the horses could be used from morning till night. Shirai opined that they would be only too glad to work, having won a last-minute reprieve from the death penalty. And so in the end we purchased some 130 horses. That was the easy part; the hard part still lay ahead.

Having been purchased separately, all 130 horses were presumably mutual strangers. Perhaps there were a few who exchanged greetings of joyful surprise at finding one another alive, enraptured to be reunited by a kind of equestrian Schindler's list—but in any case, all would now have to come together as one to work on the film, laying all other concerns aside. In other words, there was to be positively no horsing around, if you get my drift: with the serious business of filming at hand, no displays of sexual attraction could be tolerated among the horses. Since the herd was mixed, unless preventive steps were taken, males were likely to get excited and suddenly run amok. The only recourse was to remove the source of their problematic passion.

Doubtless this was a fate preferable to death. Even so, it seemed rather cruel that our film should deprive horses of one of the joys of living. But Dr. Okita, the veterinarian, made light of it as a commonplace event; I heard afterward that he thought nothing of doing five or six castrations a day.

In the hands of such a veteran, the operation was lightning-quick. After anesthetic was applied, snip snip and the job was done, the offending articles cast straight into a bucket. A little tincture of iodine and then, after an adjustment period of a week or so, any former stallion would be as good as new, ready for a new life as a eunuch. Apparently, however, it would take two months for the procedure to take full effect.

From the beginning, every effort was made to avoid purchasing males, but even so we ended up with about thirty stallions. Each one underwent the above procedure, and so in the end we mustered a herd of mares and geldings.

The next problem was the riders. Here we enlisted the cooperation of the local equestrian club, a college riding club, and the staff of the Hidaka Ranch, among others. We conducted a successful casting call from the public for *Kagemusha* and then, drawing on cast members who could already ride, we organized a group of youths called the "Thirty Knights" who came to Hokkaido a month early to help begin training the horses.

One problem was the banner each samurai wore fastened to the back of his armor, which flapped in the wind and terrified the horses. If anyone so equipped tried to mount them, the horses would buck and protest with expressions of great distaste. It would take time to accustom them to the banners and get them to realize that they were nothing but pieces of cloth.

The horses were also put off by the lances their riders carried, which tended to strike them on the side and get in the way. Again, it took considerable time to calm the horses down and demonstrate to their satisfaction that the lances were fake, with rubber tips that could do no harm.

Once horse and rider could manage to function as a team, the next challenge was to get all the horses to run fast together as a unit. If even one horse separated from the rest or failed to keep up, it would not be caught on screen.

In the last scene of *Kagemusha*, the army of Takeda, once celebrated as "swift as the wind, quiet as the forest, merciless as fire, and immovable as a mountain," goes on the attack in repeated waves, only to be mowed down and annihilated by the gunners of Oda Nobunaga's army.

I have always been moved by the sight of the dead and dying horses lying in heaps on the battlefield at the end of the film. Some foreign journalists have expressed disappointment, complaining that they had expected glorious battle scenes in the style of earlier Kurosawa films, but I in turn was disappointed by such petty commentary. Has any other film ever portrayed a battlefield heaped with the corpses of horses on such a vast scale, or with such terrible beauty?

At a press conference, a female journalist asked, "How did you film those horses? I'm sure you didn't really kill them, but I can't help worrying." Kurosawa gave her a big smile and told her to rest easy. "They were all fast asleep, knocked out with sleeping medicine. Why, we even spread cloths on the ground so they wouldn't injure their eyes when they fell." A relieved murmur spread through the room.

During filming of the scene, the careful coordination by Shirai, Hasegawa, and Dr. Okita paid off brilliantly. The trickiest part was making a judgment call about the weather. All 130 horses had to be injected with anesthetic at the same time; once that had been done, whatever might happen with the weather, there could be no retakes that day. Nor would it be possible to do the scene the next day, either, since doping the horses on successive days would have been too much for them.

To prevent the horses from acting up dangerously when the anesthetic was administered, they had to receive a mild tranquilizer first, thirty minutes beforehand.

Across the wide battleground, the 130 horses were put in

place at suitable intervals; stationed next to each was a warrior scheduled to play dead who would, at the signal "Ready!" smear his armor with gore.

On top of the *intore-dai* platform was the A camera. Kurosawa was seated there, alternately looking up at the sky and gazing around at the scene. One level below him was Shirai, megaphone in hand, waiting for instructions without ever taking his eyes off the director's face.

The wide grassy plain was utterly still, filled with tension. Here and there among the 130 horses were some fifteen veterinarians in white coats, also waiting for Kurosawa to give the word. Each vet was responsible for ten horses. The veterinarians, and their apprentices, had been especially recruited for this urgent occasion. None of them had ever experienced anything like this before. None of them had any idea what might happen.

"Looks like this weather will hold," Kurosawa commented, looking up at the sky.

Straight away Shirai called up from the level below, "Is that a go?"

"Uh . . . " Kurosawa consulted with the cameraman before announcing, "Okay! Let's do it."

"All right, I'll have them give the tranquilizers." Shirai put the megaphone to his mouth and cried, "Begin injecting the tranquilizers!"

The white-coated veterinarians began weaving their way from one horse to the next, running around till all the injections were done.

Shirai said through the speaker, "Okay, everybody, thirty

minutes from now you will administer the anesthetic, so remain in your places."

Those thirty minutes seemed to take forever. Kurosawa spent them looking up anxiously at the sky.

This time it was Shirai who spoke first, telling Kurosawa, "I think it's time."

Kurosawa's voice rang out. "All right, cavalry, in your places!" The assistant director instructed the riders, "Listen up! If you feel endangered by your horse, you may leave your place and retreat to safety, but try not to attract attention."

"Start the anesthetic!" boomed Shirai. Once again the white-coated veterinarians darted in and out among the horses.

Shirai looked up at Kurosawa and told him, "The effects will wear off in half an hour, remember, so that's how long you've got to shoot the scene." Kurosawa appeared to give instructions to the cameraman behind him to change his lens and start rolling. Quickly, Shirai grabbed his megaphone and shouted in an impassioned voice, "All veterinarians, please get out of camera range immediately! The cameras are rolling!"

Snatching up their medical equipment, the vets raced off the field as fast as they could—not as easy as it may sound, given the huge size of the field.

Individual horses responded differently to the injection; they didn't just all topple over at once. Some did, but others stood swaying on their feet, while still others fell down and then writhed, struggling to get up again. It looked, as far as I could tell, like a real battlefield.

What surprised us was that the fallen horses snored loudly.

The three cameras kept rolling until the effects of the anesthetic wore off and the horses got up and began walking around again. The huge operation was a success.

When filming was done, the horses were led off the field, each one following after its warrior. Some were still groggy or even snoring loudly as they walked off.

A few days later, Kurosawa looked at the rushes and declared that he needed more shots of fallen horses. Hokkaido was already deep in snow, however, so it was decided to do the shooting in Gotenba. It wouldn't do to use horses from Mago's riding club, as the procedure was not after all good for the horses' health, so instead, Hasegawa brought down seven of "Kurosawa-san's horses," all the way from Hokkaido. While Kurosawa was busy editing, a separate team in Gotenba administered anesthetic to our horses once again, and filmed fallen horses over a period of several days. Come to think of it, those horses who escaped death by the skin of their teeth worked really hard for us.

After filming, the lucky horses went off to spend the rest of their lives with new masters, taken in by riding clubs or other places. Even so, they must all be long since dead by now. This all happened many years ago.

CROWS

Kurosawa intended to be a painter in his youth, as is well known. He had such talent that when he was only eighteen, one of his paintings was accepted for display in the prestigious Nika Exhibition.

Later, both family and social conditions changed, so that in 1936, at age twenty-six, he applied at PCL Films (forerunner of today's Toho Studio) for a job as assistant director. He won the job and so embarked on his career as a film director.

Kurosawa always loved painting. Even late in life, he painted whenever he had the chance. If coloring materials or felt pens were laid out on his desk, he would happily sit and wordlessly draw picture after picture, like a child.

Among his favorite artists were Cezanne, van Gogh, Rouault, and Tessai. In *Dreams* (Yume, 1990), a movie consisting of eight discrete dream episodes, one of the characters is his beloved Vincent van Gogh. The episode in which the famed artist appears is number five, entitled "Crows."

The protagonist, an art student, attends an exhibition of van Gogh paintings. Seven works are featured, including the well-known "Sunflowers," "Starry Night," and "The Langlois Bridge at Arles." All are of course reproductions. Abstract painter Yoshi Hamada carefully duplicated the paintings, but when it came time to shoot, it became necessary to emphasize the raised texture of the paint, and so Kurosawa himself took up the brush and worked on them further. I remember that as he painted, he muttered in acute embarrassment, "Imagine that—me, touching up a van Gogh! Well, this is my dream, after all, so maybe he'll forgive me."

The art student, played by Akira Terao, pauses in front of the painting of Langlois Bridge and then approaches it. Suddenly the horse on the bridge begins to move and the washerwomen begin scrubbing their laundry; stepping into the painting, the student addresses one of them, inquiring if she knows where van Gogh lives. That washerwoman, incidentally, was played by Catherine Cadou, Kurosawa's longtime French interpreter. Great pains were

Assistant director Sugino making ripples in the water from underneath the laundry platform.

taken to see that the costumes and shapes of the other women also matched van Gogh's painting exactly.

Nor was it only the people who had to be matched to the original. A reproduction of van Gogh's painting was at the cameraman's side, and both he and the director kept an eye on it as they issued various demands. They made a great fuss.

In the original painting, the surface of the river is covered with great circling ripples, but that effect proved hard to duplicate. A situation like that is where the assistant director proves his worth. Tsuyoshi Sugino put on a wetsuit and dove into the water. Hidden under the platform where the women were gathered to do their laundry, he stood in the water with a basketball in his hands, and succeeded in creating the right ripples by slowly raising and lowering his arms. The water was so high that it came up to his chin, leaving very little breathing space. It was a version of water torture, but Sugino put up with it.

This much of the episode was filmed in Gotenba. From that point on, after the student ("I") spots van Gogh and shares an encounter with him, until the painter disappears beyond a wheat field with crows flying over it, every scene was shot on location in the town of Memanbetsu, Hokkaido.

Jiro Tanimoto, director of Memanbetsu commerce, industry, and tourism, was an ardent movie fan who worked with us wholeheartedly for six months. Our most important challenge at this location site was to recreate the conditions of van Gogh's last painting; the script called for *"a wheat field over which flies a flock of crows under a troubled sky."*

This was the painting "Wheat Field with Crows," praised by critic Hideo Kobayashi (1902–83) in his "Letters of van Gogh." On seeing a superb reproduction of the famous painting completed by van Gogh shortly before his suicide, Kobayashi wrote, he was so overcome that he crouched down before it in awe.

First, Tanimoto gave us his opinion that the wheat in the painting was actually the barley used in making beer, technically known as "two-rowed barley." For the crop to be ripe and golden for our planned filming in early August, he said we would have to plant the seeds in early May, and go over the field with a roller when the plants were five or six centimeters high. In the old days, people did this with their feet, so it was called "barley treading"; the point was to strengthen the roots so that the plants would not easily topple over. Tanimoto spent the interim months visiting the barley field daily, a book of van Gogh's paintings in hand, anxiously keeping watch over our crop to see whether it would grow to resemble the painting.

We had one other serious problem to contend with: crows.

On Kurosawa's staff, far and away the best person for handling animals was assistant director Toru Tanaka. He had a gift for tenaciously finding ways to work things out when it came to animals.

The number of crows in van Gogh's painting is 42. This meant readying at least 150 crows for the shoot, since once set free, they wouldn't be coming back. A supply of 150 crows would allow us only three tries, at that. We contacted Animal Productions and were told it would cost 70,000 yen ($510) per crow, each time we released them. That added up to some 3 million yen ($22,000) per try.

Tanaka was indignant. Weren't crows to be found all over the place, raising a racket? He made up his mind to go out and see what he could do on his own. And yet, our location site was in distant Hokkaido. The task was no easy one.

On contacting the Wildlife Management Laboratory in Tsukuba, we received the glad news that a man who had invented a machine for capturing crows lived in the city of Rumoi, Hokkaido. The idea was to bait a large box so that the crow entered from the top, through a funnel-shaped device. Once in the box, it could not get out. The city of Abashiri used this method of trapping crows, we learned.

At last Tanimoto and Tanaka saw a glimmer of light. But if we were to assemble 150 crows, we would need a full-time keeper for them. That's when we turned to Shoji Oe (67), a self-styled Jack-of-all-trades and local celebrity in Hokkaido.

First, in a larch forest near the location site, Oe set up a huge detention camp for crows, made of wire mesh. For the next month or so he and the others made the rounds of garbage dumps in Abashiri, Bihoro, and other Hokkaido cities, collecting scavenging crows. They succeeded beyond our expectations: in mid-July, word came that they had accumulated 250 birds.

On July 31, we entered Memanbetsu to start shooting. August 5 was D-Day, the day the crows would be called on to perform. Tanaka had gone up two days ahead of time to huddle with the others and work out a plan for releasing the crows over the wheat field in such a way as to resemble van Gogh's painting.

To begin with, they decided that fifty crows, roughly the number in the painting, were too few to show up well on screen. It was decided to divide the 250 birds into two groups, and risk everything on only two shots. To get the 125 birds to rise simultaneously from various parts of the field, they would be divided into smaller groups and set in place ahead of time. The staff made twenty wooden boxes, each of which held seven or so crows. The top of the box was made with hinged doors that opened right and left. Merely opening the top of the box would not be enough to get them to fly out, so the bottom of the box was also made so that it would slide up. Two people were needed for each box, so Tanaka set to work coaching forty local workers hired especially for this task.

This was the plan. Once the boxes were in place, Tanaka would give the signal, yelling "Crows!" The boxes would all open at once. Then the two men standing on either side of each box would raise the bottom as, off-screen to the left, blank firecrackers were set off to scare the birds. The birds would then fly up into the sky and scatter, as in the painting.

When the crows were divided into small groups and put into the boxes, they panicked, so as soon as the boxes were in place, to calm them down we played a tape of crows cawing. It had been lent to us for the occasion by a hunting association, with the explanation that it contained the sound of crows calling to each other. On hearing this cawing sound, the crows in the boxes would think they were being summoned by crows on the outside, and prepare themselves to fly off quickly in the direction of the voices.

But according to Tanaka, catching the crows just to put them into small groups was difficult. They were so big that even if you could catch them with a net, you had to transfer them to the box with both hands.

August 5 dawned, a clear, scorching hot day. The field was ripe and golden, rippling in the breeze. We made a road through the center of it, in exact accordance with van Gogh's painting. The effect was perfect.

Oe nervously muttered, "Okay crows, fly for me now, okay? That's all that's left to do." Tanimoto couldn't utter a word.

There were two cameras, and one high-definition camera (for creating special effects later). Kurosawa called for the crows to be gotten ready, and from beside the cameras, Tanaka directed the crow operatives to take their places.

Out into the yellow field marched a row of assistants visible only from the waist up, including older women in white hats and college students in T-shirts. They carried the crows out, two people per box, like a caravan carrying precious objects. When they reached their assigned locations, each pair squatted down, disappearing from sight. All we could see then was the tranquil, pastoral scene of a golden field stretching on and on before our eyes. No one would ever have suspected that it contained forty people waiting with bated breath for the signal to release their crows.

From his position high in the air by the mounted camera, where he could supervise the whole operation, chief assistant director Takashi Koizumi was conferring carefully with Kurosawa about the signal for the release of the crows.

The cut started with a narrow road in the distance, down which van Gogh, seen from behind, strode rapidly away. As Martin Scorsese, who was scheduled to play van Gogh, had not yet arrived in Japan, the scene was shot with an understudy. As "I," played by Akira Terao, ran after him through the wheat field, a flock of crows rose out of the field all of a sudden as if to block his way. "I" stopped still, dumbstruck. That was it.

The timing of the birds' flight was extremely tricky: if it didn't go right this time, there would be only one more chance. Everyone felt the tension.

Kurosawa turned to Tanaka and asked, "Ready?"

"Yes," said Tanaka, "but we're playing the tape for them now, so wait another minute."

"What are they doing, singing?" said cameraman Takao Saito, and everyone tittered.

Tanaka gave chief assistant director Koizumi the okay sign.

"All right, Kurosawa-san, we're ready for a take."

Kurosawa was composed. "Good, let's do it."

Shouts echoed across the field. "This is a take!"

The Italian assistant director Vitorio Dalle Ore struck the clapperboard.

Van Gogh walked off into the distance. Terao ran after him.

"Crows!" Chief Koizumi's voice rang out. At the same time, off to the left, off-screen, the members of the hunting association set off firecrackers: BAM BAM BAM BAM BAM.

There they go, there they go!

Released at long last from captivity, the crows flapped their wings, soared up into the sky, and vanished. Tanimoto, Oe, and Tanaka watched them off, speechless with emotion.

Terao gazed up at the sky and stood stock still. All of this had taken perhaps forty seconds.

"Cut!" yelled Kurosawa. "How'd it go?" he asked, looking around at the cameramen.

"Um, well, pretty good," said one. "They sure took off in a big hurry," said another. "One was walking instead of flying," somebody pointed out. Cameraman Masaharu Ueda wore a discontented look. Even Tanaka declared himself unsatisfied.

Since there were enough crows for another take, it was decided to try again, following the same procedure. The second time, everything went close to perfection. "Cut!" yelled Kurosawa, then immediately added, "Print!" He jumped up in delight from his chair and turned to Tanimoto and the rest, applauding.

Shouts of triumph arose. Amid a storm of applause, Oe took off his hat and approached Kurosawa with excitement on his face. "Thank you very much," he said, and bowed from the waist. Tanimoto also came forward, asking earnestly, "Was it really all right?" Tanaka stood bowing profusely to Tanimoto and Oe.

Shouts of "That was great!" and "Thank you!" rang out on and on and on.

Such moments are the true joy of filmmaking. For the sake of the forty seconds just filmed, preparations had begun way back in February, continuing through the sowing of the field in May, the gathering of the crows and all the other challenges, to culminate in the reward of this moment. Of course we were happy!

The crow battalion lined up for a commemorative photo with Akira Kurosawa. When the pictures were taken, there was another round of long applause. Kurosawa turned to everyone and thanked them, then doffed his hat and bowed.

The arrival of Martin Scorsese, who was to play the part of van Gogh, had been held up by the filming of *Goodfellas*, but on August 14, having briefly torn himself away, he landed at Memanbetsu Airport. He went straight to the location site and greeted Kurosawa rapidly, adding, "The crew of *Goodfellas* looked happy when I told them I was off to Japan for a little while. They all send their best."

That day we lost no time doing a makeup test and costume coordination there in the hotel, as Kurosawa looked on. Later, Kurosawa said to me with a laugh, hunching his shoulders, "He's good, Scorsese, don't you think? He's got the feel of van Gogh. He really made a strong impression on me that time."

By "that time," he was referring to the time in 1980 when he went to New York to promote *Kagemusha*. Martin Scorsese had come to visit Kurosawa in his room at the Plaza Hotel. His arms overflowing with papers, he had come to enlist support in a signature-collecting campaign. Unless something was done to improve film preservation, sooner or later all color prints were doomed to fade, Scorsese had explained. The thing to do was to get started now making new negatives using the three-strip Technicolor dye transfer process, he stressed, his words so rapid-fire that the interpreter could barely keep up.

After talking nonstop, Scorsese collected signatures, then packed up and promptly disappeared.

Kurosawa had been bowled over by the man's cyclone-like power and energy. Though taken aback at the time, he thought later that the fanatical expression on Scorsese's face that day would be perfect for playing van Gogh.

On August 15, after the second cut of the scene, Martin Scorsese hastily tore off his costume, headed straight for Memanbetsu Airport, and flew back to New York.

"I'm busy. I have no time. I can't stay around here." Afterward, we laughed that it was just like these lines of van Gogh's from the film.

Later, a Frenchman mentioned that it was somehow strange to see the Dutchman van Gogh played by an Italian-American who spoke New York–accented English to a Japanese. He may have had a point.

When asked if it was all right to use English in this scene, Kurosawa had replied, "It's a dream, after all. No problem."

Still, after all was said and done, it was painful to think of the anguish van Gogh must have felt as, leaving behind that "wheat field over which flew a flock of crows under a troubled sky," he shot himself in the chest. According to one theory, he had borrowed the pistol in order to scare off the noisy crows.

As van Gogh lay dying, he said to his younger brother, Theo, who came rushing to his bedside, "You mustn't cry. I did it because I thought it would be best for everyone." He thought that the fifty francs Theo sent every month was a burden that only his death could lighten, leaving everyone in his brother's household better off.

In all his life, he sold only one painting.

In 1987, ninety-seven years after van Gogh's death, his painting "Sunflowers" was sold at a London auction to the Yasuda Fire and Marine Insurance Company of Japan for the then-world record price of 5.3 billion yen ($49 million).

The absurd injustice of it all fills me with unending rage.

7

Kurosawa and Music

A SOLO CONDUCTOR

I will never hear Kurosawa's live voice again, but it was a good voice, with a low sweetness to it—even when he was yelling. It seems that from the time he was a schoolboy, he was fond of singing. I can easily picture him, a bright young man standing erect by the organ, singing with all his heart.

On location for filming, every night Kurosawa would eat dinner with the main crew and cast. Having the meal at the same time and place was indispensable to him. If anyone had kept a nightly record of those dinner parties, it might have gone far toward explaining what Akira Kurosawa the director was all about.

The dinners always went on till late at night, until he announced the end with these words: "All right, then, see you tomorrow, everybody." This was usually around one or two in the morning. Until then he would put on a virtual solo performance, in a display of energy that was nothing short of amazing.

Should someone chance to incur Kurosawa's wrath, however, the pleasant atmosphere would abruptly change. A chill tension would envelop the scene, like a dousing of cold water. People

183

would sit motionless, unable even to lift a fork, as Kurosawa's voice rang out in a harsh dressing-down.

Usually, though, he was in a good mood. He was such a great storyteller that even if we had heard the tale before, no one ever stopped him; we laughed with every telling till our sides ached.

Every so often the conversation would turn to songs taught in elementary school music classes in the Meiji Period, and Kurosawa would burst into a rendition of a song officially designated by the Ministry of Education for singing in schools, such as "The Battle of Tsushima":

> Enemy ships have appeared and drawn near,
> The destiny of our land lies at stake.
> Summoning each one to give his all,
> On the flagship mast the signal goes aloft.

As he sang these words, Kurosawa appeared like a little boy. His cheeks would flush as he lifted his voice with gusto: "Enemy *ships* have ap-*peared* and *drawn near!*" Then, a little embarrassed, he would stop. In his autobiography, he comments, "To this day I am fond of the songs 'The Battle of Tsushima' and 'Shuishiying.' The melodies are light and simple, the words are clear, and each song narrates events with surprising precision and accuracy, without any forced emotion."

The lyrics and music of the song "The Meeting at Shuishiying," which describes the 1905 ceasefire conference between Generals Nogi and Stoessel at the end of the Russo-Japanese war, are by tanka poet and scholar Nobutsuna Sasaki (1872–1963).

Kurosawa would tell us,

It starts out like this:

> Port Arthur fallen,
> the enemy General Stoessel
> and General Nogi
> met in Shuishiying

Sounds exactly like a film script, doesn't it? Starting with a long shot. Then it goes on, "In the garden, one jujube tree." Now the camera closes in on the jujube tree.

> In the lone private house
> still left standing,
> walls full of bullet holes,
> the generals face-to-face.

See how the words paint a picture?"

Sure enough, the song even goes on to include fragments of dialogue between the two men. It could easily be filmed as written.

While we were filming *Seven Samurai*, the nightly dinners were in traditional banquet style, in one great room. We sat on the tatami floor in long facing rows, each person with a small low table in front of him or her. Everyone would socialize with those on either side, taking turns filling each other's sake cups, but those across the way were too far off for extended conversation.

That circumstance may partly explain why Kurosawa often

called for everyone to sing. Nowadays it's an everyday occurrence to go out for drinks and karaoke, but this was altogether different: we sang in chorus. He was partial to the sort of singing people might do in music class or at a school festival, but never at a drinking party. Specifically, he had us sing in rounds.

"Let's do 'Ding-dong!'" Kurosawa would declare. Then actor Minoru Chiaki would jump up and divide the room into sections: "Okay, everyone from here to here is group one, group two is from here to here, and the rest of us will be group three."

"We'd better do this standing up," Kurosawa would say, rising, and everybody would follow suit—even those who were dismayed by all this, and would rather have gone on drinking—until we were all on our feet. By this time, gripping wooden chopsticks in lieu of a conductor's baton, Kurosawa would be looking around the room with a stern face, looking for all the world like a conductor surveying his performers as they tuned their instruments.

"Are you people over there ready? We'll start with Mifune's team. After that, Nakai's team join in. All right, Nakai, eyes on me, now." With a flourish of chopsticks, he would call, "One, two, three, go!" and motion to each group in turn like a fisherman casting his line.

"Listen, listen, the sound of bells, ringing in the sky." Group one would start off, and group two would chime in: "Listen, listen, the sound of bells, ringing in the sky." Then group three. By then group one would be winding up—"Ding-dong, ding-dong, ringing in the sky"—but because it was a round, the singing would continue endlessly, on and on.

Kurosawa would preside over this with a look of great solemnity, like the scene in *One Wonderful Sunday* (Subarashiki Nichiyobi,

"And a one and a two . . ." The profession of film director is something like that of orchestra conductor.

1947) where actor Isao Numasaki pretends to conduct. If one of the parts was the least bit slow coming in, he would wave his chopsticks vigorously and yell, "No, no, no! What's wrong with you people? Watch me for your cue!" He carried on just as if something had gone wrong in a shoot.

  The late Fumio Yanoguchi, the sound man, would pull on my sleeve and whisper in my ear, "Hey, I'm going out for a little while. All this has nothing to do with work. Okay? I've had all I can take." Then he would sneak out of the room. No doubt while the rest of us were still hard at it, going "Ding-dong, ding-dong," he was at a bar somewhere nearby, nursing a drink and telling a sympathetic barkeep how stressed out he was.

  Kurosawa used to say, "You want to know what the job of film director resembles most? I'll tell you. Conducting an orchestra."

  That could well be. In both cases, a large number of strangers work together to express one person's will and vision; therein lies the similarity, it seems to me.

FUMIO HAYASAKA

In movies, there were three things that not even Akira Kurosawa could control: weather, animals, and music. For these three, there was nothing to do but wait until the situation improved, or give up. Of course, Kurosawa was never one to give up. He waited.

For weather, he would hold out as long as the money lasted; his motto might have been, "All things come to him who waits." Waiting for weather was the number one reason why his production costs soared. With animals, it was possible to bring in a substitute, and as a last resort Kurosawa could always fall back on his trump card, editing. But music was different: he could neither do without it, nor spare any time waiting for it.

Once during editing Kurosawa said with a sigh, "I should have studied composing." He probably wasn't serious, but in any case, that would certainly have been too much. If on top of everything else he had taken on the task of composing the scores, he would never have finished his films, even if the man had lived for centuries.

Kurosawa was always listening to recordings, even in the middle of a shoot—not to enjoy the music, but to search for something that would go with the movie he was making.

This was a man whose mind was not of a strictly logical turn. He had little aptitude for abstract reasoning, and when it came to music, he could convey his wishes only by offering concrete examples. In his autobiography, he touches on the time he conferred with composer Fumio Hayasaka about the music for *Drunken Angel* (Yoidore Tenshi, 1948). Kurosawa suggested that during the scene when yakuza Mifune walks down the street through the black market, the music coming out of the loudspeakers should be "The Cuckoo Waltz." Hayasaka smiled right away. "Ah yes, counterpoint," he said. "That's right," I affirmed, "sniper." This expression "sniper" was something only Hayasaka and I understood. It referred to a Soviet film of that title containing a superb example of counterpoint between image and sound. We used the term as a handy abbreviation for the use of music to that effect.

Although I have never seen that Soviet picture, I have heard the scene described so many times that I can imagine it vividly.

The front in World War I, with German and Russian forces face to face. It's night. Heavy rain is falling. In the shadow of a dead horse, a German sniper is shooting. Russian soldiers crawl out and stab the sniper, killing him. Suddenly, from a trench across the way come the strains of a record playing "Ça C'est Paris." The contrast of that gay music with the gruesome action, Kurosawa stressed, is powerful.

Kurosawa was fond of saying that music should not just add to the movie, but multiply it. The contrapuntal technique he often employed is perhaps an ideal example of such multiplication.

Ikiru was made the year after *Rashomon* took the Grand Prize at the Venice Film Festival, and both Kurosawa and Hayasaka were in high spirits.

When Kurosawa met with Hayasaka to discuss music, he came with an armload of records. Hayasaka lived not far from the Toho film studio, in Kinuta. The assistant directors and I would often follow along as Kurosawa called at his house. We would all sit in a spacious room there, listening as one record after another was played—but unfortunately I cannot recall one word of the conversations the two men had.

When Hayasaka made tea for us, he would pile a mound of finest-quality green tea in the teapot, and discard the leaves after every use; I do remember how scandalously wasteful this seemed to me.

What I will never forget about *Ikiru* is what happened after the first screening. As usual, the release date was just ahead, breathing down our necks. By the time we had finished watching the film, it was late at night. As the film ended and we filed out of the screening room, the mood was tense. Photography, lighting, and sound engineers, as well as producers, gathered around Kurosawa to gauge his reaction as we made our way back to the anteroom. Kurosawa walked along wordlessly, deep in thought. The crew, too, kept silent as we entered the freezing cold anteroom, switched on the light, and sat at the table. Hayasaka sat next to Kurosawa, eyes on him.

Finally Kurosawa spoke: "Listen, everyone. I miscalculated. It's completely my fault . . . but it was a mistake to put music in that wake scene, during the flashbacks." He looked at Hayasaka, who remained silent. "I'm sorry. But the music overwhelms the scene. Kanji Watanabe's tireless efforts to make the park before he died are somehow undercut. I never thought it would turn out like this."

Hayasaka thought for awhile, and then said with a chagrined smile, "You're probably right. Let's get rid of it."

At once the room was a hive of activity: the production and editing crews jumped up and tore out of the room, and others telephoned the film lab or made other necessary arrangements. If the sound for that scene was not remixed immediately, the film would not be ready in time for its projected release.

Kurosawa apologized over and over to Hayasaka, and finally sent him home with instructions to get some rest.

Hayasaka later wrote about the incident in a letter to Ichiro Saito:

> So they took out about fourteen rolls and redid them all with sound effects. It took a bit of courage . . . For two or three days I was depressed and stayed cooped up at home, but Kurosawa came over to comfort me, and finally I recovered my spirits. Working on *Ikiru*, I was happy, I experimented, I lapsed into mediocrity and then had to pull myself out of it, I got discouraged . . . there were all sorts of emotional ups and downs.[27]

Fumio Hayasaka was born in Sendai in 1914. He moved to Hokkaido early in his childhood, and later taught himself composition; at twenty-four he won the Weingartner Prize for *Ancient Dance Music*. Besides composing for Kurosawa's films, he also did the music for major films by Kenji Mizoguchi. He contracted tuberculosis at an early age, and died suddenly on October 15, 1955, during production of *Record of a Living Being* (Ikimono no Kiroku). He was only 41 years old.

Six days before he passed away, Hayasaka wrote to Kurosawa what would be his last letter. He gave his impressions and opinions after seeing the rushes for *Record of a Living Being*, venturing that in the scene where Jiro (Minoru Chiaki) talks late at night about his father, the actor's voice is too loud. Would it not be more poignant to have the father (Toshiro Mifune) listen as his children spoke about him in hushed tones? The scene was later redone accordingly. The thought of faithful Hayasaka in his sickbed, screwing up his strength to write these words, is heartrending. He closes the letter this way:

> This may be the comment of someone unable to grasp your thoughtful direction, and if so, I apologize. I have not expressed myself fully, but the above [is my feeling]. That is what happened to strike me. Everything else is superb and needs no comment. Sincerely, Hayasaka. To Akira Kurosawa.

Those were the last words he ever wrote.

Fifty years ago, we went to Nara together on location for *Rashomon*. We were all still young then, so we often climbed Mount Wakakusa, which was near our lodgings. Hayasaka came down from Tokyo, and one day he too climbed the mountain with Kurosawa and the rest of us. I was very fond of Hayasaka, so I stayed close by him.

The "mountain" is not much higher than a pancake, but with his weak chest Hayasaka became out of breath about halfway up. He said he needed to stop and rest, and sat down on the grass. I sat down beside him and we looked down at a restaurant and sword shop below. I seem to recall that he talked about Chinese ink for calligraphy.

Already at the summit, Kurosawa turned and called down to us in a loud voice, "You two, don't bother coming up!" He said it to express concern about Hayasaka's physical condition, and to see that he did not overexert himself. Hayasaka and I looked at each other and smiled. I remember it all vividly, even the warm, golden light, like a scene from an old-fashioned movie about youth.

Hayasaka wrote lyrics for the famous "Samurai Theme" from *Seven Samurai*. Later, the song was recorded by Yoshiko Yamaguchi and put on the market. The lyrics are incomparably beautiful, like the man himself. There are three verses in all, but I will quote only the second.

Kurosawa was fond of singing this song.

> Like the wind, the samurai
> Blows across the earth.
> *Cho ryo furyo hyo furyo*
> *Hiyaruro arayo hyo furyo*
> He who was seen yesterday is no more today.
> He who is seen today will be gone tomorrow
> Unaware that tomorrow is his last,
> How sad he is today.

MASARU SATO

Record of a Living Being was never intended to have much music in the first place. Hayasaka had left behind a sketch for "Music of the Stars," which his student Masaru Sato was called upon to flesh out.

Two years later, Kurosawa asked Sato to do the music for *The Throne of Blood*. Sato was clearly excited to be tapped for the assignment. Later he wrote, "Now I felt I could really buckle down and do something. And so what was for me the stormy year of 1955 came to a close, and in came the year 1956, when I felt I would fly solo for the first time, taking off suddenly into the wide skies."[28]

Masaru Sato was born in 1928 in Rumoi, Hokkaido. After graduating from Kunitachi School of Music, he approached Hayasaka and became his student, learning how to compose music for motion pictures. He did the scores for eight Kurosawa films, from *The Throne of Blood* to *Red Beard* in 1965. The last was *After the Rain* (Ame Agaru, 1999), directed by Takashi Koizumi from a script by Akira Kurosawa. In all, he worked on 308 films. Koizumi was one of 98 directors he worked with.

I told him he couldn't die until he had worked with two more directors to make it an even hundred. And yet on December 5, 1999, at a congratulatory party for an official decoration he had received from the government, he suddenly collapsed and died.

It was shortly after beginning preparations to film *After the Rain* that Koizumi told me he wanted Sato to do the music. The state of Sato's health was a major concern, however, and so I was the one to phone Sato with the offer. I can still hear his voice on the other end of the line, expressing happiness over and over again: "I'm so happy! I'm very happy to be asked. I'll pour everything I have into this project, make it my legacy. My health? Fine, fine. I go in for dialysis every other day, but that's nothing to worry about. Anyway, thank you so much!"

Then he added: "It was worth waiting eighteen years for this."

I caught my breath. Was it really eighteen years since, after agonizing over the decision, Sato had walked off the set of *Kagemusha*? He must have marked off the intervening days, months, and years with a mixture of pride, humiliation, and keen regret. Let me go back eighteen years to the beginning of the story.

Until then, conferences about the music for a film consisted simply of Kurosawa playing a number of recordings for the composer and saying, "Something like this." He could do no more.

However, after magnetic audio tapes came on the scene, it became possible to record famous performances of all times and places (although obtaining permission from the copyright owner was another matter). During the editing process, there would of course be one tape with dialogue to match the picture, and then another of music to mix in. That gave the editor control. Kurosawa was fascinated by the possibilities. Music had always been out of bounds to him, but now, at last, he could manipulate it directly.

At home, it would seem he spent all his time listening to records—not for pleasure, but to find appropriate music for his movies. When he had found something good, in the morning his step would be different as he strode to the editing room. Clasping five or six albums in his arms, he would call out a buoyant "Good morning!" in the hallway, and issue instructions for which tracks of which CDs he wanted transferred to tape. The assistant editors would fly to the sound mixing studio. While Kurosawa took a short break, Bach and Beethoven would be transferred onto oxide 35mm recording tape and then laid out on the editing bench.

For Kurosawa, what followed was sheer bliss.

Wearing white gloves, he faced the synchronizer (the machine that matched sound and picture). He would set up the film, and then lay out alongside it the tapes of dialogue and Bach in parallel lines, like swimming lanes in a pool. As he turned the handle, he would hum to himself.

He used the classics only to convey his ideas to the composer, he would always say, explaining that this was a mere interim stage. Even so, he would end up editing the film to match the sound, altering the flow of pictures to accord with transitions in the music. Then he would show this rough cut, edited with soundtrack, to the composer and say, "Nice, isn't it? Something like this is what I had in mind."

The brilliance of his selections always filled me with admiration. Kurosawa had a gift for finding music that perfectly matched a given scene.

In *Red Beard*, Terumi Niki as Otoyo is caring for the ailing Yasumoto (Yuzo Kayama), and she opens the window to find snow falling heavily outside. This is, I believe, one of the most beautiful scenes of falling snow ever filmed. As she opens the window, Kurosawa chose to play Haydn's Symphony No. 9, the "Surprise" Symphony. The effect is superb. It is impossible to imagine any other music that would be as fitting for that beautiful scene.

In the most innocent of voices, Kurosawa told Sato, "Nice, isn't it? Isn't it perfect? Write me something like that."

"Why not just go ahead and use the Haydn?" suggested Sato, smiling stiffly.

"You want to know why? Because everyone in the audience already has a different image of this music, and that would get in the way. I tell you what you do: write me something better than the Haydn."

Carried away, I chimed in idiotically, "Haydn would be a worthy adversary to measure yourself against, after all."

Sato glowered and clammed up.

In the end, Sato produced a sort of musical paraphrase of the Haydn. When Kurosawa heard it, he said dismissively, "Hmph. It's no different from the Haydn."

This was too much. There was no pleasing the man. Sato bit his lip in chagrin.

* * *

After the days of *Red Beard* the movie industry entered a period of decline, and Kurosawa, too, was tossed on rough seas for a time. He resurrected his career in Russia, filming *Dersu Uzala*.

Back in Japan, *Kagemusha*, which had suffered from a lack of funding, finally went into production at Toho in 1979.

Music by Masaru Sato—the Kurosawa unit took that for granted. Sato came to the location site, and joined in consultations about the project.

On June 26 we started filming at Himeji Castle, and we rehearsed in July at the Toho studios.

On July 18, lead actor Shintaro Katsu suddenly withdrew. On July 25, filming resumed with Tatsuya Nakadai in his place. On October 3, filming on location in Hokkaido began, but on November 19 we returned to Tokyo because of heavy snows. The next two weeks Kurosawa spent at the Toho studio, rough-cutting the dailies.

Some of the scenes had been filmed in Hokkaido, including the scene of Takeda's army retreating along the Sanshu Kaido. For that scene, a beautiful panorama of silent troops silhouetted against a crimson sky, Kurosawa chose "Solveig's Song" from Grieg's *Peer Gynt Suites*. The lovely, plaintive melody further enhanced the lyrical emotion of the scene.

It was not long after viewing the rough cut edited with "Solveig's Song" that Sato phoned me to say it would be impossible for him to continue working on this film. I met with Sato to try to persuade him to stay, but it was he who ended up persuading me he had to leave. Later, Sato wrote as follows:

> At the end of that year (1979), I dropped out of Akira Kurosawa's film *Kagemusha* (1980). You might say that I dropped out of the Kurosawa School. There was too great a gap between Kurosawa's goals and what I was thinking. . . . To come up with something that not just resembled an impossibly famous piece, but surpassed it, was beyond me.[29]

With a heavy heart I went back to Kurosawa's home to talk the situation over with him. On the way, over and over I rehearsed how best to break it to the director. In the end, I told him, "Sato-san is not feeling well, and so he cannot undertake this job. To prevent greater trouble from occurring later, he is determined to bow out now while it's still early."

Kurosawa listened to this in silence, but he was a man of sharp instincts. I have no doubt he saw right through me.

"If he's sick, he's sick," he said shortly. "Who else is there? What's Takemitsu up to?"

I explained that composer Toru Takemitsu was currently working in the U.S., but that I would see about contacting him.

With that, I excused myself. With *Kagemusha* behind schedule due to bad weather on location, the release date already extended, there was no time to waste.

Takemitsu recommended Shinichiro Ikebe as his replacement. Today Ikebe makes frequent appearances on NHK, and his name is well known. Born in Mito, Ibaraki Prefecture, in 1943, he went on to graduate from Tokyo National University of Fine Arts and Music in the department of composition. Besides films, he also composes for theatrical and TV productions. Hearing from Takemitsu that Ikebe was well versed in traditional Japanese music came as an apparent relief to Kurosawa.

I lost no time in meeting with Ikebe in a Shinjuku coffee shop to give him a copy of the script and formally request his services. I found him to be a frank and open young man with a cherubic face. Honesty compelled me to tell him that it was Kurosawa's custom to add ready-made music to the rough cut for the composer. Ikebe's reply was so casual it amazed me: "No problem. That won't bother me at all."

And so, after many ups and downs, *Kagemusha* was completed early in the New Year.

On April 23, a gala premiere was held at Yurakuza Theater, attended by many foreign directors and journalists.

For Sato, eighteen years would lapse until his next assignment on a Kurosawa film.

After Sato died, Kenji Tokoro, former director of music at Toho and a friend of Sato's, sent me a copy of a letter Sato had written. He sent me only the part having to do with *After the Rain*. I read it and wept.

> At last I can go back to the Kurosawa School that I
> once dropped out of. When I took in my hand the
> screenplay marked "Akira Kurosawa," my heart
> beat faster with the love of film. The screenplay is
> short but well made, and between the lines I can
> feel Kurosawa's warmth. (May 5, 1999)

Memories of December 5, the day of the party to celebrate Sato's government decoration, summon feelings of bitter regret, but these days I try to tell myself that at least the whole Kurosawa group was there.

Sato felt ill quite suddenly. As we all tried to get him to lie down, he lifted his head and looked at me. "Do I look that bad?" he asked.

I nodded vaguely and was about to tell him to rest quietly, but those were the last words that passed between us. Still, Sato never thought he was dying. He probably wanted to say that it happened all the time, that if he just lay down for a while he'd be fine.

After that, I waited in a room next to the intensive care room at the hospital, but the next time I saw Sato was in the mortuary. The room was stark and empty, with no shrine set up. Sato's body lay on a gurney, covered in a white sheet. His face was peaceful, seemingly graced by a slight smile. His eyes were slightly open, so I reached out and gently lowered the lids. The chill, rubber-like feel of those eyelids still lingers on my fingertips.

I have not yet recovered from the sadness of losing Masaru Sato.

The sadness envelops me. It is all but unbearable.

TORU TAKEMITSU

The first draft of the script of *Ran* was written by the triumvirate of Akira Kurosawa, Masato Ide, and Hideo Oguni, at Kurosawa's villa in Gotenba, from February 15 to March 30, 1976. As so often happened, the movie was then shelved for lack of financing; not until seven years later, after considerable wrangling and ado, were arrangements for production in place and the final draft of the script ready. By then it was December 1983, going on four years after the April 1980 completion of *Kagemusha*.

Kurosawa often played recordings while writing a script. Perhaps having music on hand so early in the process helped him build the drama of the story. He wrote *Red Beard* while listening to Beethoven's Ninth Symphony; for *Kagemusha*, it was Toru Takemitsu's *November Steps*, composed for *biwa*, *shakuhachi* flute and orchestra. When Takemitsu heard that, he would urge Kurosawa with delight, "Hurry up and make the film, won't you!"

But shooting did not get underway till June 1984. Almost a decade had elapsed, during which time Kurosawa managed to film *Kagemusha*. For those nine years with the script on hand, Takemitsu's plans for the score must have swelled and grown.

There was an important scene in the script of *Ran* where, during the destruction of the third castle, music would play without any sound effects whatsoever. Kurosawa declared, "I'll leave it up to Takemitsu." The script describes the scene this way:

> Now, during the fall of the castle, a dreadful
> picture-scroll of Hell unfolds ... The music accompanying these pictures pulses with deep anguish,
> like the heart of Buddha, and has a melodic line

> filled with sadness. Beginning with stifled sobs, the
> music repeats like the wheel of transmigration,
> gradually intensifying until eventually it sounds like
> the bitter wails of untold Buddhas.

Having to meet such a difficult request would be a challenge for any composer, I thought, but the time came for Takemitsu to have Kurosawa listen to what he had been working on for nine years. That one scene alone was six minutes long.

Takemitsu begged me not to let Kurosawa view the rough cut with music the way he usually did. I conveyed this request to Kurosawa, but he was equally adamant that Takemitsu ought to hear his vision. Kurosawa chose Mahler's "The Farewell" from "The Song of the Earth." Ever since Mahler's "Giant" Symphony No. 1 had played as background music during the introduction of actors at the production announcement of *Ran*, Mahler had become Kurosawa's default music for the film.

During that decade of waiting, Kurosawa's vision may well have shifted from *November Steps* to Mahler. During an interview, Takemitsu commented as follows:

> At first, not knowing anything about Mahler, I
> wrote my own music for the scene. I wrote it using a
> synthesizer, and I took it over when the dailies came
> out. Then Kurosawa said casually, "Oh, I put music
> on it, too." [*laughter*] He'd already edited the whole
> scene with music.[30]

It was a replay of the same problem that had arisen before

with Sato. A warning light was flashing to indicate that trouble lay ahead.

February 24, 1985, was the long-awaited day when shooting wrapped. Ordinarily, this was a happy occasion, but at the thought of the coming editing process, my heart sank.

As I had feared, during recording of the score in Hokkaido with the Sapporo Symphony Orchestra, the two geniuses had a difference of opinion. All might have been well even then if Kurosawa had only come straight out and said what he thought, but opposite a man of Takemitsu's stature, he seemed to have difficulty in doing this. In our Hokkaido hotel, I was summoned to Kurosawa's room several times. Kurosawa would hand me a piece of paper with instructions to give it to Takemitsu; since I have no memory whatever of what the messages said, they may have been enclosed in envelopes.

It would not have done to awaken the composer early in the morning, so I would quietly slip the message under his door—and then take off posthaste, afraid the door might swing open to reveal him bellowing, "What is it now!" In this way, two or three times I delivered secret messages from one genius to another.

One morning, as I was breakfasting with Kurosawa in the hotel restaurant, Takemitsu came along with his manager in tow, and the two men seated themselves at our table. Takemitsu was in an extraordinary state. Beneath that great forehead, his eyes were fixed in a cold and penetrating gaze.

"Kurosawa-san. What have I done wrong? If something is wrong, come out and say so in plain language. Otherwise, I want out of this job."

Caught off-balance, the director mumbled, "Well, I never

said anything was wrong," or words to that effect, but I cannot recall anything after that. By launching a surprise attack, Takemitsu came out the victor.

The battle between the two great men continued from Hokkaido to Tokyo. But as the day of completion neared, a decisive clash took place as the finishing touches were being put on the film. On the fourth day of sound mixing, it all came to a head.

Records indicate that dubbing took place from April 24 to May 8 at the Toho recording studio, using four channels. The blow-up occurred April 27.

Scene number 36, in front of the great gate. Already driven out of the first castle, Hidetora (Tatsuya Nakadai) is rejected anew by Jiro in the second castle, and leaves through the gate. "Close the gate! I don't want to look at you!" Jiro stands motionless as, urged on by Kurogane, the castle soldiers close the gate.

This was one of Kurosawa's favorite scenes.

Behind Hidetora, the great doors creak shut. At that moment, Hidetora's hauteur crumbles, his shoulders sag, and he reels. As he stumbles, there is a shrill blast from a flute, characteristic of Takemitsu's music, and an immediate cut to the blazing sun. Beneath the flute music sounds a rumble of low tympani.

The balance of these two highly symbolic tone colors was the source of the disagreement.

Kurosawa said, "Can't you increase the low notes? Make it hit you in the pit of the stomach. It's got to have more weight."

Takemitsu said nothing. He sat so silently that it was as if he had not heard Kurosawa's words. He disliked the tympani to begin with, and had introduced it here only reluctantly, at Kurosawa's request.

Takemitsu was seated on the sofa nearest to the screen, so that only his back showed. In front of machinery that looked like the cockpit of an airplane was a row of recording technicians and Ichiro Minawa, in charge of sound effects. Kurosawa sat near them, issuing orders to the technicians. They replayed the scene with the low tones higher in volume.

"No good. You can't hear them. Make it stronger, make it grab you."

Afterward I heard from one of the assistant recording engineers that Takemitsu's shoulders were shaking with the effort to control his anger. Unaware, Kurosawa issued a request directly to Seihachi Ando, who was manipulating the music track: "Slow the tape down, would you? I want the sound good and deep."

Later, Ando regretted that he did not stop to ask Takemitsu's permission. Yet with the great director looming in front of him, telling him what to do, he probably had no choice but to obey.

Takemitsu finally found his voice. "Kurosawa-san! You can cut and paste my music. You can use it as you please. But I want my name off the credits. That's all. I quit. I'm leaving!"

With that, he gathered up his sheets of music and his briefcase and walked out. His manager, Mr. Uno, followed behind him with a look of sadness. I rushed after them to see about transportation.

Everyone else was thunderstruck. They watched us off, frozen.

It was like the sudden, dramatic end of a scene.

In front of the studio, I found the great man waiting for a taxi in high dudgeon.

At the time, I was driving a small Subaru, but the trip from

Everyone watching aghast as Toru Takemitsu exits stage left in a rage.

there to Seijo Station was a mere five minutes. I swung my Subaru around and offered them a ride, assuming they wanted to get away from there as fast as they could.

Those five minutes were inordinately long. Neither man spoke, but from the passenger seat beside me I could feel the emanations of Takemitsu's seething anger. As I pulled up to the bank across from the station, he finally spoke, as if he'd been saving the words up: "It's all the fault of the people around Kurosawa!"

"I'm so sorry," I said, and stopped the car.

Takemitsu put one foot outside and glared back at me. "I mean you, too!" he spat out, then got out and slammed the door. Uno scrambled out of the back seat and followed after him.

The shock of that final blow made the five-minute ride back seem longer than it was, and my spirits plunged.

Back at the studio, for some reason the door wouldn't open.

I rattled the knob helplessly until someone came to open it. When whoever it was recognized me, he gravely let me in.

The interior was dimly lit, with only the security lights on. I could just make out the figures of about thirty crew members sitting on the floor, arms around their knees. The mood was heavy and ominous, as if this were the night before a peasants' uprising—with Kurosawa, of course, as ringleader.

As soon as I came in, he turned abruptly, gave me a stern look, and barked, "Where have you been!"

"I took Takemitsu-san to the station," I answered, and he roared back, "You didn't have to do that!"

Whatever I did, apparently, I was going to get yelled at. I sat behind the rest of the peasants and Kurosawa resumed speaking to the group, picking up where he had left off. His tone was one of studied calm:

"I'll give it some more thought, but one option is to do without music altogether. Just handle it with sound effects. I'll have to consult with Minawa, but it might also be possible to get by just with Japanese instruments."

I thought to myself, *Oh boy, now we're in for it.* The movie's premiere was set for May 21. We had not just the Japan Herald producer to worry about, but the hard-to-please French producer Serge Silberman as well. Delaying the release date any further was not an option.

Later I learned that after I followed Takemitsu out, Kurosawa had ordered the recording crew to turn off the intercom and lock all the studio doors. After what happened when Shintaro Katsu walked off the set (see chapter 9), he had probably feared the media getting wind of this incident and writing something libelous.

Minawa's notes end that day, but according to him the crew was back at work as usual the next morning at 9:30. They worked on only two reels of film, and wrapped up by 1:30 in the afternoon, however, so it is possible that they dubbed only scenes requiring no music.

The producers no doubt spent the day scrambling to put out peace feelers in hopes of calling an end to hostilities.

Producer Masato Hara succeeded in winning over Takemitsu. He, Takemitsu, and Takemitsu's manager all called together at Kurosawa's home. It was after dark when I got a phone call from Kurosawa.

"Takemitsu came by and apologized. Apparently he wasn't feeling well. Now that I think about it, his color wasn't good, was it? Anyway, he'll be back at work tomorrow." He could barely conceal his pleasure.

I do not believe for a minute that Takemitsu was ill, but that excuse worked best with Kurosawa. Of course, he did not seriously believe Takemitsu was ill, either. That was the outcome of the peace negotiations.

Despite the late hour, I lost no time in calling Minawa. I will never forget the enthusiasm in his voice when he heard the news. It must have been a huge load off his mind.

"Really? That's good news. That's really good news. When he said we'd make the movie using only sound effects, I didn't know what to do. Ah, this is great news!"

And so peace was restored.

Ran was released nationwide on June 1, 1985—right on schedule.

Born October 8, 1930, in Tokyo, Takemitsu studied composition with Yasuji Kiyose; later, with surreal poet Shuzo Takiguchi and others he formed the Experimental Workshop. He also served as assistant to Fumio Hayasaka, who wrote music for many Kurosawa films. Starting in 1956, he composed roughly one hundred distinguished film scores. Following the 1967 publication of his composition *November Steps*, he received international recognition and was awarded numerous prizes. On February 20, 1996, he died of cancer.

It was the final day of the sound mix. In the studio, we all drank a toast to the movie. After Kurosawa had thanked everybody and departed with a wave, Takemitsu was still in high spirits, holding a can of beer.

All at once, he went over to the piano and did a jazz improvisation on lines something like these:

> Yesterday's sadness, today's tears
> Will tomorrow be cloudy or fine?
> Yesterday's sadness, today's distress
> Will tomorrow be cloudy or fine?

Takemitsu then said with a laugh, "I dedicate this song to Kurosawa."

He seemed to be in high spirits. But I suspect that inside, he might have felt downcast.

8

Sentimental Recollections

DEATH NOTICES

This year, 1993, has been a year of death notices arriving one after another. The sudden death of director Ishiro Honda on February 28 was swiftly followed by the passing of the great actor Chishu Ryu on March 16. Then on June 7 my old friend Kazuko Kawakita of the Shibata Organization (known in Japan as France Eiga-sha), a leading distributor of European and art films in Japan, died suddenly of a brain hemorrhage. This series of blows has been devastating, and I am still knocked out.

Also in June came word from Moscow friends of the sudden passing of Maria Dorya, on the twenty-eighth. Anyone in Japan who made movies with the former Soviet Union is bound to have worked with the bilingual Ms. Dorya, who had a Russian father and a Japanese mother. A stout woman of sturdy build, she seemed to exemplify the Russian working woman.

Films shown at Moscow film festivals and screenings usually have no subtitles, and so Ms. Dorya was in high demand as an interpreter. She had to change her voice to suit each character, a daunting feat the equal of performances by *benshi* (narrators) in the era of silent cinema in Japan. "That must be a tough job," I would say sympathetically, and she would quickly counter, "But fascinating. I get paid for doing what I love, and what could be better than that?"

On July 10, at 11:40 in the morning, writer Masuji Ibuse, author of *Black Rain* and many other works, died. He was ninety-five.

For once, I had been prepared. His wife had told me, "He's getting steadily weaker, as if each day he goes one step lower on a flight of stairs." Every time the phone rang after that, I felt a wave of apprehension. Now, finally, the day had come.

"Sensei has passed away": After hearing this message left on my answering machine in a sad voice by the wife of writer Shotaro Yasuoka, I hurried to the hospital in Ogikubo together with Yasuoka and a representative from Shinchosha Publishing Company. We were shown into the mortuary at the rear of the hospital, where gathered in front of the coffin we found several of Ibuse's intimates, sitting in chairs exactly as if they had come to wish him a speedy recovery. Looking into the coffin at Ibuse's face, his eyes closed, I realized that never again would I see him smile, or listen to his witty conversation.

Around 1948, when I was still a know-it-all beginning editor at the publishing company, I would often call at the Ibuse home to receive his latest manuscript. He would greet me by saying, "Let's step out, shall we?" and take me to a street stall near Asagaya Station for a drink. It was a lively place frequented by neighborhood literati such as Mizuho Aoyagi, the scholar of French literature, as well as writers Akatsuki Kanbayashi and Shigeru Tomura. Ibuse would tell me, "Aoyagi here hasn't read even one of my books," and Aoyagi would grin back, "Oh, I may have read one." In this era when we were at last free from war, men of letters would gather in such places to enjoy the pleasures of debate or a meeting of minds.

Many of Ibuse's works were made into popular movies after the war, such as *No Consultations Today* (Honjitsu Kyushin, 1952); *Bill-collecting Trip* (Shukin Ryoko, 1957); *The Hotelman's Holiday* (Ekimae Ryokan, 1958); and *The Curio Shop Owner* (Chinpindo Shujin, 1960). *The Hotelman's Holiday* (a literal rendering of the title would be "Station Inn") was such a hit that it spawned a whole series of films with similar titles—twenty-four in all, and some of them rather queer-sounding: *Station Teakettle, Station Clerk, Station Horse-racing*, and what have you.

The only ones that managed to capture something of the flavor of Ibuse's writings, I would say, were *Ornamental Hairpin* (Kanzashi) by Shochiku, directed by Hiroshi Shimizu, and the last work from Nano Eiga, director Mikio Naruse's *Hideko the Bus Conductress* (Hideko no Shasho-san). Both masterpieces were made in the year 1941. The latter was based on the story "Okomasan," serialized in a magazine the year before, and the lead part was written for movie star Hideko Takamine, whose popularity was at its zenith following the previous year's hit movie *Hideko the Cheerleader* (Hideko no Oendancho).

Ibuse wrote in detail about this film in an essay.[31] In the film, the part of a writer very like Ibuse himself is played by Daijiro Natsukawa. There is a scene in which, as Natsukawa's character leaves town to return to Tokyo, Hideko Takamine—or "Deko-chan," as she was known—stands with Kamatari Fujiwara, waving, at a railroad crossing. The scene was shot on location in

Sakaori, Yamanashi Prefecture. Ibuse, who was waiting for a bus to a teahouse in the mountain pass, happened to come across Natsukawa's car and so ended up watching as the scene was filmed. He told me later that while they were waiting, Deko-chan looked into the bag that the bus conductress wore around her waist and declared, "I could never figure out all this money!"

Before this movie was completed, Ibuse was conscripted into the army, and sent south that December. However, he chanced to see the film in a Singapore movie theater. In the above-mentioned essay, he wrote, "*Hideko the Bus Conductress* is the simple story of a sixteen-year-old girl named Hideko whose job it is to describe the passing scenery to passengers on a rattletrap bus as it goes through the mountains. The bus company is on the verge of financial collapse, but she, knowing nothing of that, carries on happily with her work. The bus is the picture of shabbiness. To make it look more rundown, director Naruse went to the trouble of using rust-colored paint mixed with reddish soil on the chassis. This was bad luck for the movie. Lieutenant Sakurai of the PR division pointed out a problem: If the Malays saw this movie, they would figure all Japanese buses were this decrepit-looking, which would be a stain on Japanese national honor. He had a point. When Lieutenant Sakurai reported this to his superior, Major Otaka, the movie was promptly banned."

I always made a point of inviting Ibuse and his editors to the advance screening of a completed Kurosawa film. I think what Ibuse enjoyed most about such events was going out drinking afterward with everyone in Shinjuku or Ogikubo. The screening of *Dreams* was the last he ever attended.

Even as I write this remembrance, death notices keep arriving without stop, as if this were a war zone. A telephone call from Paris relayed news of the July 19 death of Mary Meerson, whose late husband Henri Langlois was the first head of La Cinémathèque Française, a Mecca for any aspiring filmmaker. "Please let Director Kurosawa know," the voice said—but I well remember that Mary always called him "Akira" with great affection.

Before meeting Henri Langlois, she was married to the late Lazare Meerson, art director for the films of René Clair. A woman with a strikingly beautiful face, in her youth she had been a top model whose face graced magazine covers, although in recent years she had grown as stout as Orson Welles. When Kurosawa went to Paris, she dressed in a beautiful new outfit specially made for the occasion and drove to the airport to meet him, but her girth made it hard for her to get out of the car. When Kurosawa went over to her car to say hello, it took awhile for her to get on her feet, but as soon as she did, she burst out happily, "Oh, Akira!" and enfolded him in her arms. Smothered against her bosom, he looked to me like a frail young man.

On July 21, Tetsuro Mayuzumi, an editor for the arts department of the *Asahi Shinbun* who used to write sharp film reviews, died at the young age of fifty-six. He used to call me every so often for news of the latest doings of Kurosawa and Ibuse. I can still hear his sweet, slightly nasal voice in my ear.

And just now (July 27) I received notice that Madame Kashiko Kawakita, the mother of my friend Kazuko, has died. It feels like an announcement of the demise of the happy, golden days of film in Japan.

KAMATARI FUJIWARA

Recently I had occasion to watch several videos of Kurosawa's works. The sight of so many actors who have passed on brought back vivid memories of the old days, and put me in a sentimental mood.

The Lower Depths (Donzoko), filmed in 1957, includes a scene in which Koji Mitsui and Kamatari Fujiwara converse in their respective roles as a gadabout and an actor, with Haruo Tanaka in the background as a cooper. Coughing in the ratty futon in the foreground is Eiko Miyoshi, whose husband, a craftsman, is played by Eijiro Tono. As Fujiwara, the actor, rouses the craftsman's wife and takes her out to a sunny spot, in comes the landlord Rokubei, played by Kabuki actor Ganjiro Nakamura, who is fuming about something. As I was watching, it hit me that all of the actors appearing thus far, in slightly more than two minutes of screen time, have gone on to the next world. How terribly sad it is that these dear faces and voices survive nowhere else but on the screen.

Nor are they the only ones now gone: Takashi Shimura, Masayuki Mori, Bokuzen Hidari, Nobuo Nakamura, Atsushi Watanabe . . . far too many names to write them all. The world will never see such actors again, I believe.

In his youth, Fujiwara struggled for an education, attending night school, and at age sixteen he became a chorus boy, then learned to play the violin and worked as a musician in movie theaters. Those early experiences surely contribute to the depth of his performances in movies such as *Horoki* (1935, directed by Sotoji Kimura), *Tsuruhachi Tsurujiro* (1938, directed by Mikio Naruse), *Hideko the Bus Conductress* (1941, directed by Naruse) and others. Now I can watch him on video, but in those days I saw him every day, yet to my bitter regret I did not ask him any questions or seek to find out more about his earlier life. And now it's too late. All I can do is gnash my teeth at my folly.

On the set, Fujiwara was always telling dumb jokes, but before finishing one he would wave his hand as if to erase it, and say, "That one was no good, no good, a failure, a failure!" That struck the rest of us as funny, so we'd burst out laughing, and tease him: "So that was supposed to be a joke?"

Fujiwara and Kurosawa were close, having worked together since Kurosawa's days as assistant director on *Horses* (Uma; 1941, directed by Kajiro Yamamoto). Fujiwara appeared in virtually every Kurosawa film from *Ikiru* (1952) to *Kagemusha* (1980). In the times spent waiting between takes, I enjoyed watching them sit warming themselves at a charcoal fire set in a tin container known as a *gangara*, talking about food or sake. The other day the French actress Françoise Arnoul came to Japan and confided to me that Jean Renoir and Jean Gabin would sit around talking about food too; it tickled me to think it's the same everywhere.

When we filmed *Yojimbo* in 1961, I remember Kurosawa telling me over and over, "That Kamatari is a fine actor," or "He has style." He was particularly referring to the scene at the end in which the actor comes out as the silk merchant Tazaemon, beating a flat drum, and kills Tokuemon with a madman's peculiar intensity.

In *Kagemusha* (1980), he played the doctor who checks Shingen's pulse as the man dies his empty death; it was a brief role, but one that again had Kurosawa praising him as a "fine actor." When I told this to Fujiwara, he laughed with surprise and pleasure.

That same Fujiwara once provoked Kurosawa to fierce

anger. It was during the filming of *Dodesukaden* in 1970. An old man played by Fujiwara visits Tanba (Atsushi Watanabe), who is about the same age as Fujiwara's character, and tells him he is tired of living, he wants to die. Tanba hands him a powder, saying, "Drink this and you'll die a peaceful death in just an hour." After ingesting the substance, while waiting for the inevitable to happen he begins telling the story of his life. When Tanba tells him, "Those memories are alive as long as you are," the old man has a sudden change of heart and begins to plead, "Help me, I don't want to die!" On finding out that the "poison" he took was actually stomach medicine, the old man weakens and collapses. All this was to be shot in one scene, as a single shot. The scene lasted approximately eight minutes.

It was a difficult scene to shoot. It put great demands on the actors, especially Fujiwara, who had trouble memorizing long lines of dialogue. Kurosawa had a basic policy of allowing no changes in the dialogue. But where the script called for Fujiwara to say, for example, "Nothing I eat tastes any good," he would say instead, "There's nothing I want to eat." Every time he did something like this, the director would boom, "No, no! Cut! Do it again!" Having written the script himself, Kurosawa was not about to put up with anyone making random changes in it.

In the beginning, he would say easily, "Kama-san, get your lines right, okay?" But the more retakes there were, naturally the more upset he became. Finally he told me to go over and feed Fujiwara his lines, acting as a prompter. To have someone else's voice come in during a take was unheard of, but that's what we did.

I went as close as I could to the set without getting in the frame, crouched down, and with the script in one hand, rapidly

The one and only time a scene was filmed using a live prompter.

called out the start of each of Fujiwara's lines. This was technically difficult, and required careful timing. In the spaces between his lines I would quickly say a few words like, "My wife took to her bed," and Fujiwara would then continue, "My wife took to her bed and died half a year later." Or I would say, "My house burned," and he would say, "My house burned to the ground in an air-raid." I felt horribly awkward, sure I was getting in the actor's way, and if I stammered the least bit, one of Kurosawa's missiles would suddenly fire off in my direction: "Read it more clearly!"

I just prayed that somehow we could make it to the end of the scene, where Fujiwara collapsed. Finally, both the seventh and eighth takes were deemed acceptable, and the crisis was over. This shot lasted for eight minutes, and was shot with two A cameras and two B cameras, so we viewed dailies four times, for just over an hour in all.

Kurosawa went straight off to the editing room, certain

that with so much material to work with he could put the scene together somehow. After that, we did battle with the four rolls of film and a mountain of sound tapes. Just removing my voice from the soundtrack was a fiendishly difficult task, and the tape had to be chopped up in a hideous state.

Kurosawa told me later that the following day he received a phone call from Fujiwara. "My wife and I are so happy it's an OK, we're drinking a toast."

"You idiot!" seethed Kurosawa. "Have you any idea how much work it took for us to edit that scene?"

I must say his anger was entirely justifiable. And yet I can sympathize with Fujiwara's point of view, too—anybody would want to celebrate after going through all that.

Fujiwara was scheduled to appear in *Ran* (1985) as well. He was cast as a peasant, and Kurosawa had already drawn a picture of him in costume, but by then Fujiwara's health was on the decline. He wanted to be in the picture anyway, though; his wife sent Kurosawa a message that her husband was eager to accept any role at all. Kurosawa was concerned that coming to Kyushu in the heat of summer in his frail state could be fatal; "Talk him out of it, convince him to look after himself," he said to me, putting me in the awkward position of mediator.

Again, I understood the feelings of both parties. Fujiwara's determination to be in the film certainly owed much to his belief that this would be his last chance ever to participate in a Kurosawa film.

He died on December 21, 1985, of heart disease. His real name was Shigeo Yasue, and he was eighty years old.

JUNZABURO BAN AND BOKUZEN HIDARI

During the five years from *Red Beard* in 1965 to *Dodesukaden* in 1970, Kurosawa struggled mightily with uncooperative American financiers. He was left exhausted in body and spirit. *The Runaway Train*, due to begin production in the United States in 1966, was canceled, and in 1969, plans for a joint production of *Tora! Tora! Tora!* with Twentieth Century Fox fell through after filming had already begun. The waste of those five years was more excruciating for Kurosawa than we can possibly imagine.

The production advisor, Yoichi Matsue, had tried hard to salvage *Tora! Tora! Tora!*, and in 1970 it was he who produced *Dodesukaden*. Kurosawa must have been eager to put unpleasant memories behind him and make a fresh start. This became his first color picture.

Filming began April 23 in Horie, a town built on landfill in Edogawa Ward in Tokyo. It ended June 29 with background shooting for the credits. The chief assistant director, Kenjiro Omori, had scheduled forty-four days of shooting, but the picture was finished with amazing swiftness, with only twenty-eight days of shooting.

The movie is based on *The Town without Seasons*, a collection of short stories by Shugoro Yamamoto. It tells the story of Rokuchan, a retarded boy in love with streetcars, and others who live in a slum. Junzaburo Ban played the part of a resident named Shima who is always dressed neatly in a suit and fedora. He carries a cane because his left leg is crippled, and he has a recurrent facial tic.

On June 17, we shot scene 80, "In Shima's house."

Shima brings home three business colleagues. He announces their arrival to his wife in the kitchen, who makes no response.

The arrogance displayed by this shrewish wife, played by Kiyoko Tange, leaves the guests aghast. Shima attempts to smooth things over, but after his wife leaves the house to take a bath, one of them erupts in fury.

"What's wrong with that woman! You ought to kick her out of the house!"

Shima responds by abruptly knocking his guest over, sitting astride him, and shouting, "That's my wife you're talking about! . . . She stayed with me when we were so poor we had nothing to eat. . . . Who are you to tell me to kick her out?"

The guest apologizes: "I was out of bounds. Forgive me." Then the trio exchange toasts with Shima.

It was a scene like a one-act play. This long scene, running to some thirteen pages in the scenario, was filmed in one cut using two cameras. In rehearsals the day before, it had gone over ten minutes; this wouldn't do, as it meant running short of film, so the dialogue had to be cut. The camera held 1,000 feet of film, or enough for only about eleven minutes. Some extra film was required on the spools, so the scene could not exceed ten minutes. Should the camera run out of film with seconds to go, then no matter how well the scene had gone, it would all be wasted.

For this scene, camera A, with a 50mm lens, would move lengthwise, capturing Shima and the rest as they came in, while camera B, with a 75mm lens, moved in a perpendicular direction, capturing Shima as he heated sake in the kitchen.

Junzaburo Ban was nervous that morning. Entering, I passed him on his way to the men's room, muttering his lines to himself with a look of such intensity that I refrained from calling out a greeting.

In a shot as long as ten minutes, avoiding mistakes in the dialogue is challenge enough. On top of that, with four actors on the move, standing, sitting and walking around the set, any time their positions overlapped in front of either camera the take would have to be scrapped. Besides that, Ban had to prepare a dish of hot tofu and warm sake for his guests. He also had to display a facial tic at regular intervals. To fulfill all of those conditions and finish the scene safely in under ten minutes, all hurdles passed, was a task of Herculean proportions.

Take 1 lasted one minute and ten seconds, Take 2, a minute and thirty-one. The problem both times was positioning. Take 3 lasted a minute and six seconds, Take 4, a minute and five. Both of these times, the gesture someone made in lighting his cigarette did not go right. Take 5, an even two minutes, was scrapped because Ban forgot to display the tic. Take 6, three minutes and eighteen seconds long, was no good because of positioning. Take 7 finally went to the end of the scene, lasting eight minutes and forty-eight seconds. Kurosawa called for a retake. Take 8 was eight minutes and forty-seven seconds. This time, finally it was an OK.

All this time, behind the scenes the camera crew was turning cartwheels. With only ten minutes of film in the camera magazine, if the director called for a retake after two minutes, there would not be enough left to finish the scene. Every retake meant replacing the magazine on both cameras. A supply of spare magazines had been loaded ahead of time, but with this many retakes, there would not be nearly enough. The cinematographer's assistants turned pale and, with the urgency of sailors rushing around to replace explosives in the Battle of the Midway, they tiptoed off the set during filming, flew to the darkroom to load fresh film stock

Behind the emotional handshake, camera crew members run around madly.

and tore back again, while the production manager telephoned Kodak with an emergency SOS.

As soon as Kurosawa's voice rang out in the hushed room, "OK!" Ban slumped weakly to the floor. Kurosawa reached out for a hearty handshake and assured him that the scene had gone well. The actor looked up, blinking, and bowed again and again, unable to muster a word. In his long acting career, few moments could have brought him as much happiness.

Junzaburo Ban began acting in 1925. From then until 1953, when he became a success based on his creation of the fad word *ajapa* (an expression of comical surprise), he was always a bit player, performing on stage as horse legs and in the movies as a character soon cut down or arrested. His private life, too, was far from happy. But when I remember him, I will always think of his face that morning as he gazed up at Kurosawa, filled with emotion.

Bokuzen Hidari is another comic actor whose life was filled with pain. Born in 1894, he was apprenticed out at age ten, and later worked his way through school in conditions of great adversity, delivering newspapers and bottles of milk.

In 1935, from around the time he took the stage name Bokuzen Hidari for his debut performance at Shinjuku Moulin Rouge, he began what would be a lifelong struggle with the severe pain of gangrenous feet. In my mind, his crutches merge with the image of his wife Ito, who always stuck to him as close as a shadow. In the studio, some people treated it all as a laugh, claiming that the crutches were fake; when the bus was coming, the joke went, he put the crutches up on his shoulder and ran. His droll demeanor as a comedian lay behind such rumors, but apparently the pain he endured was beyond words.

Hidari let on only to his wife what torture the filming of *Seven Samurai* was for him. During the battle in the rain where he ran through the mud holding a bamboo spear, he endured such agony that he nearly passed out. His wife wrote this: "Whenever I picture my husband's scenes in *Seven Samurai*, his face seems to me to be contorted in pain. The illness he bore in secret brought him enormous suffering."[32]

But Hidari showed no outward sign of such trauma, and none of us had any inkling. When I visualize his face, I always see him with his eyebrows lowered and his mouth wide open in a great big laugh.

Hidari died in 1971 at the age of seventy-seven and Ban in 1981 at the age of seventy-three.

TAKASHI SHIMURA AND TOSHIRO MIFUNE

"I'm Shimura. How do you do?"

In 1943, by the fountain at Toho Studios, Takashi Shimura introduced himself to Akira Kurosawa, and the two men exchanged greetings for the first time. Shimura had been recommended for the part of jujutsu instructor Hansuke Murai in Kurosawa's directorial debut, *Sugata Sanshiro*. Later, after coming across Kurosawa's description of the incident in a film magazine, Shimura incorporated it into his memoir, *The Autobiography of My Heart*:

> Shimura-san was standing on the grass dressed in a suit. At first I was taken aback, having no idea who he might be. He was wearing a thin hat that was old and scruffy and yet suited him perfectly; a great hat.[33]

Maybe it was the doing of the Stetson: Shimura got the part.

It was producer Nobuyoshi Morita, Shimura's old friend from the Shingeki Theater, who recommended him to Kurosawa. Even though Shimura was still under contract elsewhere, Morita scurried around and got him to transfer to Toho, which would have an enormous impact on Shimura's career. Nor was that the only dramatic turning point Morita helped to bring about in his friend's life: In 1934, as Japanese movies entered the sound era, Shimura joined Shinko Kinema under the auspices of Morita, who was a producer there. The timing was perfect. Shimura passed the dialogue test for *Chuji Uridasu*, which became the first talkie for both Shinko Kinema and for director Mansaku Itami. This was Shimura's first real acting role, and it led directly to his appearance in Itami's 1936 acclaimed masterpiece, *Kakita Akanishi*.

In that film, Shimura's character Tsunomata slips poisoned buns to an imprisoned assassin. The man's death is not shown on screen, but indirectly, through the look on the face of the watching Tsunomata. Shimura describes it this way in his memoir: "I understood then the depth and fascination of cinema. In that sense, *Kakita Akanishi* was the film that opened my eyes to cinema. I can never forget it."

Shortly after New Year's, 1952, preparations got underway for what would become Shimura's signature film, *Ikiru* (1952), the story of a man who struggles with the knowledge that he is dying from cancer. Before shooting could begin, however, Shimura was hospitalized with appendicitis. As he convalesced after surgery, Kurosawa visited him in the hospital and told him not to gain back any of the weight he had lost, as "a cancer patient ought to be a little underweight." Only a director would say such an outrageous thing.

When Shimura was finally released from the hospital, Kurosawa called on him at home, accompanied by cinematographer Asakazu Nakai and recording engineer Fumio Yanoguchi. Kurosawa's account of that visit was so entertaining that I shall attempt to recreate it in full:

> There the man was barely out of the hospital, and we sat around his bed having a drinking party; really shameless, we were. At first there was no alcohol. Neither Shimura nor his wife are big drinkers, so she brought out tea and cookies, but nobody

wanted them. Finally she figured out the problem, and brought out some Suntory or something. Pretty soon we were having a regular drinking bout in the middle of the afternoon. Nakai feels strong when he drinks, and so he said, "Let's do some sumo." We all agreed and trooped out into the garden. Shimura came too, saying, "I'll have a go." It was crazy. When it was his turn, Nakai squeezed himself into a tiny space, and came bursting out of there. While Yanoguchi and Shimura wrestled, the dog started yapping in its master's defense. Now that's one loyal dog. To protect Shimura, it went over and bit Yanoguchi on the leg. We laughed uproariously. Then Mifune came by, and we started up drinking again. There was no stopping us. After awhile Mifune got up, went out to the entranceway, and brought back a big bundle wrapped in a *furoshiki* cloth. I figured it was some sweets or something like that, but to everybody's amazement, it was a baby. His wife had had a baby, and he'd brought it over to show us, he said. So then we drank to the baby.

I can almost hear the laughter and banter of these motion picture greats. I love this story.

Apparently, Mrs. Shimura was so worried that the film with her husband's first starring role would not be a box office success, she couldn't sleep nights. But *Ikiru* was released on October 9 of that year and became a great hit. It also won numerous awards.

Kurosawa was moving from strength to strength: by the following May, he had already started filming the epic *Seven Samurai*.

* * *

Let me close with a word about Mifune's charm. Without Toshiro Mifune, the films of Akira Kurosawa could never have come into being.

During the writing of the script for *Seven Samurai*, when Kurosawa, Hideo Oguni, and Shinobu Hashimoto were holed up in Atami, every so often Mifune would drop by. At first there were to be six samurai, and Mifune was intended for the part of Kyuzo, played in the film by Seiji Miyaguchi. But Kurosawa was convinced that the story needed a totally unconventional character to succeed, and thus was born the rakish Kikuchiyo, the fake samurai of peasant stock, which Mifune took over.

Kurosawa told him to play the part any way he liked, completely naturally. Mifune did not disappoint, rising brilliantly to the challenge and coming up with all sorts of ideas of his own. One of the most interesting of these came in the scene in which he catches a fish in his bare hands. On the occasion of the issuing of the laser disc version of Kurosawa's works put out by Toho, I interviewed Mifune for the accompanying commentary, and he shared this story with me:

> The samurai are sitting on a rock eating rice balls. Kikuchiyo has nothing to eat, so he goes fishing. The scene was a single cut from the time I went in the water till the time I came back out, so I had to have the fish with me already when I went into the

Catching fish bare-handed: hiding them in his loincloth first was Mifune's idea.

river. I had no clothes on: the only place to hide a fish was in my loincloth. I was supposed to yank the fish out of the water and hold it up to show everybody, laughing in triumph. The props man warned me not to grip the fish too tightly or it would thrash around and get away. Keep a light grip on it, he said. At first we used a couple of crucian carp, but I didn't hold on tight enough and they both got away. The next time I squeezed too hard, and the fish flew right out of my hands. We did it over and over until all the fish we had were gone, and we couldn't shoot the scene.

All right, I said, hand me a fishing pole and I'll catch the ones I let go. I fished that river up and down like a madman, but you know, catching fish isn't all that easy. While all this was going on, the props man got in his car and drove to Numazu to buy some more fish. He bought back trout, and so the scene was shot with trout. It figures—knowing it was going back in my loincloth, what self-respecting fish would let itself get caught again! Ha ha ha!

As soon as the director yelled, "Cut! Print!" we all dissolved in laughter.

Toshiro Mifune has done such a marvelous body of work that I want him to sit back, relax, and enjoy the rest of his life. At one point he was ill and entered the hospital, but he seems as fit as ever now.* When I told this to Kurosawa, he said happily, "The next time I see Mifune I'll tell him what a great job he did. I want to praise him."

Visions of Mifune's superb acting must have surfaced and resurfaced in Kurosawa's mind. The past is limitless.

MIFUNE'S EMBARRASSMENT

After six years in the military, Mifune was in Kumamoto on the southern island of Kyushu when the Pacific War came to an end. His parents both dead, he made his way to Tokyo and called at Toho, where someone he knew from the military worked, to ask if they could use an assistant cameraman. Whether intentionally or by some fluke, his resume was sent around to the "New Face" talent hunt, and he made the cut.

---

*Translator's note: Mifune died December 24, 1997, weeks after this was written. See chapter 9, p. 276.

He had never intended originally to be an actor. When director Senkichi Taniguchi negotiated for him to appear in a film, Mifune, who was then in actor's training, explained that he would soon be transferring to the camera department. He was not going to be an actor. "The idea of a man making a living from his face just doesn't sit right with me," he said firmly.

In 1946, demonstrations wound through the burned rubble of Tokyo with banners reading, "Give us rice." Toho was embroiled in a labor dispute, and ten of their top stars finally had enough and broke away. As if to say, "Who needs stars? We'll compete with sheer ability!" the directors left behind took a script co-authored by Akira Kurosawa and Senkichi Taniguchi and produced *Snow Trail* (Ginrei no Hate, 1947) for Taniguchi's directorial debut. They convinced Mifune to appear in it alongside Setsuko Wakayama, and so came up with a fresh masterpiece of postwar Japanese cinema built on the combined efforts of newcomers.

Released in 1947, *Snow Trail* is the story of three bank robbers holed up in the Japan Alps. Mifune got the part of the youngest and most violent of the three. His glowing eyes and indomitable spirit contributed to an outstanding debut performance.

Even so, Mifune saw acting as a mere temporary diversion; ultimately he was determined to work in the camera department. On location in Hakuba he carried the tripod, battery, and other heavy camera equipment more than fifty kilometers (thirty miles) and was always at the head of the line, striding for hours through the snow.

I believe that Mifune never lost his sense of embarrassment at ending up an actor; it clung to him to the end.

The year after *Snow Trail*, Kurosawa chose Mifune for the lead role in *Drunken Angel*. That movie's success established Mifune overnight as a new star representing the finest in postwar Japanese cinema. However embarrassed he may have been as an actor, he was never allowed to go back to the camera department.

The first time I ever saw Toshiro Mifune in person, he had just arrived at Daiei Kyoto Studio with Takashi Shimura and Akira Kurosawa. I was an apprentice script supervisor. Toho was sealed off then, but Kurosawa was brought over from another company, and he swept into Kyoto with all the vigor of the rising sun. The year was 1950. Filming on *Rashomon* was about to get underway. By good fortune, I was included in the crew.

One hot midsummer day, we filmed the kissing scene out behind the temple Komyo-ji. Due to the necessity of capturing sunlight filtering through the trees behind them, Mifune and actress Machiko Kyo had to climb up onto a two-meter platform. The camera was positioned to capture them from below.

Kurosawa called out, "Test!" Mifune stood straight, heels clicking like a soldier, smiled, and bowed his head before Miss Kyo, saying, "Begging your pardon." I can still see that shy, innocent smile.

Around then Mifune was not yet weighted by the burden of international stardom and was newly married to Sachiko, a fellow "new face" from the Toho talent hunt. That was probably the happiest time of his life.

Later, even after he became a huge star and an international figure, or rather especially then, he was embarrassed to be an actor. He had no retinue, never relied on the script, always knew his lines cold, and was unfailingly considerate to the crew; all of this was a token of his self-reproach, I think, and his determination never to cause trouble for others even if he *was* an actor.

Working on a Kurosawa film was something like being in a regiment; from start to end, we crew ate our meals with the director and cast, even if there was no filming that day. At such times, even if he was laughing heartily, Mifune's sensitive nerves must have worn to a frazzle, like silken threads. Sometimes late at night, after the rest of us had gone to sleep, the threads would snap.

Recklessly—even granting there were few cars on the road in those days—he would get drunk and race his beloved MG around at high speed. It was so dangerous that no one dared go near him. Only Kurosawa could bring him in line then. Somebody would go and awaken the sleeping director, and bring him out. According to Kurosawa, "A yellow blur [the MG] would fly past with a loud roar, turn to a tiny dot in the distance, and then before I knew it, fly past with another roar heading back in the opposite direction."

"Mifune! Go to bed!" Kurosawa would yell, standing in the middle of the road with his arms waving as if he were trying to stop a runaway horse. Whatever state he was in, Mifune would recognize the director and come to a sudden stop. That seemed to sober him up. Afterward Kurosawa would say with a strained smile, "That's taking your life in your hands. I might as well be a wild animal tamer."

Even so, the next morning Mifune would be up before anyone, sitting in front of the hair stylist's mirror and muttering that he had had too much to drink the night before.

Takashi Shimura's wife, Masako, was on close terms with the Mifunes, having known them ever since his debut. Two days before Mifune died, she went to visit him in the hospital. He was surviving on injections, his body wasted away, but he gazed steadily at her with those beautiful eyes. Overcome, she cried out, "Mifune-chan! You have got to pull yourself together!" and slapped him smartly in the face. Then, she said, a tear came trickling from the corner of his right eye.

"I'd known him for dozens of years, and that was the first time I ever saw Mifune-chan cry," she told me.

I wondered what Mifune wanted to say. I wondered what he was grieving about. Suddenly I felt very sorry for him, and tears filled my eyes.

REMEMBERING JUZO ITAMI

The first time I met Juzo Itami, he was a middle-school boy of thirteen named Takehiko. Back then he was still shorter than me, and his head was shaved, as was the custom for schoolboys.

After his father Mansaku Itami died, I visited their residence in Kyoto. I walked with Takehiko on the way back from a shopping trip and told him, "Tomorrow I go back to Tokyo. Shall I take you with me?" I'll never forget the way he looked up at me, snapped the fingers of his right hand, and beamed, "Nice!"

The following year, after the rest of the family packed up and returned home to Matsuyama, it was arranged that I would live with Takehiko for a year in Kyoto, and cook his meals. But my job as script supervisor with Daiei Kyoto Studios went from early in the morning till late at night, and since it was my first job, I struggled with it and left Takehiko pretty much to his own devices.

Why I went to Kyoto, I don't know. Afterward it occurred to me that the reason for Takehiko's stubborn refusal to leave was that he had a crush on a certain young lady in his class at school. I once met her and her mother, a very appealing woman, and I suspect that many of Takehiko's meals that year came from their kitchen.

The two of us led such irregular lives that finally the landlord ordered us out, and we moved to an apartment by Katabiranotsuji Station. The building leaned like the tower of Pisa, perhaps because of the vibrations from passing trains. We took two second-floor rooms, one with six mats and the other with eight. The rent was 900 yen ($2.50), my monthly salary around 4,000 yen ($11). In no time, I got to know the neighborhood pawnbroker quite well. The landlady, who lived on the ground floor, was a fiftyish widow. Sometimes she'd have a man, an electrician or that sort of person, come over and we'd hear them laughing together till late at night.

Takehiko attended school, I commuted to the studios. Again, I have little recollection of our sharing any meals together. At home we would listen to records and do sketches in the manner of Bernard Buffet on the paper *fusuma* doors. One day, as he was listening to the radio, Takehiko commented, "Hey, they just said, 'The Hattori clock brings you ten o'clock.'" (The Hattori clock tower, a Ginza landmark, tolls every hour in silvery tones.) That was the start of commercial radio.

I remember he would sing "Buttons and Bows," the popular song from the 1948 Bob Hope movie *The Paleface*, and proudly point out the correct pronunciation of the title: "It's not *batten bo*, you know," he'd say, "it's *botan ando bo*."

After that year, Takehiko went back to Shikoku to attend Matsuyama Higashi High School, and I went to work for Toho in Tokyo. After graduating from high school, Takehiko came to

Tokyo to look up the producer Seiichiro Eida. A very caring man, Eida got the boy a position on the editing staff at Shin-Toho. I'm sure the experience he gained there, cutting and splicing film, proved useful in his later career as director.

I may have been an abject failure as Takehiko's cook, but as I shall relate, by an unexpected turn of events I was able to act as his Cupid.

Kurosawa Productions was launched in 1959. Toho calculated that making Kurosawa responsible for production costs might prove a restraining influence. From then on, Toho and Kurosawa Productions split profits and losses right down the middle.

The first picture from Kurosawa Productions was *The Bad Sleep Well* (Warui Yatsu hodo Yoku Nemuru, 1960). Around that time Kazuko Kawakita, the only daughter of Towa founder Nagamasa Kawakita and an aspiring director, returned from London where she had been studying and requested permission to join the Kurosawa crew. Her mother, Madame Kashiko Kawakita, accompanied her to the studio to put the request formally to Kurosawa, who said, "I'll leave her to Non-chan." In this way, Kazuko was more or less dumped in my lap to begin with; as it turned out, for the next thirty-three years—until her untimely death in 1993— she would be my dearest friend on earth.

Back then she was barely twenty, and her immediate goal was to get her driver's license. Before long, she was using her brand-new license to drive a Hillman from the Kawakita home in Kojimachi to Toho in Setagaya. Few people owned cars in those days, and so the roads were clear. After work I often rode with her to Shibuya, where we would park right in front of the Kirin Beer Hall and go in for a beer. Today such a thing is unimaginable.

While drinking our beer, we would talk about movies. *Daughter of the Samurai* (Atarashiki Tsuchi, 1937) was the first-ever Japanese-German collaboration, produced by Nagamasa Kawakita and directed by Arnold Fanck and Mansaku Itami. Made under a grueling schedule that required separate filming of Japanese and German versions, it ended up a peculiar work conforming to the official state line, but as sheer entertainment it proved a great success. Itami never offered a word in defense of this film, writing only, "On *Daughter of the Samurai* I learned a little about my own foolishness, and that is its only significance."[34] His comment is splendid.

As Kazuko and I discussed such things, eventually it came about that I introduced her to Takehiko. In the beginning the three of us would go out drinking together, but it wasn't long before I realized I was definitely in the way. I became the intermediary whom Takehiko would call at the studio to ask when we were getting off work, or to leave a message for Kazuko telling where he would be at a certain time.

The Bad Sleep Well was completed in August of that year, and released on September 4.

In due time Takehiko (whose birth name was Yoshihiro Ikeuchi) and Kazuko Kawakita were married. For the wedding, Mansaku's widow, Kimi, came up to Tokyo and met Kashiko, the mother of the bride, for the first time. Dressed alike in elegant kimonos, they said things like, "Well, this was simply meant to be, wasn't it!" and laughed graciously, each with a ladylike hand covering her mouth.

Kazuko had intended to become a film director, but watching Kurosawa at work convinced her that she could never do it, and she gave up. She was always one to accept the inevitable with good grace.

The newlyweds set up housekeeping in Towa housing, in the central Tokyo district of Kojimachi. Downstairs was a garage, upstairs was a bedroom and a large living room. The main Kawakita home was in Kamakura, but due to the demands of her work, Kashiko, Kazuko's mother, would often spend the night in Kojimachi.

The windows in the living room were very large; outside, the leaves of a plane tree blowing in the wind would brush up against the glass.

Producer Eida began to boost Takehiko as an actor with Daiei, thinking perhaps to balance his career with that of Kazuko; in 1960 he pushed him into the picture *I Hate You, I Hate You, I Hate You* (Kirai, Kirai, Kirai), directed by Hiromu Edagawa. Takehiko's stage name was then Ichizo Itami. He changed his name from Ichizo to Juzo in 1969, after his second marriage, to Nobuko Miyamoto. The difference between the two names was based on the addition of a single stroke to the first character: in "Ichizo" the first character is a straight horizontal line meaning "one," while in "Juzo," a perpendicular line has been added to form the character for "ten." He summed it up nonchalantly: "I changed a minus sign to a plus sign, that's all."

In private, we continued affectionately to call him "Take" or "Take-chan."

The time he spent living in Kojimachi corresponds to his years as an actor. The house there functioned as a salon, and was filled with a continual flow of guests. Journalists, actors, writers, musicians, and directors would engage in heated discussion of Jean-Luc Godard's *Breathless* (A Bout de Souffle, 1959), or lie stretched out on the floor listening over and over to recordings of The Modern Jazz Quartet.

Takehiko and his friends put together a short 16mm film called *Rubber Bullets* (Gomu Deppo), a sketch of daily life. Though little more than a student exercise, it was released by the Art Theater Guild as an appendage to full-length movies. It is likely that Kashiko's influence had something to do with that.

Kazuko was an excellent cook and a devoted wife, but as is so often the way with men, Takehiko did not want to be tied down. She began confiding in me that he was seeing another woman, staying away nights—and then, after seven years, the marriage was over. As a result of their breakup, however, he went on to become the great director Juzo Itami, and she to form the Shibata Organization (France Eiga-sha), a major importer and distributor of specialized films, so they each did find their calling.

Yet on June 7, 1993, Kazuko suddenly succumbed to a subarachnoid hemorrhage. She was only 53 years old. The morning of the day she died, I spoke with her on the telephone.

On what corresponded to the third anniversary of Kazuko's death, I was in the bar of the Imperial Hotel in Tokyo, meeting with Juzo Itami and producer Yasushi Tamaoki to discuss building a memorial hall in honor of Mansaku Itami in Matsuyama. When I happened to mention that it was the anniversary of Kazuko's death, her former husband looked thoughtful, and spoke feelingly about his last glimpse of her: "I saw her in Venice the last time. As I was going down a canal in a gondola, I saw her standing in the prow of another gondola as it came gliding past. She didn't see me. That was the last time I ever saw her."

She could never have dreamed that four years after her death, Takehiko would take his own life. The god of death lurks in unexpected corners.

In September 1995, after completing *A Quiet Life* (Shizuka na Seikatsu), director Juzo Itami returned to Matsuyama with his family to attend services marking the fiftieth anniversary of the death of his beloved father, Mansaku. The services were also attended by Itami's son-in-law, the writer Kenzaburo Oe and family; guitarist Kiyoshi Shomura and his mother, Mansaku Itami's younger sister; Mansaku Itami's chief assistant director for many years, director Kiyoshi Saeki; producer Yasushi Tamaoki and his family; and myself. In all there were nearly twenty of us, and we set off for the temple cemetery in a microbus.

Before the service began, as we were all gathered in a reception room, Takehiko, as I shall continue to call him, hung a framed bit of writing on a pillar and explained it to us. The previous night, he said, he had selected a quotation from his father's writings and copied it out for today. He had written this: "To offer people comfort must be the noblest role possible for cinema. Mansaku Itami, age 30. Juzo."

The elder Itami had written this in a manuscript occasioned by the production of his film *Beyond the Spring Wind* (Harukaze no Kanata e, 1930).

Takehiko went on to address remarks to us, prefacing them by saying, "Mansaku Itami wrote these words when he was thirty years old. In other words, offering comfort to other people is the greatest thing we can do in our lives, through our work. The impact of these words to me is overwhelming."

Takehiko was fifty-one when he took up his father's work

as film director. He had already lived longer than his father, who passed away at forty-six. How he must have longed to talk with the older man about cinema and about being a director! I can well understand why these words of his father impressed him, as he—director Juzo Itami—consistently sought to entertain viewers in his films. He must have wanted to embrace his father and share these sentiments with him.

Takehiko lost his father when he was thirteen. (The name "Juzo" is written with the characters for ten and three, a combination that can also be read *jusan*, "thirteen.") From then on, he lived surrounded by women. It seems to me that he was constantly seeking among his male friends and acquaintances for someone to hold in esteem. This too may have been an expression of yearning for his father.

That night, we all went to a Japanese-style restaurant for dinner. As the evening began, Takehiko called his children over and spoke to them about their grandfather, Mansaku. Everybody present was a relative or intimate, so what he said then must have been the thoughts he truly wanted to pass on:

> Usually when we talk about generations, the relation between parents and children is expressed in a two-beat rhythm: parent, child, parent, child. But a Frenchman named Jacques Lacan said no, there's a father, and a father, and a child. So it's a triple progression. The role of the father, Lacan said, is an intermediary one. He transmits to the child the words of his own father, the child's grandfather.
>
> Today is the fiftieth anniversary of the death of

> Grandpa, your father's father. And as his son, it's my job to transmit his words to you.
> Your grandpa, Mansaku Itami, died the year after the end of the Pacific War. I was thirteen. Grandpa was true to himself. He was very strict. He was incapable of telling a lie. But during the war, remaining true to yourself was very hard to do.
> What runs through all his films is this: the question of how the individual can live truthfully in an age when totalitarianism oppresses human freedom and dignity.

And then he proceeded to go through all of Mansaku Itami's films, beginning with his debut work, *Wandering Revenge* (Adauchi Ruten), and to explain them one by one to his children. As I watched and listened, I was moved by Takehiko's ardent love for his father.

On the morning of December 21, 1997, I was awakened around seven by the ringing of the telephone. I picked up the receiver, assuming it was an overseas call, and the line went dead. Well, I'm up now, might as well watch the news, I thought, and switched on the tube. What I saw was chilling.

On the lower right quadrant of the screen was a photo of Juzo Itami. A female announcer was briskly summarizing his career. At the end she said, "Itami-san was sixty-four." The finality of the past tense plunged me into despair.

It was all over something so trivial that had he lived longer, surely he would have come to brush it aside with a snort of derisive laughter.[35]

Had he lived longer, he might have made more of his fascinating movies.

In the few seconds it took for you to fall to earth, Takehiko, did you feel regret, did you think, "Ah, what have I done"?

On the TV screen, Juzo Itami, in the middle of a shoot, was laughing as he talked eagerly about something.

9

Observing the Kurosawa Group

DIRECTOR TOSHIRO MIFUNE

In 1962, Toshiro Mifune set up Mifune Productions. I don't know what inspired him to do it. He was bursting with energy in those days. If I ran into him in the studio, he would declare with deep conviction, "If we make good movies, audiences will come."

The following year, Mifune Productions came out with its first film, based on an original scenario by Ryuzo Kikushima called *The Legacy of the 500,000* (Gojumannin no Isan). Mifune took everyone by surprise by directing it himself. This was his first and only venture into directing. He was such a shy man by nature that I cannot imagine it was his own idea. More likely, he reluctantly allowed himself to be talked into it by producer Masazumi Fujimoto, or by Toho itself.

The story concerns a cache of gold worth seven hundred million yen ($200,000) that was sent from Japan to the Philippines (then under Japanese occupation) and abandoned in the hills of Luzon by General Yamashita's troops when Japan lost the war.

It was promoted as a "stylish action drama" exploring people's lust for gold with thrills and suspense. The production staff were straight from the Kurosawa team, including cameraman Takao Saito, art director Yoshiro Muraki, and sound engineer Fumio Yanoguchi; I myself took part as script supervisor. The only exception was Mikio Komatsu, the director's aide, who was from the Hiroshi Inagaki team.

Mifune Productions lacked its own studio, so filming took place at Takarazuka Films, affiliated with Toho. When anybody called Mifune "director," he would squirm and say, "No, don't call me that! I'm the president and errand boy of Mifune Productions, that's all."

In my opinion, Mifune was never suited to be a director. And for this movie, he had to wear three hats, as director, lead actor, and president of the production company. He wore himself out.

In the first place, no one as considerate of others as Mifune was can possibly function as director. The best film directors tend to have a strong streak of willfulness, pay no attention to what others say, and go to any lengths to get the picture they want. Mifune was incapable of behaving like that. For example, one of the director's most important jobs is deciding the number of cuts for a given scene, but Mifune, fearful that the staff wouldn't like it if there were too many, would suggest, "What if we go all the way to the end in one take?" And he couldn't bring himself to call for close-ups of his own face.

When we were on location in the Philippines, soon after arriving in Manila, someone from a local clothing store came around to our rooms. When we asked what he wanted, he explained that Mr. Mifune had ordered formal Filipino wear for everyone, and he had come to take our measurements. Mifune must have assumed that showing up at parties dressed in local style would make a better impression. Called *barong tagalong*, the magnificent see-through garments were made of banana fiber or something. I remember one party where we all wore ours. None of us looked good in formal wear, so we were all a little embarrassed in front of each other.

Nor was that all. Around the end of filming, Mifune paid out of his own pocket for the families of the crew to go to Takarazuka to see the revue, and then to visit Arima Hot Spa. Naturally, the families were ecstatic. They still talk about it. This happened because Mifune was incapable of inviting only his own family to come celebrate.

Then there was the matter of Mifune's TV commercial for an energizing drink called Arinamin. His tag line, *Nondemasu ka* ("Are you drinking it?"), had made the commercial a big hit. In deference to Takeda Pharmaceuticals, the sponsor, he announced he would work a plug for the drink into the film. I was in stitches at the thought, asking him why in the world a Japanese ex-soldier out hunting for General Yamashita's hidden gold would be carrying Arinamin. Mifune felt he had no choice but to shoot the bit anyway. It was bizarre: Mifune, playing the former soldier, is riding along in a jeep when suddenly, for no discernible reason, he pulls a bottle of Arinamin out of his pocket. This scene would end up causing him difficulties later.

Having arranged from the first to receive the cooperation of his mentor Akira Kurosawa for post-production, he issued an invitation to the director and his family to come down from Tokyo for the editing.

During the editing, Mifune's jitteriness was painful to behold. He would wait in a corner of the room, agonizing over Kurosawa's every move and jumping up periodically to make him coffee. Appalled by the Arinamin take, Kurosawa lost no time in discarding it. When Mifune sputtered a protest, he told him flatly, "It's weird." Mifune resisted feebly, but he was no match for Kurosawa. Later, he shot a new Arinamin commercial in Tokyo.

Kurosawa also commented that there were not enough close-ups of Mifune where they were needed, and ordered more. The extra footage was shot in a nearby woods.

As I said, Mifune was not cut out for directing.

The Legacy of the 500,000 was a big box-office success. Mifune went straight out and had imitation gold coins like those in the movie made for everyone who had worked on the film. They were by no means cheap, either. I still have mine.

THE PETITION

From my years of observing a great director in action, I know that the job of film director is certainly not as easy as it appears to outsiders. It is like walking along a precipice at the risk of one's life. The rest of us on the crew have all we can do just to maintain our positions on the mountainside; we never get near the precipice.

Should a movie by good fortune win a Grand Prix, it is the director who is in the spotlight, as well he should be. Some may cite the Japanese proverb "A general climbs to fame on the bodies of ten thousand nameless soldiers" and feel resentful, but when a production flops, it is the director who comes in for all the flak, while the nameless soldiers emerge unscathed.

Kagemusha was the first movie Kurosawa had made with Toho in ten years, since *Dodesukaden*. Toho insisted on a cap of 1 billion yen ($2.5 million) on production costs, and Kurosawa battled for more. Today the idea of making a movie on that grand scale for such a pittance seems unbelievable, but in the end they settled on a budget of 1.1 billion yen. Filming started June 27, 1979, on location in Himeji. Toho probably intended to wrap up the film before the end of the year and release it at New Year's.

As it happened, disasters befell us one after another. It all started with the abrupt departure of our star, Shintaro Katsu. By the time we got going again with Tatsuya Nakadai in his place, it was late July. Next came the sudden illness of cameraman Kazuo Miyagawa. On location in Hokkaido we were swamped by a blizzard so we scurried back to Tokyo with our tails between our legs, like the defeated German army leaving Russia. After that we shot on location successively at Kumamoto Castle in Kyushu, in Iga Ueno in the Kansai region, and in Kyoto, winding up the year at Gotenba.

From the first of the New Year we were beset by bad weather again in Gotenba, but we had to film the scene where the identity of the double is revealed. It was already the end of February, and all of us, including of course Kurosawa himself, were worried sick about the amount of work still left to be done. We congratulated ourselves that at least it was a leap year, so there was one extra day.

On February 26, a press conference was held to explain to the waiting audience the reasons for the delay. Members of the press corps flocked around.

The next day, Kurosawa, production coordinator Ishiro

Honda, and six others left for Nagoya on the bullet train to scout out a site by the Kumano River as a candidate for the last scene.

There was yet more bad news on the way. Aboard the train, Kurosawa opened the evening paper and found an article mocking the previous day's press conference. "*Kagemusha* gobbles money," it claimed, and showed an unflattering cartoon of Kurosawa eating a bowl of noodles and exclaiming "*Nobiru, nobiru!* (Longer and longer!)"[36]

Of course, Kurosawa was incensed. I'm sure he felt like lashing out: "Who do you guys think you are? You're a bunch of know-nothings. Have you got the slightest idea what I go through every day to get this picture made? I'm the one who wants the picture finished most of all, you numbskulls!" After all the trouble he had gone to the previous day to explain himself, it must have been terribly frustrating.

I remember watching from behind as Kurosawa, dressed in jeans and sneakers, crossed the broad street in front of Nagoya Station on the way to the Grand Hotel. He kicked at a stone and swore mightily.

The hour was late. In an attempt to mollify the director, knowing he was fond of steak, producer Toshiaki Hashimoto chose a steakhouse for dinner. The interior was dimly lit, however, and Kurosawa's mood only grew blacker. We sat around the table, but no one spoke. The air was heavy with tension. Clearly, Kurosawa was seething.

Finally, in a voice of controlled rage, he spoke up. First, he demanded that Toho persuade the newspaper to issue an apology. Not just some small disclaimer, either. It was Toho's fault that such a mocking article had come out, anyway. Until he received an apology, he was not setting foot out of there. "You're all with me on this, right?" He looked around the table, appealing to us for our approval. He wanted us to sign a petition and submit it to Toho in protest, he said. Having been through a number of disputes in the past decades, Kurosawa was forged of hardened steel. Sitting at the end of the table, I thought privately he might be overreacting, but of course I agreed to his proposal. Kurosawa made one exception, I'm told, excusing producer Toshiaki Hashimoto, our intermediary with Toho, from affixing his name; if true, this was a samurai's compassion, but I don't remember it.

My memory is also fuzzy as to whether or not the petition itself was drawn up on the spot. I cannot even say whether I ate my steak or not that night. The way cameraman Masaharu Ueda remembers it, he was too upset to eat. "I never touched my steak," he says—but Hashimoto recalls that we all had good appetites. Memory is fallible.

Hashimoto quickly informed Toho of this new emergency situation, and that night's scheduled departure of the crew for the location site was put on hold.

The next morning, as we were having breakfast in the hotel dining room, wondering what would become of the Nagahama location shoot, all of a sudden Kurosawa came out with his traveling bag in hand. We jumped up in amazement: "What, are we leaving?" Kurosawa sat down next to cameraman Ueda, saying, "It's childish to get angry about every little thing." He himself had worried the most over the problem.

Kagemusha was released April 26, 1980. Box office revenues were a record 2.6 billion yen, or the equivalent of $6.5 million.

WHAT REALLY HAPPENED WITH SHINTARO KATSU ON *KAGEMUSHA*

I remember with absolute clarity riding with Kurosawa in his Mercedes Benz on the way to Toho's main offices one day when he suddenly turned to me and said, "Want to hear an interesting idea? Shintaro Katsu and Tomisaburo Wakayama are brothers, right? They look a lot alike, too. Why not have Wakayama be Shingen Takeda, and have Katsu play his double? Might be interesting."

To be honest, I had hardly seen any movies by either of the two; I answered that the idea sounded like it had possibilities. I doubt whether Kurosawa had seen many of Katsu's movies, either. His idea was based on gut instinct.

The idea must have appealed to Toho, as they relented somewhat in their insistence on holding production costs to 1 billion yen, and compromised at 1.1 billion. *Kagemusha* was on its way.

Later Wakayama withdrew on grounds of ill health, leaving Shintaro Katsu to play both the warlord and his double. Tsutomu Yamazaki was cast in the role of Nobukado, Shingen's younger brother.

The opening words of the script were *"There are three identical human beings."* Yamazaki would have to be made up to resemble Katsu. Kurosawa drew sketch after sketch, trying to figure out what sort of makeup would work best. To do the job properly he needed a photograph of Katsu, and it fell to me to ask Katsu's manager, Masanori Sanada, to send over some promotion stills of the star.

Sanada was a model of devotion to his client; we used to marvel over it, calling him the "faithful retainer." Eventually, a large package of photographs arrived from Katsu, who was shooting another film on location in Kyoto. He had attached a note asking us to use the one marked with a circle on the back. Kurosawa picked it up and said irascibly, "What's he talking about? It's my job to pick the picture *I* want."

Looking back, it seems that this event was an omen of what was to follow. If this were a Kabuki performance, it would have been accompanied by a sinister roll of the drum.

While we were scouting for a location site in Kyoto, Katsu said he would treat Kurosawa to one of the steak dinners he loved. Cameraman Kazuo Miyagawa and I were also invited along. I have forgotten the name of the restaurant, but it was evidently a top-class *chaya* or teahouse where guests are entertained by geisha. When we opened the door, the *okami*, or proprietress, bowed down formally, hands on the floor, and greeted Katsu in the soft Kyoto dialect, her voice husky: *"Ma, sensei. Okoshiyasu.* Why, Sensei! Welcome." She radiated dignity and authority. Katsu told us to make ourselves at home, acting like the lord of the castle. He was in an ebullient mood, and entertained us in inimitable style with humorous talk about acting, his own shoulders shaking with laughter.

After a time two young geisha appeared in the doorway. *"Konbanwa.* Good evening," they chirped and, lifting the skirts of their kimonos, came traipsing in. Their faces were painted so white it was impossible to tell what they might look like underneath. As one of them came near Kurosawa, flashing yellow teeth in a smile and holding out a container of hot sake, saying, *"Do dosu.* Would you like some?" the director moved away from her in seeming panic, which set us all to laughing.

In the car on the way back to our hotel, Kurosawa said, "I can't stand that stuff, it gives me the creeps. They were painted solid white all the way down their necks, did you see? I don't know what Katsu's thinking. I'm willing to bet he owes money there. I saw the look that *okami* gave him. I never miss those things. It comes with being a director." After having been treated to a fine dinner, I'm sorry to say he was unsparing in his criticism.

In short, the two men simply had different styles. They were as unalike as two Japanese folk heroes from the Edo period: if one was Jirocho Shimizu, a powerful gangster boss who reformed late in life, the other was Kinjiro Ninomiya, a peasant who rose to greatness by constant diligence and conscientiousness.

Filming got underway with a scene at Himeji Castle in which Katsu was not scheduled to appear. Day One was June 27, 1979.

On July 17, at the Takeda mansion, constructed on a mammoth Toho set, it was finally time for Katsu to appear in the role of Shingen Takeda's double. It was a rehearsal for the scene where Tsutomu Yamazaki, in the role of Nobukado Takeda, shows the double around the premises and explains how they are built.

Katsu had a single line. In response to Nobukado's "Well done!" he was to reply, "Well done or not, there was nothing else I could do." It was easy enough to remember, and yet he said the line a different way every time. He probably felt he was nobody's puppet, and wanted to show he needed creative freedom to be himself. At first Kurosawa remonstrated mildly with a grin, but gradually his tone grew more severe. Once again, the sinister drum roll was sounding.

Finally came the fateful day of their falling-out.

It was the second day of rehearsals, a rainy day.

Hearing Katsu had arrived an hour earlier, I headed for the makeup room. As I walked down the hall, I could hear the shrill voice of the head of Yamada Wigs, whom we always referred to as "Old Man Yamada." I couldn't make out exactly what he was saying. Old Man Yamada, though barely more than a meter and a half tall, was famous for the resonance of his voice.

No one else was yet in the makeup room except for Katsu, who was sitting before the mirror in costume having his wig adjusted by Old Man Yamada. As soon as he caught sight of my reflection, Old Man Yamada said loudly, "Katsu here says he wants to make a video recording of his performance, but I was just telling him it's not a good idea. The director would never approve. Why don't you go see what he says? If you ask me, it's a bad idea."

Now Katsu addressed my reflection. "You see, this is something I always do. Otherwise I can't see what I am up to. I study the video and learn from it."

Old Man Yamada told me again that I'd better go seek Kurosawa's permission first.

"Never mind," said Katsu. "I'll ask him myself. Is he on the set?"

Saying I would go check, I stepped out of the makeup room and took a look in the wardrobe room. Actor Jinpachi Nezu was inside. He'd gone to the makeup room, but finding Katsu already seated there, he'd come to the wardrobe room instead. Nezu himself was usually first to have his makeup on, but since today Katsu had beaten him to it, he must really be gung ho, Nezu marveled, telling me all this when I interviewed him later. When he arrived, Katsu had apparently announced to him too, "Hey, Nezu! I'm videotaping the rehearsal today."

By the time I reached the set, Katsu was already standing talking to Kurosawa. The lighting crew was just getting set up, calling back and forth in loud voices, and the surroundings were dim; I could only see Katsu from behind, in silhouette, but from his gestures it was clear he was talking about the video. Kurosawa remained seated in his director's chair, smoking a cigarette as he looked up at Katsu, twisting to see him better.

Afterward Kurosawa told me, "At first I had no idea what he was going on about. All I could think was that his makeup was laid on too thick. I couldn't pay attention to anything else."

When he finally understood, Kurosawa's face turned grim. "Absolutely not! If you did that, it would be a huge distraction. All you need to do is focus on your role. Nothing else!"

For those of us used to Kurosawa's outbursts, this was on the mild side, well below average, at most a two on the Richter scale. For an unaccustomed actor, however, it was enough to knock you for a loop. Katsu stood motionless for a few seconds, stunned.

"Never mind that, hurry and get ready now," he was told, and at that he snapped back to his former state. Turning his back indignantly on Kurosawa, Katsu stomped off the set.

"What's eating him?" said Kurosawa in irritation, watching him depart. "Go see what the matter is," he told me, motioning with his chin.

Outside, rain had turned the road and buildings a somber gray. Amidst that dripping gloom, the sight of Katsu's bright yellow *hanten* jacket swaying back and forth far ahead is imprinted on my memory. As he strode along, his anger suddenly seemed to erupt, and he hurled his oiled paper umbrella to the ground.

What happened next, I learned from actor Jinpachi Nezu. In a July 26, 1993 interview, he said, "All at once, Katsu came storming into the wardrobe room. He was sullen, and started ripping his clothes off furiously without saying a word. I wondered if he had to take a leak. Then he pulled off his wig, flung it on the pile of clothes, and went out, looking pretty agitated. There's no way he would have taken off his wig just to go to the toilet, so I figured something must have gone wrong with that video idea of his."

Word that Katsu had walked out in a fit of anger spread rapidly, throwing the production unit into chaos. "What's going on?" "The director's fit to be tied." "No, no, it's Katsu who got mad and flew the coop." Some people ran to the phone, others scurried around like chickens with their heads cut off. I headed for the main gate, where the security guard reported that Katsu's vehicle had yet to go by. At that point, I was still planning to try and placate him and get him to come back.

Just then, the car from NHK pulled up at its usual time. Producer Kiyoshi Watanabe, who was supervising NHK's complete coverage of the filming of *Kagemusha*, smiled and nodded his head as he said a leisurely "Good morning." I told him something unfortunate had come up and we didn't want him doing any filming today. Without even waiting for me to finish, Watanabe said obligingly, "Okay, I'll take off then." He swung the car around in a U-turn and drove out. Later, he gnashed his teeth at having missed filming this historic moment by seconds.

Katsu's van appeared, so we figured he was finally leaving, but it pulled over by the fountain in front of the production division. Somebody from the actors' department ran up to the van, alternately tapping on the door and shouting, but the door stayed shut. The actors' representative gave up and ran splashing through the rain back into the building. Meanwhile, producer Tomoyuki Tanaka came rushing up in his car. I held out an umbrella and filled him in on what had happened as we went over to the van.

Apart from the chauffeur, whose duties included opening and closing the doors, Shintaro Katsu was alone inside the vehicle. Thinking back, it seems obvious that he was waiting for his faithful retainer Sanada to appear. Later, Sanada would lament bitterly that he was not around when all this happened, calling it the gravest blunder of his life. In my opinion, however, his presence could not have saved the situation. The signs had been there all along. Even if things had been smoothed over that day, a clash between the two men still would have been inevitable.

When I returned to the set, I found rehearsals proceeding as if nothing was amiss. An assistant director was filling in for the actor, going through his moves, and the camera was practicing dolly shots. Kurosawa was supervising the proceedings with apparent unconcern, and yet clearly the business about Katsu was on his mind. When I approached him, he turned toward me right away. I explained that producer Tanaka was presently trying to talk Katsu out of his ill humor, but that Katsu seemed determined to leave.

Kurosawa said, "Okay, I'll go now." He stood up, instructed the cameraman to keep on with what he was doing, and walked off the set. I held out an umbrella for him, but he brushed it impatiently aside, deep in thought as he walked quickly toward the van. I followed behind, half-running to keep up.

In his heart he must have been thinking that the time for a decision had come, that this might just be the right opportunity. The other guy had started this fight, after all.

As Kurosawa drew near, the van door opened, and he bent his tall frame and squeezed inside. Looking in, I saw Katsu and Tanaka both turn their eyes to the director. Tanaka smiled and said diplomatically, "I was just asking Katsu-san if he wouldn't be so kind as to reconsider and go back to the set."

Katsu was apparently not about to soften his position simply because Kurosawa had come. Pursing his mouth, he told the director, "This is the kind of actor I am. I cannot perform under these circumstances," or words to that effect.

After a pause, Kurosawa said with incredible sangfroid, "Then there's nothing for it but to have you step down, Katsu-san." With that, he turned and climbed out of the van. As he went past me, inside the van Katsu lurched to his feet, glared at Kurosawa with eyes that looked ready to pop out of his head, and moved as if to attack him.

"Katsu-san, Katsu-san, you mustn't!" Though slight of build, Tanaka pinioned Katsu's arms from behind, turning bright red and managing somehow to hold the other fast even as he was dragged about inside the van. Though he could surely hear the commotion behind him, Kurosawa paid it no mind, never looking back as he strode away. As I watched him go, I almost thought I heard him mutter, "Good riddance! I can't have these goings-on."

When I arrived back at the set, I found the staff sitting in a circle around Kurosawa, listening to him speak. He was telling them that he expected each of them to use this time carefully to check and recheck their work so that they knew exactly what to do.

This was July 18.

The media then was much less frenzied than it is today, but still the incident quickly came to light and caused a major commotion. This was very big news. Something had to be done to get a handle on it, and quickly, especially since Katsu was also trying to be first to get his story out.

Whether Kurosawa knew it or not, inside the van a dramatic struggle was taking place.

At 6:00 on the evening of July 20, a press conference was held in a second-floor meeting room in the new building at Toho Studios to explain why Shintaro Katsu had dropped out of the production of *Kagemusha*. The room was packed with reporters; TV cameras and still photographers had been there all day, getting ready.

As I recall, Katsu's news conference came first, sometime in the afternoon.

We showed off our unruffled composure by having the lighting crew continue with preparations on the set.

Before he went out to start the press conference, Kurosawa motioned me over and said in a low voice, "I wonder if Nakadai is free. If it looks like he might have time, broach this with him. Tell him I'm sorry he'll be coming in as a replacement."

I tensed, realizing that amidst all this turmoil, I was being called upon to undertake these highly sensitive negotiations.

The room was filled to bursting with reporters, and an overflow crowd had set up camp out in the corridor. Some were standing on stools, craning their necks to see inside. I entered a small room across the way and, leaving the door slightly ajar so I could keep an eye on what was happening, sat down and picked up the phone.

The publicity department was explaining the background behind the incident; fragments of their talk came to my ears. Reporters were firing questions one after another, but I couldn't make out exactly what they were saying. Watching all of this take place, I dialed the home phone number of actor Tatsuya Nakadai.

Kurosawa's confident voice boomed out: "It's Katsu's loss. He himself quit, after all."

Nakadai's voice came on the line.

"As you probably know, he's holding a press conference about that right now," I said, shielding the receiver with my hand as I proceeded to negotiate with him about taking over the role.

Sounds of laughter drifted in from the other room. I stuffed a finger in one ear, pressed the receiver up against the other, and listened to Nakadai's low voice.

"Okay. Tell him if I can be of service, I'm happy to do it."

Clutching a memo in my hand, I went out of the room, bent on handing the news to Kurosawa just as soon as the press conference ended.

FOOTFALLS OF A GIANT

The other day I had a look at a new video released by Toho. Entitled *Footfalls of a Giant*, it consists solely of trailers of Kurosawa films. Speaking as a member of the staff on eleven of the films in question, I found each trailer brought back fond memories, but beyond that, they were interesting in and of themselves. I was impressed with the way each one made me want to see the movie again.

But then it only stands to reason that the trailers should be interesting: they were all made by Kurosawa himself. His name does not come up in the credits, but he did everything hands-on, from the editing to the script for the narration, the music, and even the publicity catch phrases splashed across the screen. (Usually the work of preparing trailers falls to the first assistant directors.) The video was, in effect, a collection of short works by the director.

At the end of the one for *Yojimbo* is a scene where Sanjuro and Unosuke walk steadily toward each other like enemies in an old-fashioned Western. Unosuke says, "Don't come any closer." Sanjuro sneers and moves his shoulder. The moment he fires his gun with a bang, the words "Powerful masterpiece!" fly onto the screen. It's marvelous.

Watching that scene made me laugh, though, as it brought back a funny memory of a crew member named Daisaku Kimura. Then a second assistant cameraman, he was known as a great focus puller (the one who adjusts the focus of the camera during filming). In any Kurosawa film, when the camera alternates cuts of two people as in this *Yojimbo* scene, it is essential that the two figures be matched in size. Kurosawa apparently asked Kimura, "What's the distance to Mifune [from the camera]?" Back then, focus was done intuitively, without any automatic measuring device, so Kimura had no idea precisely how many meters it might be. He was forced to answer, "I don't know." The director pressed, "Then how many meters is it to Nakadai?" When he got the same answer as before, he blew up. "How do you expect me to shoot the scene if I don't know the distances!" Fed up with the young Kimura's halting answers, Kurosawa said, "Never mind, I'll do it myself. Hand me the measuring tape." By rights, the assistant should have grabbed the end of the tape and scampered over to where the actor was standing, but poor Kimura was so confused he just stood there blankly by the camera, holding the tape measure. It was Kurosawa who grabbed the end of the tape and ran to Mifune to make the necessary measurement.

Today a brilliant cinematographer, Kimura likes to brag that he is probably the only man on earth who ever made Kurosawa run.

At the beginning of the trailer for *Ikiru*, two swings are shown in a dimly lit park, swinging slowly to and fro in counterpoint. Then a somber voice intones, "When someone is told of his impending death, how should he live out his remaining days?" It's a very effective presentation.

In the trailer for *The Throne of Blood*, a helmet is laid symbolically on top of a coffin as the narrator says, "The seat of power, and those who fight for it." Taketoki and his helmeted military commanders then appear, circling around the coffin to suggest the coming bloodbath.

Scenes like these were often shot on the set especially for the trailer, as part of the initial camera tests, along with still photographs for publicity. A lot of directors want nothing to do with publicity, feeling it is not their job, but Kurosawa was very involved with the smallest details. I suspect that he found it was a way to develop and clarify his ideas and feelings.

Since the purpose of the trailer is to introduce the full-length film, usually the trailer is made when the film is close to being finished. It draws on footage that didn't make it into the final version, or scraps from the cutting room floor. Since Kurosawa usually shot with two cameras, there was a wealth of material from which to choose—which made coming up quickly with the section he requested all the more of a challenge.

The editing crew would receive a "trailer memo" from the director, marking the start of the project. Here is the memo from *Rhapsody in August*:

- Organ
    "The story of one strange summer"
    "A charming grandma and her charming grandkids"
    (these are suggested titles)
- The letter from Hawaii
- Grandma and grandkids in the moonlight

The editing staff uses notes like these to ready the film.

Kurosawa had a sharp memory, so we had to be on our toes. "You know, that outtake, the one where things didn't get moving properly and I cut it off in the middle!" he would shout, or "That take we edited that's in the scrap heap, that one!" He gave us no time to search by leafing through the script. Once in a while the dependable chief editor Ryusuke Otsubo, after coming under constant fire, would return a salvo of his own: "No, sir, we used that take in the film, so it's not here."

In any case, I would venture that Kurosawa was the world's fastest film editor. Swift and decisive, in barely an hour or two he could make light work of a one- or three-minute trailer. All that was left to do was to survey the results and say, "That should do it. Thanks, everybody." I'm sure he had it all thought out in his head beforehand, but even so, he had a golden touch.

The trailer for *Red Beard* shows a scene of music being recorded in the dubbing room at Toho, which then boasted the finest recording facilities in the country. This too was Kurosawa's idea. He brought in lights and set it up to look like the real thing. Putting tape on all the machines and running them at once was strikingly new at the time. The titles for *Red Beard* were also effective.

The final duel in *Sanjuro*, not included in the trailer, is extremely well known. The props man in charge of the cylinder of compressed air responsible for that spectacular explosion of blood from Nakadai's chest was Shoji Jinbo, currently managing director of Toho Eizo Bijutsu (Toho Art Division). When I talked with him about the challenges involved, he commented, "If Nakadai-san had known how it worked, I was afraid he'd be unable to act, always worried about what was coming, so I didn't tell him anything. All I said was 'don't worry, it's perfectly safe.'" A very astute move.

According to Nakadai, there was a hose under his kimono, the tip of which lay against his chest. He admitted to being surprised by the huge geyser of blood that erupted, and added that he nearly got blown into the air by the force of the explosion.

During the long pause as the two men stood confronting one another, my job as script supervisor was to crouch right by the actors with a stopwatch and count off the seconds out loud ("Three seconds! Four seconds!") for Jinbo. I've forgotten now how many seconds it was supposed to be, but I well remember that as soon as I reached the end of the count, I got drenched with spray. We were in the middle of a take, so I couldn't jump up; I scrambled sideways to get away, but my head and my jacket were soaked with bright red fake blood. Nakadai continued steadfastly to hold his position opposite the other man, sword in hand, but he told me afterward that out of the corner of his eye he could see me leaping away, covered in gore. It is amazing that he could register all that and still play the part so perfectly.

Kurosawa was satisfied with the take but Jinbo wanted to do it again: apparently the powerful pressure had weakened a joint of the hose at Nakadai's feet so that the color red had seeped into the ground. Kurosawa said, "I think it's all right. Let's take a look at the dailies and decide." In the end they never did redo the scene. Cuts like that generally don't come out very well when you do them a second time. As usual, Kurosawa's instinct was sharply honed.

When I look at the trailers for his movies, I am struck by the thrilling rhythm, lucid themes, and underlying humanity of Kurosawa's work—all of which, I think, came from the character of the director himself.

PARTING SADNESS: DIRECTOR AKIRA KUROSAWA

"The regent lies gravely ill."

With this solemn refrain from a famous poem by Bansui Doi

(1871–1952) about the death of a great Chinese minister echoing in my mind, I longed to see Kurosawa. On September 5, 1998, I sent a letter to his chief assistant director, Takashi Koizumi, asking when would be a good time. The next day was a Sunday, and when I got home late at night, I found some thirty calls on my answering machine. The first was from Kurosawa's daughter Kazuko: "Please come right away to see Jiiji [her name for her father]." The tone of the messages gradually became more urgent. In the latter half, when I came to one from Koizumi announcing, "Mr. Kurosawa died at 12:45," my blood drained away. I felt myself crumple up. It was all over.

I threw down what I was carrying and tore out of the house, over to the Kurosawa residence. I was shown into the room where the body lay, with Koizumi and the other assistant directors gathered at the foot of the bed.

He appeared to be peacefully sleeping. I leaned over him carefully, the way you do when you are fearful of waking someone. To keep his mouth from falling open, a three-cornered cloth had been tied around his jaw and fastened on the top of his head; he looked as if he were in bed with the mumps. His face was calm.

Once he had told me, "I can picture my own funeral. I'm a director, after all. Non-chan (his name for me), you'll have your hands full." Had he imagined himself laid out like this?

By his pillow was a "bird of happiness," carved from birch by a Siberian peasant, that I had delivered at the request of Russian conductor Vladimir Fedoseyev. It was Fedoseyev who conducted the "Caucasian Sketches" suite by Ippolitov-Ivanov at the end of *Dreams*. I had delivered get-well gifts from people around the world, all sent as encouragement for Kurosawa to get well quickly and begin work on a new film.

On his birthday the year before, when his staff all gathered in the parlor to wish him well, he had come out in his wheelchair and said, "Next year I'd like to get back to work." We responded, "Why not come back in your wheelchair, the way you are?" I told him about the Italian filmmaker Michelangelo Antonioni, confined to a wheelchair since a stroke in 1985, who continues to work: "He made a film even though he is far more physically challenged than you."

I remember vividly something he said that day. "I don't yet have a good grasp of what cinema is, but these days, I have begun to think that the secret of cinema lies in the connection between one cut and the next."

It was very unusual for him to discuss cinema in theoretical terms that way. I wish he could have taught us more. That he didn't is something I will always regret.

He always used to say, "I can't do anything but make movies. Times when I'm not working are the hardest for me." How painful the last three years of his life must have been, confined to a sickbed as he was. Freed at last from all suffering, he seemed to me to have fallen into a deep, untroubled sleep.

Of Kurosawa's thirty films, I had participated in the making of nineteen, beginning with *Rashomon*. I could only consider myself extremely fortunate. In my heart I expressed silent gratitude for that long association.

On September 13, a farewell gathering was held at the Kurosawa Studios in Yokohama. Members of the general public came from morning till after dark to pay their respects.

A great star had at last fallen. Our sense of huge loss matched the mood of the elegiac poem by Bansui Doi, "A Star Falls in the Autumn Wind on the Wu-Chang Plain."

Akira Kurosawa, a name forever fair.

KUROSAWA AND MIFUNE AFTER *RED BEARD*

Whenever Kurosawa gave a press conference abroad, this question would invariably come up: "Sir, you haven't worked with Toshiro Mifune since *Red Beard*. What happened between the two of you?" Kurosawa always gave the same smiling reply: "Mifune and I haven't quarreled. It's just that I've already done everything possible with him. There's nothing left to do."

Red Beard (Akahige) was finished in 1965. Kurosawa's final film, *Madadayo*, was finished in 1993, while the last film Mifune ever appeared in—Kei Kumai's *Deep River* (Fukai Kawa)—came out in 1995. In the intervening three decades, the careers of the two men followed starkly diverging paths.

I will never forget something Kurosawa told me at the party celebrating the completion of *Red Beard*. Speaking softly, in a subdued tone of voice, he said: "[Scriptwriter Hideo] Oguni told me Mifune is all wrong." A shadow of regret crossed his face, as if he had committed a serious error.

Oguni apparently meant that Mifune had not correctly understood the eponymous leading role.

When the scenario was being written, Shugoro Yamamoto, author of the novel on which the film was based, cautioned Kurosawa: "Don't forget that Red Beard is someone with a deep wound in his soul." On viewing the completed film, Yamamoto praised it, saying, "You did a good job. It's better than the original." Notwithstanding this praise, the comment from Oguni was strangely telling. It was like a splash of cold water that gradually soaked through Kurosawa's heart.

Prior to that, Kurosawa had made sixteen films with Mifune, never voicing any complaint about the actor's performance. Indeed, he was completely sold on him: Once, asked what he would do without Mifune, he replied simply, "I would no longer be able to make films." During a shoot he never asked Mifune to change his style of acting or seemed in any way critical of him.

Red Beard was probably the first time that Kurosawa had ever evinced any dissatisfaction with Mifune's acting. Even so, he did not talk it over with him, but seemed rather to retreat diffidently, distancing himself from Mifune.

At that point an unexpected development invaded his world like a virus, starting Kurosawa on a completely different tack: a producer who had been off studying in the United States sounded him out about making *The Runaway Train* jointly with the U.S. company Avco Embassy Pictures. This man had never worked with Kurosawa and lacked the necessary experience to serve as liaison between him and an American film company. Yet, taken in perhaps by the man's glibness and facility with English, Kurosawa trusted him implicitly.

The script by Kurosawa (eventually filmed by Andrei Konchalovsky) was appealing, and plans proceeded as far as scouting a location—but in the end terms could not be worked out and the project was scrapped. From then on a black cloud began to settle over Kurosawa's fortunes. This was in 1966.

That same year, Mifune set up his own studio in Setagaya

and devoted himself to producing films; everything seemed to be coming up roses for him. He expanded into Hollywood, appearing in John Frankenheimer's *Grand Prix* in 1967 and John Boorman's *Hell in the Pacific* in 1968.

Kurosawa, meanwhile, still blind to the producer's limitations despite the *Runaway Train* misadventure, once again listened to him and jumped headlong into a misbegotten war. This was the *Tora! Tora! Tora!* debacle.

On April 28, 1967, producer Darryl F. Zanuck of Twentieth Century Fox held a conference to announce a Japan-U.S. joint production entitled *Tora! Tora! Tora!* The name was taken from the Japanese code words used in launching the attack on Pearl Harbor.

The Japanese director was to be Akira Kurosawa and the U.S. director, Richard Fleischer. After prolonged delay, filming commenced on December 3, 1968, and continued for some twenty days, but there was no end of trouble. Finally Fox dismissed Kurosawa on the grounds that he was having a nervous breakdown. While hunting for a replacement, Fox asked Mifune to take the role of Admiral Isoroku Yamamoto. Mifune agreed on two conditions: one, that Kurosawa direct, and two, that production be turned over completely to Mifune Productions. Undoubtedly, Mifune sought to take this opportunity to renew his collaboration with Kurosawa and help his old friend out of a tight spot.

Mifune claimed he telephoned Kurosawa to encourage him, and invited him to play a round of golf.

But Fox rejected the proviso that Mifune Productions should have control over the film. Nor did Kurosawa have any further interest in working with Fox: it had come home to him that the

American studio system was completely at odds with his unique auteur style of filmmaking.

In an interview, Mifune commented about the movie that "one factor leading to this result could have been Kurosawa's casting of amateurs." This remark was widely reported, and many people assume that it incurred Kurosawa's wrath. Mifune may have regretted making such a heedless remark and thereby further widening the distance between himself and Kurosawa. But I don't believe that was the case: Kurosawa was far too engrossed in attempting to forget his troubles with filmmaking and heal his wounded soul to have been reading the newspapers.

In any case, Mifune missed what was literally the chance of a lifetime to restore his relationship with Kurosawa. Yet even if things had gone differently, I strongly doubt that Kurosawa would have cast Mifune as Admiral Yamamoto.

Kurosawa always liked documentary-style realism. This led to a paradox: The ideal performance he sought from professional actors was for them to become the same as amateurs, the original characters on whom the material was based. And so for *Tora! Tora! Tora!* he hired nonprofessional actors, all of them war veterans. Adjusting the schedules of so many working adults was not easy, and it took time to help them overcome their stage fright, making it impossible to shoot the film with Hollywood-style efficiency. Mifune's suggestion that this style of casting factored into Kurosawa's dismissal is no doubt valid.

Battered by rough waves and cast away by the U.S. movie industry, Kurosawa joined with three colleagues to establish a new production company called Yonki no Kai or "Club of Four Knights." He made a fresh start writing scripts for movies and

TV. In 1970, to prove to the world he was in full possession of his powers he made *Dodesukaden*, managing to wrap shooting in only twenty-eight days. By this unprecedented swiftness he demonstrated his acuity, but the film did poorly at the box office.

In 1971, the news that Kurosawa had attempted suicide at his home sent shock waves around the world.

Meanwhile, Mifune's situation was much more glamorous: He was then in France shooting Terence Young's *Red Sun* (Soleil Rouge), in which he starred alongside Alain Delon and Charles Bronson. Yet thereafter, from 1972 through 1975, Mifune did not appear in a single movie. What could he have been doing during that four-year hiatus?

In 1972, Yoichi Matsue, the producer of *Dodesukaden*, received a communication from the All-Soviet Union of Filmmakers stating their readiness to commit to a Soviet-Japanese project long in the works: a film version of *Dersu Uzala*, to be directed by Akira Kurosawa. At New Year's, 1973, Matsue and I flew to Moscow. While the production would be entirely a Soviet enterprise, to prevent a repetition of the sorts of problems that had occurred in the abortive collaboration with Hollywood, producer Matsue signed the production agreement on the condition that Kurosawa should have full creative and artistic sway.

Actually, at this stage the name of Toshiro Mifune was in top consideration for the title role!

The film tells the moving story of the coming together of Captain Vladimir Arseniev, leader of an expedition to Siberia, and expedition guide Dersu Uzala, a denizen of the Siberian forests. But it struck me as illogical to cast Mifune as a member of the Gold tribe; on questioning Matsue about this later, I learned that it was a Soviet suggestion. The Soviets may well have thought that by reuniting Kurosawa and Mifune they could make a big splash internationally.

It is beyond imagining how much Mifune must have ached to work again with Kurosawa. But apparently Kurosawa thought that Mifune was not the best choice to play Dersu, the Gold tribe member and man of nature. Matsue talked the Soviets out of the idea by telling them it would be impossible to tie Mifune down in the wilds of Siberia for two and a half years.

The role of Dersu was hard to cast, but in the end it went to the unknown actor Maxim Munzuk.

Not only had Mifune missed out on another opportunity to work with Kurosawa, but he spent the next four long years idle; his position was truly pitiable. During this time he did go to Moscow as a judge for the 1973 Moscow International Film Festival and there encountered Kurosawa, who was at Mosfilm, busy with preparations for filming.

The following year, Kurosawa struggled with the rigors of the Siberian climate and finished shooting his masterful *Dersu Uzala*. In spring 1975 he was back at Mosfilm in post-production when Mifune came by to interview him for a Japanese TV show to be called "Movie Director Akira Kurosawa." Producer Matsue made the arrangements to help publicize the movie, and had of course obtained Kurosawa's prior consent. Video footage of the interview shows how awkward and strained their conversation was. When Mifune held out his lighter to light Kurosawa's cigarette in front of the Mosfilm studios, the gesture seemed somehow different from usual, as if he were saying farewell.

Dersu Uzala took first prize at that year's Moscow International Film Festival and was awarded the 1976 Academy Award for Best Foreign Language Film as well. Rising phoenix-like out of the depths of misery, Kurosawa went on to further glory that same year, as he received an Award for Cultural Contribution from the Japanese government.

Mifune made just two movies in 1976, appearing in the British movie *Paper Tiger*, directed by Ken Annakin, and the U.S. movie *Midway*, directed by Jack Smight. After that he cut back production at his company, appearing in period films with Toei Kyoto Studios as well as a spate of foreign productions, including Steven Spielberg's *1941* and Terence Young's *Inchon*, both in 1980; the TV mini-series *Shogun*, also in 1980; and John Frankenheimer's *The Challenge* in 1981. It seemed as if Mifune was attempting to heal his wounded spirit by plunging into overseas work.

Despite Kurosawa's artistic resurrection through *Dersu Uzala*, Japanese film companies were uniformly loath to fund his next expensive project. From 1976 to 1979, Kurosawa eked out a living by appearing in TV ads for whiskey. Finally, in 1979, he came to an agreement with Toho over production costs and began shooting *Kagemusha*—fourteen years after making *Red Beard* with Toho.

Financed through the cooperation of American directors Francis Ford Coppola and George Lucas, *Kagemusha* had excellent domestic box office sales and won the Golden Palm at the 1980 Cannes Film Festival. Fortune was smiling on Kurosawa again.

After that, from *Ran* in 1983 to *Madadayo* in 1993, he made four more films. Overseas, a number of events were held honoring his achievements. Rewarded in his later years for all the troubles he had gone through, I believe Kurosawa was happy.

Meanwhile, in 1989 Mifune appeared in Kei Kumai's *The Death of a Tea Master* (Sen no Rikyu—Honkakubo Ibun, a.k.a. *Sen no Rikyu—Honkakubo's Student Writings*), which won the Silver Lion Award at the Venice Film Festival. Mifune earned rave reviews for his portrayal of Sen no Rikyu, who served as grandmaster of the tea ceremony to Hideyoshi Toyotomi, the ruling warlord of Japan, during the sixteenth century. Famous as a man of extraordinary cultivation and depth, Rikyu stood high in Hideyoshi's favor until the day he was peremptorily banished, for reasons that remain unknown, and ordered to commit *seppuku*. Rikyu died in 1591 at the age of 71.

Kurosawa was no tyrant on the order of Hideyoshi, so the comparison cannot be taken too far; still, amid Mifune's stern portrayal of the tea master, when an occasional shadow of loneliness darkens his features, it is as if his role had overlapped with the true feelings of a man who never comprehended his swift fall from favor with Akira Kurosawa.

Following that performance, Mifune's health deteriorated, and he weakened in appearance as well; but he loved acting so much that he would ignore his doctor's orders and take on film roles even if they consisted of a single scene.

The last time Kurosawa and Mifune saw each other face to face was February 28, 1993, at the funeral for Kurosawa's sworn friend, director Ishiro Honda. Catching sight of a spectral Mifune standing with difficulty in the line of mourners, Kurosawa went over to him and said, as he told me later, "Are you okay? Don't overdo, now." Mifune replied, "I'm okay." That was their last exchange.

In 1995, while writing a scenario at a Kyoto inn, Kurosawa

fell and broke a bone. That injury was the beginning of the end of his career; he never returned to directing.

That same year, Mifune exerted his last bit of strength to appear in director Kei Kumai's *Deep River*. Since he was playing the role of an invalid ex-soldier, it was not unnatural for him to be weak, but seeing him strain to mumble his lines was pitiable. By then his internal organs were already ravaged by disease.

Toward the end, when Mifune was in the hospital, I called one day at Kurosawa's house. Kurosawa came into the parlor in his wheelchair. I had gotten word of Mifune's condition, and when I reported this, Kurosawa said in a tone of nostalgia: "If I ever see Mifune again, I want to tell him what a good job he did. I want to praise him."

How Mifune must have yearned to hear those words.

But without his ever having had that chance, on Christmas Eve, 1997, at the age of seventy-seven, the turbulent life of Toshiro Mifune came to an end.

Nine months later, on September 6, 1998, the death of the great filmmaker Akira Kurosawa was reported around the world, marking the end of an era. He was eighty-eight years old.

10

Akira Kurosawa and World Filmmakers

After achieving worldwide acclaim overnight with *Rashomon* in 1951, Akira Kurosawa brought out in quick succession another pair of masterpieces, *Ikiru* (1952) and *Seven Samurai* (1954). He became the talk of film festivals around the world, and was showered with prize after prize. His first foray abroad, however, did not come until October 15, 1957, when *The Throne of Blood* was screened at the opening of the first National Film Festival at London's National Film Theatre (NFT). Kurosawa was then forty-seven years old.

The array of prizewinning directors gathered for the screening of their representative movies was extraordinary: John Ford for *Stagecoach*, René Clair for *Le Million*, Vittorio De Sica for *The Bicycle Thief*, Laurence Olivier for *Hamlet*, Akira Kurosawa for *The Throne of Blood*. All the directors were introduced, and actress Gina Lollobrigida was there to lend glamour. Princess Margaret presented everyone with an award certificate on stage.

Afterward, Kurosawa returned to Japan on October 23 by

way of Paris. When we staff members went to meet him at the airport, no sooner was Kurosawa through Customs than he took us straight to the airport restaurant. Sipping whiskey, he talked excitedly about his first experience in a foreign country: how charming the foreign directors were, how eagerly journalists and young people had listened as he discoursed on cinema, and so on. He seemed particularly keyed up about having met John Ford. I heard him tell the story many times.

JOHN FORD

It was the day of the award presentations at NFT. In his anteroom, Kurosawa waited nervously. One reason for his restlessness was his getup—for the first time in his life he was wearing formal Japanese attire: crested kimono, baggy pleated trousers known as *hakama*, *zori* sandals. What added to his nervousness was that no interpreters were allowed in the room.

Someone came up to him all of a sudden, stuck out his hand, and said: "René Clair." Hastily, he blurted, "Akira Kurosawa," and shook the man's hand. That's the way it went.

John Ford came up, thumped him on the back, said, "John Ford," and shook hands, then jerked his thumb as if to say, come this way. In broken Japanese, Ford invited Kurosawa to have a drink. Before the award ceremony, Ford made gestures to indicate his heart was pounding with nervousness, and then did warm-up stretches until De Sica teasingly threw a handkerchief at him from the side. Thanks to Ford, Kurosawa was able to relax a bit even though he knew no English. Besides, neither the Kawakita family (who had accompanied him to London) nor anyone else he knew was there to see, so it wasn't as embarrassing as it might have been, he told us afterward.

The following day he went to call on Ford, who was then filming *Gideon's Day* (1958) in the MGM studios. On stage, Ford seated Kurosawa in a chair that he had brought out and placed next to the camera. When the take was finished, he told Kurosawa *"Arigato"* (Thank you) and bowed. Then he turned to the cast and crew and introduced Kurosawa in a loud voice. Everyone saw him off with thunderous applause. Kurosawa told us that the tribute had moved him to tears.

Actually, John Ford had once watched Kurosawa direct a scene. It was just after the war, during the filming of *They Who Step on the Tiger's Tail* (Tora no O o Fumu Otokotachi, 1945). Ford was in Japan as an officer in the Occupation, and he visited Toho. Kurosawa remained unaware of the visit as he was up high with the camera on a crane. Ford left saying, "Give the director my regards."

"John Ford is really great," Kurosawa said, like a little boy. "When I'm old, that's the kind of director I want to be."

Concerning Ford's films, Kurosawa had this to say: "I've watched them from way back. I think the first was *3 Bad Men* (1926). It was scary. *How Green Was My Valley* (1941) and *The Grapes of Wrath* (1940) were good too, but when you come down to it, Ford is best at Westerns. I would say his greatest Western is *My Darling Clementine* (1946). It's a model of what cinema should be."

Word of John Ford's death came by telegram during the filming of *Dersu Uzala* in Moscow. We couldn't bring ourselves to tell Kurosawa the sad news until filming was over.

LAURENCE OLIVIER

At the time of the NFT opening, Kurosawa had a memorable conversation with Laurence Olivier, the great British actor and director. Concerning *The Throne of Blood,* Olivier told him, "That interpretation of Macbeth is wrong. Macbeth is a man who suffered in a very human way." Kurosawa responded, "I think *Macbeth* is the tragedy of a simple man who was manipulated by others."

Olivier went on to mention four things about *The Throne of Blood* that had impressed him:

1. That Lady Macbeth was pregnant, and went mad after giving birth to a stillborn child.
2. The evocative impact of the horses' stampede.
3. That the night before the forest moved, a flock of birds flew into the castle.
4. The scene where Macbeth was killed by arrows.

Olivier then asked, "The next time I do *Macbeth*, would it be all right if I made Lady Macbeth pregnant?" To which Kurosawa replied, "Certainly."

Olivier continued, "Instead of a stillbirth, I want her to give birth to a deformed monster." With this, he screwed up his face like a strange monster and made everyone laugh.

To be in the homeland of Shakespeare, discussing *Macbeth* with Laurence Olivier, was a precious experience, Kurosawa said.

JEAN RENOIR

Kurosawa was extremely fond of *Grand Illusion* (1937). He read Renoir's autobiography and found it moving. Until then he had always refused to write his own autobiography, but after reading Renoir's, he decided to go ahead and try his own.

On the way back from London, Kurosawa met Renoir in Paris. Since they both had made film versions of Gorky's *The Lower Depths*, Kurosawa wanted to talk about that—only to have Renoir tell him, "Mine is not *The Lower Depths*. It is completely different from the original work."

"After treating me to a delicious French meal, when it came time to leave, Renoir came out to the front of the restaurant to see me off, and he kept standing there until the car went around a curve. The sight of him standing there is something I'll never forget. He's really a warm and broad-minded person. A marvelous person. I'm glad I was able to meet him." Kurosawa would reminisce in this way.

FOREIGN FILMMAKERS OFFER SUPPORT

After *Red Beard* and the subsequent failed collaboration with Hollywood, Kurosawa lost his way for roughly ten years; it was owing to the encouragement of Soviet film director Sergei Gerasimov that he made a comeback with *Dersu Uzala*. Again with *Kagemusha*, Toho's commitment to producing the film came about because Francis F. Coppola and George Lucas announced they would produce the overseas version. In the case of *Dreams*, Warner Brothers agreed to finance it as a presentation of Steven Spielberg. In this way, Kurosawa's later movies were made possible through the support and cooperation of foreign filmmakers.

In 1980, when Kurosawa traveled to the U.S. to receive an honorary Academy Award for lifetime achievement, a party was held in celebration of his eightieth birthday. The image of a tearful Kurosawa saying, "I am truly a lucky man" aired on Japanese television as well, and all of us who saw it were moved.

After *Kagemusha* won the Grand Prix at that year's Cannes International Film Festival, until 1982, Kurosawa traveled extensively in Europe and the United States, meeting with filmmakers everywhere he went and being warmly welcomed. While he was staying in New York's Plaza Hotel, he received many surprise visitors, including film greats Jean-Luc Godard, John Milius, Werner Herzog, and Martin Scorsese.

JEAN-LUC GODARD AND JOHN MILIUS

The combination of Godard and Kurosawa was unusual. Probably he was invited along by Milius and went out of curiosity. Producer Tom Luddy might have come with them as well.

We had heard that Milius was a Kurosawa fan, and Kurosawa also had good things to say about his *The Wind and the Lion* (1975). Milius asked Kurosawa to teach him the martial art of *kendo*, or Japanese fencing, and did Mifune impersonations, but Godard only sat looking on, smiling, and never spoke to Kurosawa.

WERNER HERZOG

Another unusual visitor was the German director Werner Herzog, whose name was then unfamiliar to Kurosawa. There was a book he wanted to give Kurosawa, said Herzog, but he hadn't been able to find it in the book store and he had a plane to catch, so he had just dropped by to pay his respects. Then the next day, I think it was, he made a special trip to hand-deliver the book—having gone to the trouble of altering his flight reservations to do so. I believe it was a book of drawings. In any case, Kurosawa found this gesture deeply moving.

Later, in Japan, Kurosawa took the first opportunity to go see Herzog's *Fitzcarraldo* (1981) and was overwhelmed by its tenacious energy.

MARTIN SCORSESE

One day, Scorsese came flying in like a whirlwind. His arms were full of documents, and he rattled on like a machine gun (or so it sounded to those of us who couldn't understand the language). Not even the veteran interpreter Audie Bock could keep up with him. It turned out he had come by to ask Kurosawa to sign on to a movement to prevent the fading of color film by preserving it in primary colors.

Kurosawa did sign the papers, I believe, but what was most interesting was the strong impression Scorsese evidently made on him that day: Later he asked Scorsese to play the part of van Gogh in his film *Dreams* (1990). The images of the two men apparently overlapped in his mind.

From then on, Kurosawa and Scorsese were like family.

WILLIAM FRIEDKIN

Once we were invited to dine at the home of William Friedkin, in the center of New York City. Kurosawa admired his *French Connection* (1971), so he gladly accepted the invitation. When Friedkin showed Kurosawa and the rest of us around his lovely home, I remember realizing with amazement that Kurosawa's residence would not fill even one floor of that house.

SIDNEY LUMET

Among the glittering panoply of guests at the dinner in Friedkin's house was Sidney Lumet. Kurosawa always used to say that his *Murder on the Orient Express* (1974) was a model of film as entertainment. On this occasion, the two filmmakers traded compliments: Having just seen Lumet's latest film, *Prince of the City* (1981), in a New York theater, Kurosawa praised the use of rain in it—whereupon Lumet came right back with, "No, sir, you are the true master at using rain."

FRANCIS F. COPPOLA

While we were in the Soviet Union filming *Dersu Uzala*, the hotel restaurant was continually filled with the haunting strains of the theme music from *The Godfather* (1972). Vodka glass in hand, Kurosawa would say, "That Coppola—what a director! I thought Part One of his *Godfather* series was perfect, and then he amazed me by surpassing it in Part Two. Usually the sequel is a poor imitation." Seated in a restaurant in a foreign land, we spoke Coppola's name with much admiration.

Coppola has said that before starting to shoot a movie, he often looks at Kurosawa's movies for inspiration. Although he has many favorites, one that he singles out for admiration is *The Bad Sleep Well* (1960), where he marvels at the directorial technique of letting the audience in on the entire setup right away, in the opening wedding scene.

While Coppola was editing *Apocalypse Now* (1979), Kurosawa called at his Zoetrope Studios in San Francisco and was treated to a special screening of a small part of the film. An unassuming man, Coppola showed him the opening scene, remarking how intimidating it was to have Kurosawa view his work. To the sublime music of Wagner, helicopters flew in formation, filling the screen.

"Wonderful," said Kurosawa. "You captured the scene well. It must not have been easy."

Coppola got up and went over to the screen, pointing to the space beside it: "Actually there were a lot more helicopters in the air, here, and here, too. They didn't get in range of the camera." He sounded rueful. Today, of course, with computer graphics the number of helicopters could be increased ad infinitum.

Coppola often traveled to Japan with his family, and always made a point of having dinner with Kurosawa. They remained close for a long time.

GEORGE LUCAS

Lucas is a quiet man. He often came to a shoot to watch Kurosawa in action, but said little, content to listen to the explanation provided. However, since he and Coppola were co-producers of the overseas edition of *Kagemusha*, Kurosawa took their opinions into consideration during editing. Lucas suggested omitting the scene in which the shadow warrior goes wandering in his sleep. I was of the same opinion, so the suggestion came across quite strongly. In the end, the issue was resolved when Kurosawa said, "That's what I wanted to film, so let me do it my way."

In 1981, we visited George Lucas's enormous studios. By then, the high-tech computer system used to such superb effect in *Star Wars* (1981) was already fully in place, and his staff demonstrated its various aspects to Kurosawa and the rest of us; impressed though we were, we couldn't make head nor tail of it.

At the studio entrance stood R2D2 and C3PO, the robot pair inspired by a pair of farmers in *The Hidden Fortress* (Kakushi Toride no San Akunin, 1958). Someone evidently told Lucas that Kurosawa had come to collect a copyright fee for their use. On hearing that, Kurosawa hastily told Lucas, "No, no!" adding with a smile, "Please use them all you like."

In the first scene of *Kagemusha*, a mud-spattered soldier rushes into the castle to make a report—a scene inspired in turn by the German film *Der Kongress tanzt* (Congress Dances, 1931), where in the midst of an elegant ball, a soldier rushes in with word that Napoleon has escaped.

JOHN CASSAVETES AND JIM JARMUSCH

Kurosawa was very interested in the work of less mainstream American filmmakers as well. He was impressed by John Cassavetes' *Shadows* (1959), which he saw in the *Cinémathique Française* in Paris. Hearing that Cassavetes was present, he wanted to convey his admiration in person and had people go look for him, but to his regret they never did get together.

And when he saw Jim Jarmusch's *Stranger Than Paradise* (1984) at a private screening by a French movie company, he raved about the talent of the young newcomer. Hearing how quickly and cheaply the movie had been made, Kurosawa said, "Maybe I'll try that next time." Those of us who knew him burst into laughter: "You? Never!"

THE DIRECTORS GUILD OF AMERICA

On October 9, 1981, the Directors Guild of America, located in New York City, held a reception for Kurosawa. The afternoon garden party was attended by many famous directors, the sun sparkled, and it was a wonderful day.

William Wyler, George Cukor, Samuel Fuller, Rouben Mamoulian and other towering figures from the world of cinema were all gathered in Kurosawa's honor, and naturally he was thrilled. When I indicated that I didn't know who Rouben Mamoulian was, Kurosawa told me, "Oh, he's the one who made that masterpiece of cinema, *Applause* [1930]." He quickly went over to Mamoulian and greeted him.

On that day, Kurosawa was as excited as any young movie fan. The excitement of that day became an unforgettable, lifelong memory. In his later years, he would frequently reminisce: "It was a wonderful party. They all were gathered there on my account— such wonderful directors. Japanese film directors should do that, too. Get together with other directors all the time, and talk about films. If we did, more good films would be made."

Afterword

The bulk of the essays in this book ran serially in *Kinema Kurabu* (Cinema Club), the bulletin of a video sales company, from July 1991 to October 1997, under the title *Tenki Machi* ("Waiting on the Weather"). The rest include essays from other publications, and some written newly for this occasion. I ask the reader's indulgence for inevitable repetitions among the various essays.

The idea for the book was suggested by Takamaro Shimaji, senior editor of the bulletin, formerly of *Kinema Junpo* magazine, whose readership includes many avid movie fans now getting along in years. Would I consider writing some behind-the-scenes stories about older movies? I would and did.

As I was starting to write about *Rashomon*, in September 1994, I was approached by Yasuo Terui of *Bungei Shunju*, also a member of Cinema Club, about publishing the essays in book form. I am grateful that he continued to support me throughout the subsequent six years, despite my lack of diligence.

During the course of those six years, on September 6, 1998, Akira Kurosawa passed away without ever making another film. Afterward, in the midst of my desolation I looked around and realized that very few of the Kurosawa group were left. It reminded me a bit of the final scene of *Seven Samurai*, in which unsheathed swords are stuck in the top of a grave-hill, and only the wind passes by.

Few people can have enjoyed as much good fortune as I: For nearly half a century, from *Rashomon* on, I was able to work alongside Akira Kurosawa. Even granting that the Kurosawa I know may only amount to the tip of the elephant's tail, it seemed to me like a good idea to leave an account of what I do know of him, however little it may be.

The new essays in this book were all written after Kurosawa's death. To be honest, I don't think I could have written about him this way while he was alive. If he saw what I've written, he would be sure to snort, "What I went through wasn't like this at all. You've got it all wrong."

At the time we filmed *Dersu Uzala*, Kurosawa was mentally and physically exhausted. To this day I regret that I did not understand the distress he was in.

To write about Kurosawa and the various composers he worked with only now, when the parties concerned have all passed on, may be cowardly. But everybody sees things differently from their own perspective, and I have merely written what I saw with my own eyes; I have tried not to write about anything that I did not personally observe.

An expression that Kurosawa was fond of using was, "Well you see, a lot of things happened." In a movie that I think was made by Hiroshi Shimizu, an old man stops on a bridge, utters that line, and laughs uproariously. It sums up my present state of mind.

AFTERWORD

I wish I could go back on location with the Kurosawa group and listen to Kurosawa talk as he warms his hands over a primitive kerosene stove. I wish we could all share a good laugh again. Those happy days will never come again.

I am indebted to two remarkable men: Makoto Wada for the book design, and Hisashi Inoue for his words of recommendation. I am sure I owe their cooperation to Kurosawa, but I am grateful none the same.

Warmest thanks to Takamaro Shimaji, who saw this project through to the end; to members of the Kurosawa group staff, who consented to be interviewed; to Kazuko Kurosawa, who gave me unflagging support; and to Rokusuke Ei, Aiko Sato, and Shotaro Yasuoka as well.

Teruyo Nogami
November 9, 2000

Afterword to the English Edition

Good things happen when you live long.

Nearing the end of my life, my hand reaching for the doorknob on the way out, I had an unexpected bit of luck come my way: the U.S. publishing company Stone Bridge Press agreed to publish my book *Tenki Machi* in English. Today there are more books about Akira Kurosawa than one could count, filling the shelves of "Kurosawa corners" in bookstores. Since my book was chosen out of so many, I can only be grateful. I realize this is the result of the goodwill of many friends and acquaintances, and I feel very blessed.

I must thank Donald Richie, who first entered into negotiations with foreign publishing houses, and Kunihiko Watanabe, who assisted him in preparing a sample translation of the "*Rashomon*" chapter and other parts. Unlike music, words require translation in order to communicate with people in foreign countries; and unless someone pays the fee, there can be no headway. Canadian filmmaker Marty Gross smoothed out this rocky road like a bulldozer, clearing the way. I have the deepest respect and gratitude for his enormous passion and energy.

In this book, I have simply written about Akira Kurosawa exactly as I saw him. In terms of understanding the great Kurosawa, this is only one small piece of the puzzle. I have done nothing but touch the tail of the elephant, perhaps, but the tail is real for all that.

I look forward with great anticipation to holding a copy of the English version of my book in my hands this fall. This gives me reason to go on living yet awhile longer.

Many thanks to translator Juliet W. Carpenter for kindly struggling with my poor writing, and to Toshiko Adilman and Kyoko Hirano for checking details.

For their generous provision of funds to support the translation and publication of this book, I am grateful to the Suntory Foundation and the Japan Foundation, as well as to the Criterion Collection—Janus Films, Peter Becker, and Jonathon Turell. I also appreciate the kindness of James Quandt and Akihide Tamura. Finally, heartfelt thanks to Peter Goodman of Stone Bridge Press for deciding to publish the book.

Teruyo Nogami
February 2, 2006

Notes and Sources

[1] *Eiga Zakki*, Daiichi Geibun Press, 1937.

[2] "Itami Mansaku no Omoide," in *Itami Mansaku Zenshu* (The Complete Works of Mansaku Itami; hereafter abbreviated as IMZ), vol. 2, Tokyo: Chikuma Shobo, 1982.

[3] Ibid.

[4] On March 3, Japanese families celebrate the Doll Festival (*hina matsuri*) with a display of oval-faced dolls representing an emperor, empress, attendants, and musicians, all in ancient court attire.

[5] "Bai," IMZ, vol. 2.

[6] Translator's note: Three knife-wielding yakuza attacked the director following completion of his movie *Mimbo: The Gentle Art of Japanese Extortion* (Minbo no Onna, 1992), which had a strong anti-gang message. This article was published in Fall 1992, five years before Itami's death.

[7] "Shinkokyuko: Byosho Zakki" (Old and New Manuscripts: Sickbed Notes), IMZ, vol. 1.

[8] "Seishin Doshin Roku" (Record of a Quiet Body and an Active Spirit), IMZ, vol. 2.

[9] Ibid.

[10] "Hajime Owari" (Beginning and Ending), *Geppo* (Monthly Bulletin), IMZ, vol. 2.

[11] Translator's note: The Japanese name of the great burnet plant, *waremoko*, is homophonous with a phrase meaning "I too, thus." The poems are from

"Record of a Quiet Body and an Active Spirit," IMZ, vol. 2.

[12] "Kabe Chomon" (Listening Walls), IMZ, vol. 1.

[13] *Eiga 40 Nen Zenkiroku* (Forty Years of Motion Pictures: A Complete Record), *Kinema Junpo Zokan*.

[14] *Eiga Nenkan* (Movie Almanac), 1950.

[15] "Kurosawa Akira Dokyumento" (Akira Kurosawa Document; hereafter abbreviated as KAD), *Kinema Junpo Zokan*, May 7, 1974.

[16] *Satsuei Oboegaki* (Photography Notes).

[17] KAD.

[18] Akira Kurosawa, *Gama no Abura—Jiden no Yo na Mono* (Something Like an Autobiography), Tokyo: Iwanami Shoten, 1984.

[19] Ibid.

[20] *Daiei Junenshi* (A Ten-Year History of Daiei), Daiei Inc., 1951.

[21] Tokuzo Tanaka, *Eiga ga Kofuku Datta Koro* (When Movies Were Happy), Tokyo: Japan Design Creators Company, 1996.

[22] KAD.

[23] KAD.

[24] "Nancho to Iu Koto ni Tsuite" (Concerning Soft Tones), IMZ, vol. 2.

[25] Kazuo Miyagawa, *Kameraman Ichidai—Watashi no Eiga Jinsei 60 Nen* (The Life of a Cameraman: My Sixty Years in the Movies), Tokyo: PHP Institute, 1985.

[26] Ryohei Yamaoka, *Kyoshinka no Nazo ni Semaru* (Mysteries of Co-Evolution), Tokyo: Heibonsha, 1995.

[27] "Kurosawa Eiga no Ongaku to Sakkyokusha no Shogen" (Music in Kurosawa Movies and the Testimony of Composers), KAD.

[28] Masaru Sato, "300/40 Sono E, Oto, Hito" (300/40: The Pictures, the Sound, the People, *Kinema Junposho*, 1994.

[29] Ibid.

[30] Yuichiro Nishimura, *Kyosho no Mechie—Kurosawa Akira to Sutafutachi* (The Metier of a Maestro: Akira Kurosawa and His Staff), Tokyo: Film Art-sha, 1987.

[31] "Zoku Choyochu no Kenbun" (What I Saw and Heard during My Draft Time, Part II), in *Ibuse Masuji jisen Zenshu* (The Self-Selected Works of Masuji

Ibuse), vol. 10, Tokyo: Shinchosha, 1986.

[32] Ito Mikashima, *Kijin de Kekko—Otto Hidari Bokuzen* (Being Eccentric Is Fine—My Husband, Bokuzen Hidari), Tokyo: Bunka Shuppan Kyoku, 1977.

[33] *Waga Kokoro no Jijoden*, *Kobe Shinbun*, 1973.

[34] "Itami Mansaku Hodan o Yomu" (Reading "Chats With Mansaku Itami"), IMZ, vol. 2.

[35] Translator's note: Juzo Itami jumped eight stories to his death after leaving suicide notes denying reports of an extramarital affair due to be published in a tabloid.

[36] Translator's note: A pun on the noodles stretching out and the length of filming time expanding.

PUBLICATION HISTORY

Portions of this book previously appeared in the following publications and were edited for the first Japanese edition.

CHAPTER ONE
"Letters": *Kinema Kurabu Kaiho*, no. 13 (Fall 1991).

"Listening to Memories": *Koza Nihon Eiga 7 Geppo*, Iwanami Shoten, January 1988.

"A Female Muhomatsu," "Images," "*The Life of a Giant*," and "Face to Face with Death": *Kinema Kurabu Kaiho*, nos. 14–17 (Winter 1991–Fall 1992).

CHAPTER TWO
Kinema Kurabu Kaiho, nos. 18, 19, 21, 22 (Winter 1992–Fall 1993).

CHAPTER THREE
Kinema Kurabu Kaiho, nos. 23–29 (Spring 1994–Fall 1995).

CHAPTER FOUR
Kinema Kurabu Kaiho, nos. 30–34 (Winter 1995–Winter 1996).

CHAPTER FIVE
"Bone-Freezing Night Shoots": *PHP*, August 1999.

CHAPTER EIGHT

"Death Notices": *Kinema Kurabu Kaiho*, no. 20 (Summer 1993).

"Kamatari Fujiwara," "Junzaburo Ban and Bokuzen Hidari," and "Takashi Shimura and Toshiro Mifune": *Kinema Kurabu Kaiho*, nos. 35–37 (Spring–Fall 1997).

"Mifune's Embarrassment": *Bungei Shunju*, March 1998.

CHAPTER NINE

"Director Toshiro Mifune": *Mainichi Mukku*, "Mifune Toshiro: Saigo no Samurai" (Toshiro Mifune: The Last Samurai), February 1998.

"The Petition": *Mainichi Mukku*, "Kurosawa Akira no Sekai" (The World of Akira Kurosawa), October 1998.

"What Really Happened With Shintaro Katsu on *Kagemusha*": *Shukan Bunshun*, September 24, 1998.

"Footfalls of a Giant": *Kinema Kurabu Kaiho*, no. 12 (Spring 1991).

"Parting Sadness: Director Akira Kurosawa": *Kinema Kurabu Kaiho* no. 41 (Fall 1998).